Authors

Elisabeth B. Booz was born in London to American parents. She grew up in England and Europe, and received her Master's degree in Political Economy from the University of Geneva. She freelances for the National Geographic Book Division as a writer and researcher. She is widely travelled; recent trips have taken her to Poland, the Orkney Islands, Iceland, Malta and China. She divides the remainder of her time between France and the USA. Her other books include the *Odyssey Illustrated Guide to Tibet*.

Andrew Hempstead has spent many years exploring, writing, and photographing worldwide; travelling extensively through the South Pacific, the United States, Canada, Europe and India. He has been writing since 1989 when, after leaving a career in the field of advertising, he took off for Alaska. Since that time he has carved out his niche in travel writing. Andrew has travelled to New Zealand numerous times on writing and photographic assignments, but also purely for pleasure, golfing the links of Northland and skiing the slopes around Queenstown. He lives with his family in Banff, Canada.

Photographer

Born in the Year of the Dragon, Ben Simmons grew up in Columbus, Georgia. He studied photography and psychology at university in upper New York State, then completed a Master of Fine Arts in photography and art history at the University of Florida. Simmons taught photography at Penland School of Crafts in North Carolina before travelling to Japan in search of adventure. His current base is a traditional seacoast retreat, *Momo-an* Studio, perched on a hill of peachtrees and bamboo above Sagami Bay south of Tokyo. Ben travels throughout Asia, America, Europe, and the Pacific specializing in graphic colour images for photo features, books, and original prints. He has worked as a photographer covering such diverse areas as Tahiti, Siberia, easter Island, Japan and Vietnam and for leading publications such as *Time, Newsweek, National Geographic* and the *New York Times*. Refer www.bensimmonsphotos.com.

(front cover) An aerial view of the Hollyford River in the Lower Hollyford Valley in Fiordland National Park in the South Island.

(page one) A Nomad sightseeing plane of Air Safaris giving a closeup view of the Southern Alps in Mount Cook/Aoraki National Park.

NEW ZEALAND
SNOWY PEAKS TO OCEAN DEEP

Elisabeth B. Booz
Andrew Hempstead

Photography by
Ben Simmons

# ODYSSEY BOOKS & GUIDES

Odyssey Books & Guides is a division of Airphoto International Ltd.
903 Seaview Commercial Building, 21–24 Connaught Road West, Sheung Wan, Hong Kong
Tel: (852) 2856-3896; Fax: (852) 2565-8004
E-mail: sales@odysseypublications.com; www.odysseypublications.com

Distribution in the USA by W.W. Norton & Company, Inc., 500 Fifth Avenue, New York, NY 10110, USA
Tel: 800-233-4830; Fax: 800-458-6515; www.wwnorton.com

Distribution in the UK and Europe by Cordee Books and Maps, 3a De Montfort St., Leicester, LE1 7HD, UK
Tel: 0116-254-3579; Fax: 0116-247-1176; www.cordee.co.uk

New Zealand—Snowy Peak to Ocean Deep, Sixth Edition
ISBN-13: 978-962-217-758-1
ISBN-10: 962-217-758-1
Library of Congress Catalog Card Number has been requested.
Copyright © 2006 Airphoto International Ltd.
Copyright © 2001, 1999, 1994, 1991, 1989 Odyssey Publications Ltd.

All rights reserved. No part of this book may be translated, reproduced or transmitted in any form or by any means, electronic, mechanical, photocopying or otherwise, without the prior permission of the publisher, except for brief passages for inclusion in critical articles or reviews.

Although the publisher and author(s) of this book have made every effort to ensure that all information was correct at the time of going to press, the publisher and author(s) do not assume and hereby disclaim any liability to any party for any loss (including loss of life) or damage caused by errors, omissions or misleading information.

Managing Editor: Helen Northey
Design: Rob Warner
Cover Design: Au Yeung Chui Kwai
Maps: Chris Folks
Photography by Ben Simmons

Grateful acknowledgement to Pierre Constant for article on pages 84–89 *Poor Knights Islands*.
c/– Le Trident–74 rond point du Pont de Sevres–92100 Boulogne–France
Tel: 331 4761 9329; Fax: 331 4621 7736; Email: calaolife@yahoo.com

Additional photography/illustrations courtesy of Andris Apse 9, 17 (middle right), 275; Bill Bachman 256; Magnus Bartlett back cover right, 107; Ian Brodie 264, 265; Communicate New Zealand 185; Pierre Constant 85, 88; Brian Enting 17 (all but middle right), 117, 132–133, 257; Andrew Hempstead 25, 49 (top left), 60, 61, 65 (bottom left and right), 93, 99, 106, 113, 120, 129, 145, 156–157, 160, 172, 192, 216 (top right), 233, 244, 253; Graeme Matthews front cover, back cover left, 1; Alexander Turnbull Library, National Library of New Zealand 35, 54, 58, 69, 71, 82, 108, 123, 139, 143, 144, 155.

Production and printing by Twin Age Limited, Hong Kong
E-mail: twinage@netvigator.com
Manufactured in China

(preceding pages) The distinctive peak of Aoraki Mount Cook rises 3,754 metres above sea level, not particularly high in comparison to the world's highest peaks but spectacular nonetheless.

Contents

INTRODUCTION.......... 10
   BIRD-WATCHING 15
   WALKING..................... 18
   FLY-FISHING 21
   GOLFING 23
   WINE-TASTING 26

FACTS FOR THE TRAVELLER 29
   GETTING TO NEW ZEALAND 29
   WHEN TO GO 29
   ENTRY REQUIREMENTS 30
   CUSTOMS..................... 30
   MONEY 31
   HEALTH 31
   CLIMATE AND CLOTHING 31
   ELECTRICITY 32
   COMMUNICATIONS 33
   GETTING AROUND 34
   MAPS 38
   INFORMATION 38
   ACCOMMODATION 38
   FOOD AND DRINK 43
   SHOPPING 46
   NATIONAL HOLIDAYS 47
   LOCAL HOLIDAYS 47
   ANNUAL EVENTS................ 47

NORTH ISLAND.......... 50
   AUCKLAND 51
      FOCUS......................... 62
   NORTHLAND 74
      WHANGAREI AND ENVIRONS 75
      BAY OF ISLANDS 76
      THE FAR NORTH................ 78
      THE WEST COAST 79
      FOCUS......................... 79

   NORTH CENTRAL 90
      COROMANDEL PENINSULA 91
      BAY OF PLENTY 94
      HAMILTON AND ENVIRONS.......... 95
      WAITOMO CAVES 98
      FOCUS 100
   THE CENTRE.................. 104
      ROTORUA 104
      LAKE TAUPO.................. 112
      TONGARIRO NATIONAL PARK 113
      FOCUS 114
   THE EAST 121
      THE EAST CAPE 123
      GISBORNE.................... 126
      WAIROA AND ENVIRONS 127
      NAPIER...................... 128
      FOCUS 130
   THE WEST 137
      NEW PLYMOUTH 138
      EGMONT NATIONAL PARK 140
      WANGANUI 141
      FOCUS 147
   THE SOUTH 150
      WELLINGTON 150
      THE HUTT VALLEY 158
      THE WAIRARAPA 159
      THE KAPITI COAST 160
      PALMERSTON NORTH 161
      FOCUS 161

SOUTH ISLAND 166
   THE NORTH 166
      MARLBOROUGH SOUNDS 170
      NELSON 171
      ABEL TASMAN NATIONAL PARK 173
      THE FAR NORTHWEST 174
      NELSON LAKES NATIONAL PARK 174
      FOCUS 175

THE WEST 182
   BULLER GORGE................. 186
   WESTPORT 186
   GREYMOUTH.................. 187
   ARTHUR'S PASS NATIONAL PARK 191
   HOKITIKA 192
   WESTLAND NATIONAL PARK 194
   FOCUS 196
THE EAST 203
   CHRISTCHURCH................. 203
   BANKS PENINSULA 211
   KAIKOURA.................... 213
   NORTH CANTERBURY 214
   SOUTH CANTERBURY............. 215
   FOCUS 215
THE CENTRE................. 223
   AORAKI MOUNT COOK
      NATIONAL PARK 223
   QUEENSTOWN 227
   WANAKA 235
   FOCUS 237
THE SOUTH 243
   DUNEDIN 243
   NORTH OTAGO................. 247
   THE CATLINS 247
   INVERCARGILL 250
   STEWART ISLAND 252
   FIORDLAND 258
   FOCUS 262

PRACTICAL INFORMATION 272

RECOMMENDED READING 285

COMMON MAORI WORDS 289

INDEX.................. 292

SPECIAL TOPICS
New Zealand's Land Mammals 33
Some Important Events
   in New Zealand History.......... 56–57
The Treaty of Waitangi.......... 68–70
The Poor Knights Islands 84–89
The Giant Kauri................. 92–93
Glow-worms..................... 98
Maori Carving 108–109
Voyager Kupe
   and Captain Cook 122–123
Maoritanga................. 142–145
From the Brink
   of Extinction.............. 148–149
Katherine Mansfield 155
The Curious Kiwi............. 184–185
Gold Rush 190–191
The Founding of Christchurch 207
Speakers' Corner 209
A Land of Sheep 220–221
Bungy Jumping 232
New Zealand's Outer Islands 254
Middle-earth Aotearoa.............264–266

Maps
Bird-watching Areas 16
Walking Areas 19
Fly-fishing Spots 22
Top Golf Courses.................. 24
Wine-producing Regions 27
North Island 52–53
Auckland 64
Rotorua 110
Wellington 153
South Island 168–169
Christchurch 205
Queenstown 229
Dunedin 245
The Outer Islands 255

Otago, an old gold mining town

Introduction

Although New Zealand is but one small speck on the world map, its diminutive size belies an astonishing diversity of attractions. The country boasts some of the world's greatest natural features, along with abundant opportunities for outdoor recreation, a colourful Maori history, a genuinely friendly population, and an excellent network of tourism facilities. All these elements combine to make New Zealand one of the world's premier travel destinations.

The country lies in the South Pacific, halfway between the equator and the South Pole. Australia lies 2,200 kilometres (1,375 miles) northwest; the United States is a distant 10,500 kilometres (6,562 miles) to the northeast. Two main islands—the North Island and the South Island—make up the bulk of the country's land area. The South Island is the larger of the two at 151,100 square kilometres (58,342 square miles). Combined, the two islands have a total land area of 266,170 square kilometres (102,772 square miles), roughly the size of Great Britain, Japan or the American state of Colorado.

Topography varies dramatically between the two islands. The warmer, emerald green North Island was shaped aeons ago by the fire of volcanoes. The process continues today, with the last major eruptions occurring here as recently as 1996. In the far north, the climate is subtropical, with lush forests broken by convoluted waterways and a ninety kilometre (fifty-six mile) beach ending at the island's northernmost point, fog-enshrouded Cape Reinga. At its narrowest point, the North Island is just 1.5 kilometres (0.9 miles) wide. Extending south from this isthmus, the east coast is lapped by the warm waters of the Pacific Ocean and the west is lashed by the stormy Tasman Sea.

The even more spectacular South Island is a land of lofty peaks, sapphire blue lakes, and deep fiords slowly carved by glacial ice. A spine of rugged, rocky mountains, snowcapped year-round, runs the length of the island. Aoraki Mount Cook dominates the Southern Alps; at 3,754 metres (11,442 feet) it is New Zealand's highest peak. The mountains slope gently to the east, through the rolling Canterbury Plains in the north and the barren, rugged Otago to the south. Across the island, the wet-and-wild west coast is buffeted by prevailing winds from the Antarctic; here glaciers descend almost to sea level. Lying off the South Island's southern tip is Stewart Island, New Zealand's third largest island.

New Zealand is often compared to other parts of the world, especially England. In fact, no place could be less like England than this land of golden, subtropical beaches, volcanoes, snowcapped mountain ranges and fern-filled rainforests. No industrial revolution ever blackened New Zealand's countryside, and no smog settles over its towns and cities.

While natural beauty is the country's greatest asset, the 3.73 million New Zealanders (known universally as 'kiwis') themselves go a long way to making the country such a great place to visit. They are a mix of two cultures: the Maori from the South Pacific (the original settlers), and the European colonists who came later, mostly from England and Scotland. The resulting blend has evolved into an egalitarian, frank, attractive society that is neither English nor Polynesian, but pure New Zealand. Where else in the world will a farmer tending his flock of sheep wave as you whiz by to destinations far afield? A hotel receptionist be genuinely interested in how your trip is going? A fruit seller throw in a few extra pieces just for the sake of it? And don't be too surprised at the cab driver who rounds the fare *down* instead of up.

The country has long had a reputation as an intellectual backwater, and back before World War II, when great distances and relatively slow communications made it difficult for New Zealanders to travel abroad, this may have been the case. Back then, writers Katherine Mansfield and Ngaio Marsh had to go to England to find a wide audience for their books describing life in New Zealand. Today, though, things have changed. The literacy rate here is one of the highest in the world, and New Zealanders are, per capita, the world's biggest book-buyers. Good bookshops with offerings from around the world can be found in every sizeable town. Books written in New Zealand by Sylvia Ashton-Warner, Alan Duff, Janet Frame, Keri Hulme, Witi Ihimaera and Margaret Mahy are much discussed in England and North America.

Through the years, New Zealand films have occasionally garnished worldwide acclaim. Examples include *Once Were Warriors* (1994), a brutal portrayal of modern-day Maori life, and the Oscar-winning *The Piano* (1993), for its insight into the life of a mute woman in the late 1880s. The latter was directed by Jane Campion, New Zealand's best-known director. Additionally, New Zealand has become a popular spot for filming Hollywood blockbusters, including the *Lord of the Rings* Trilogy, *The Last Samurai, King Kong,* and *The Lion, The Witch, and The Wardrobe*.

New Zealand is equally well represented in the world of music. Dame Kiri Te Kanawa, a Maori, is currently riding high as one of the world's great opera singers. In the contemporary music scene, Split Enz (which re-formed as Crowded House in the mid-1980s) has been the country's most successful export. Dunedin is often compared to Seattle as a breeding ground for talented musicians.

Exhibitions of New Zealand art, such as Te Maori, travel the world. Public galleries from Auckland to Dunedin mount an endless stream of major shows, while dozens of smaller galleries in the cities and provincial towns exhibit the works of local painters, printmakers and sculptors. The country's performing-arts scene is vibrant. Handicrafts, particularly those using ceramics and wool, are widely practised, appreciated and used throughout the country. Maori arts and

(following pages) A cattle and sheep station in the Wairau Valley

crafts flourish in both their traditional and modern forms. The output is amazing, considering New Zealand's relatively minuscule population.

As for the familiar image of New Zealanders as sheep farmers, times have changed. Sheep still outnumber humans 20 to one, but only a small percentage of people actually farm full-time. Although New Zealand's economy rests solidly on agriculture, its population has become mainly urban and suburban.

Although it may seem hard to believe when travelling around the country, tourism is as important as agriculture to New Zealand's diversified economy. Tourism New Zealand has done an excellent job of developing facilities, promoting the country's natural beauty and making events of cultural interest accessible. The board runs the Visitor Information Network (VIN), comprising over 100 official information centres in cities, towns and villages. As well as providing information on local attractions, these centres sell stamps and phonecards, make accommodation and transportation bookings, and help plan onward itineraries. New Zealand is still new enough to the tourism game for visitors to be treated as individuals, although this is slowly but surely changing. In the most intensely developed sites, such as Rotorua and Queenstown, the commercial tourist-trap hype is definitely apparent.

The Department of Conservation (DOC) was established as a Cabinet-level ministry in 1987, combining under one authority the administration and protection of wildlife refuges, forests, wilderness areas, marine reserves and national parks. New Zealand's watchdog against the kind of environmental damage that is occurring in many other parts of the world, the Department of Conservation runs well-managed field centres in most national parks and forest reserves and maintains offices in all major cities. For visitors interested in nature, the DOC can be an invaluable source of information and help.

New Zealand offers so much to see and do that your challenge as a visitor will be trying to decide which sights and activities to concentrate on. The aim of this guide is to focus your attention on five specialities worth travelling halfway around the world to sample. Any one, or any combination, will lead you through both islands, taking you off the beaten track and into easy, friendly contact with New Zealanders with similar interests and tastes.

Bird-watchers will encounter a rich diversity of bird life, including many unique species, to make this the bird trip of a lifetime (see page 15).

Anyone with a love of nature and a pair of good shoes will find New Zealand unique in the world for its network of wonderful walkways, well frequented by a population that walks for pleasure and health (see page 18).

Anglers the world over have long known about New Zealand's trout-filled lakes and streams. Many of the best spots, while still pleasingly remote, are within reach and well supplied with good facilities (see page 21).

 Golfers will find a true paradise in New Zealand, where the descendants of Scots have created more golf courses per capita than anywhere else in the world. Green fees are relatively inexpensive and visitors are welcome everywhere (see page 23).

 Sophisticated wine connoisseurs are becoming increasingly intrigued with New Zealand's fast-growing wine industry, and the country's cool-climate wines are making impressive showings on the international scene (see page 27).

This guide is organized in two parts: the North Island and the South Island. Both parts are divided in turn into chapters corresponding to the regions of each island. Each chapter begins with a brief overview of places, sights and local history, followed by a more comprehensive description and travel tips. At the end of each chapter is a 'Focus' section marked by the symbols given above. These provide detailed information on the five specialities, gathering together your options in each region.

Bird-watching

New Zealand's unrivalled bird life is a consequence of the country's unique, solitary natural history. Eighty million years ago, the primal landmass near the South Pole slowly broke apart to form the seven continents, with a lone sliver of land adrift on the rim of a tectonic plate later becoming the islands of New Zealand. Only birds, one mammal (a bat), a few lizardlike reptiles and three kinds of frog inhabited these islands.

New Zealand was a paradise for birds. Without fear of predators, many bush birds lost the power of flight. Some developed strange feeding habits; the ostrichlike giant moa, for example, grazed on the grasslands. Evolution continued in isolation, producing about 250 species of birds, many of them unknown outside New Zealand. From time to time, strong winds blowing in from Australia brought seeds, insects and birds to add new variety to New Zealand's ancient forests. The first mammal predator to endanger this unique and fragile ecosystem was man.

Bird-watching Areas

Rangaunu Harbour
godwit, knot, turnstone, red-necked stint, banded dotterel, pied stilt; also crake, pukeko, harrier and swamp birds

Bay of Islands
northern blue penguin, giant petrel, cape pigeon, white-faced storm petrel, fairy prion, shag, heron

Tiritiri Matangi Island
saddleback, takahe, stitchbird, brown teal, parakeet, bellbird, pigeon, petrels and little blue penguin; also watch on any Hauraki Gulf sea trip for shearwater, gannet, arctic skua, giant petrel, white-faced storm petrel, cape pigeon, fairy prion

Little Barrier Island
wildlife sanctuary (permit required) stitchbird, saddleback, kokako, kakapo, black petrel, Cook's petrel

Firth of Thames
godwit, knot, South Island pied oystercatcher, wrybill, sandpiper turnstone, red-necked stint, gull, tern, shag, heron, banded dotterel, pied stilt

Muriwai Beach
gannet colony

Auckland Zoo
aviary has kaka, kereru, blue duck, saddleback, kakariki

Manukau Harbour
spotted dove, pheasant, finch, whimbrel, other waders

Rotoehu State Forest
North Island kokako, kaka, wattlebird, forest species

Otorohanga
Kiwi House and Native Bird Park

Waikato Wetlands
bittern, heron, egret, spotless crake, kingfisher, pukeko, shining cuckoo, brown teal, fernbird and waterfowl

Urewera National Park
shag, swan, blue duck, scaup, shoveler, robin, tui, morepork, falcon, pied tit, bellbird, long-tailed kaka, rifleman

Cape Kidnappers
gannet sanctuary with three large colonies

Marlborough Sounds
sea and shore species, king shag breeding ground

Farewell Spit
godwit, knot, turnstone, whimbrel, black swan, pipit, goldfinch, California quail, waders and shorebirds

Mount Bruce
National Wildlife Centre

Nelson
waders and shore species in estuaries

Kapiti Island
sanctuary (permit required) whitehead, North Island robin, pied tit, grey warbler, tui, bellbird, little spotted kiwi, brown teal, blue penguin, kaka, stitchbird, takahe

Paparoa National Park
Westland black petrel (winter breeder), tomtit, tui, pigeon, bellbird, silvereye, grey warbler, kaka, brown creeper, rifleman, yellow-crowned parakeet, blue duck

Rakaia River
banded dotterel, black-fronted dotterel, wrybill, plover

Okarito Lagoon
(permit required) white heron sanctuary and spoonbills

Avon-Heathcote Estuary
spotted shag, godwit, white-faced heron

Lake Ellesmere
pukeko, black swan, duck, golden plover, pectoral sandpiper, curlew sandpiper, sharp-tailed sandpiper, greenshank, stint, wrybill, other waders and waterfowl

Milford Sound
Fiordland crested penguin, banded dotterel

Lake Pukaki & Godley River
waterfowl, wrybill, pied stilt, white-faced heron, spur-winged plover, banded dotterel, black stilt, chukor, falcon, kea, morepork, little owl

Otago Peninsula
royal albatross, yellow-eyed penguin spotted and Stewart Island shag nesting area

Te Anau Wildlife Bird Reserve
takahe, falcon

Eglinton Valley
yellowhead, kaka, robin, tomtit, rifleman, brown creeper, yellow-crowned parakeet, long-tailed cuckoo, kea, rock wren, grey warbler, bush species; watch for kea and rock wren at the Homer Tunnel's western end

Stewart Island
little spotted kiwi, Stewart Island brown kiwi (diurnal), kaka, red-crowned parakeet, New Zealand pigeon, shearwater, little blue penguin, southern pelagic species

© Airphoto International Ltd.

(clockwise, from top left) Native pigeon, kea (alpine parrot), royal albatross, kaka (forest parrot), blue duck, gannets

The Maori, a Polynesian race, came to New Zealand about 1,200 years ago. Flightless birds made easy prey, and the many species of moa were soon hunted into extinction. A thousand years after arrival of the Maori, Europeans colonized New Zealand, and in the space of one century inflicted more damage on the local bird life than the Maori had in a millennium. They felled and burned forests, drained swamps to create farmland, and systematically introduced all kinds of flora and fauna from 'home'. About 30 European birds became established in the wild, but these generally did not invade the habitats of native birds, choosing instead man-made environments such as farmland and gardens, to which no endemic species had adapted. Other imported animals, including predators of birds, produced ecological havoc. By 1900, controls had been imposed; since then, awareness of the need for conservation has reached national proportions. These developments arrived too late, however, for the roughly half of New Zealand's native bird species that are now extinct. And many other species are still endangered, amongst them the kakapo, a unique flightless parrot, and the black stilt, the rarest wader in the world. Today, the Department of Conservation carefully oversees the country's environment.

New Zealand's climate ranges from subtropical in the north to cool-temperate, verging on subantarctic, in the south. The diversity of terrain—alpine regions rising above treeline, highland and lowland forests, native 'bush', open grassland and a long, variegated coastline—creates habitat for an astonishing range of bird species and makes the islands a delight to anyone with a pair of binoculars. New Zealand celebrates its wealth of birds by opening its national radio programme at 7 am and 9 am every day with bird calls!

Walking

For any lover of the outdoors, walking, or tramping as it is known in New Zealand, is one of the country's greatest attractions. The spectacular national parks (four on the North Island, ten on the South Island), numerous forests and countless scenic reserves all provide well-marked paths ranging from short nature walks with plants and trees labelled for identification to long, hard hikes lasting several days. A system of national walkways legislated into being with the Walkways Act of 1975 has created an imaginative network of walking trails across public and private land all the way from the Cape Reinga to Stewart Island.

Walking is a national pastime in New Zealand. During school holidays whole families set out together with backpacks, food and sleeping bags to tramp one of the famous tracks. However, now that the population is 80 per cent urban or suburban, shorter day walks within easy driving distance of towns have soared in number and popularity.

INTRODUCTION 19

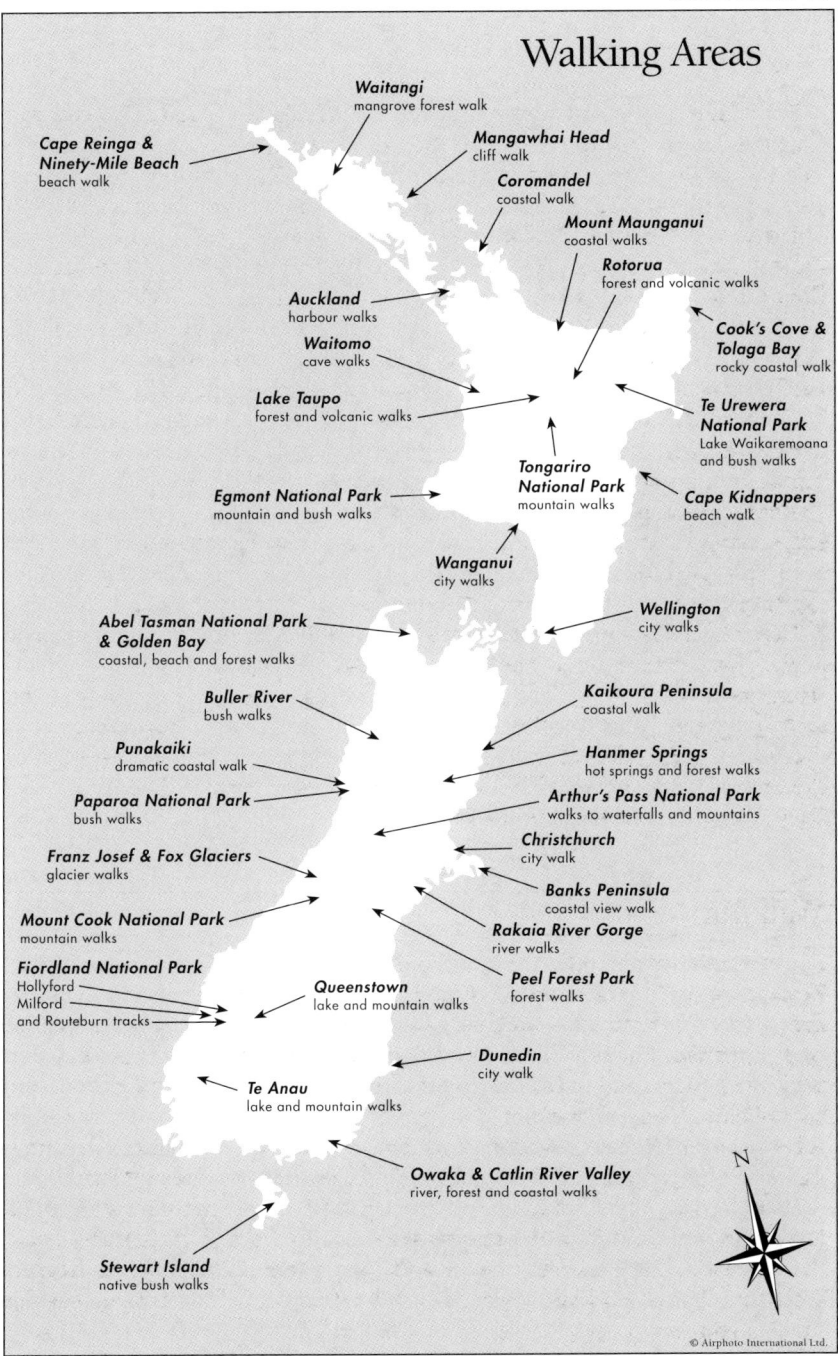

School-zone sign along Highway 1

Walkways in New Zealand have four classifications: a *path* is a well-formed track suitable for the average family; a *walking track* is a well-defined trail, suitable for people of good average physical fitness (New Zealand's standard of average is higher than in most countries); a *tramping track* is a lightly marked trail, usually through wilderness and often with steep grades; and a *route* is lightly cut and often unmarked, has steep grades, and is to be used only by well-equipped and experenced trampers.

This guide concentrates on some of the many wonderful walks throughout New Zealand that require no special equipment other than a pair of stout shoes and a light day-pack. They may vary in length from one or two hours to a full day's excursion, but in all cases the walker can get back to a hot shower, a good meal and a bed by the end of the day. The walks described here collectively offer a wide variety of scenery: mountains, rivers, forests, coastline, lakes, cityscapes, beaches, volcanoes, caves and, best of all, the 'bush', which is the misleadingly dull name for New Zealand's ancient, magnificently towering and fern-filled indigenous forest. Many fine walks are beyond the scope of this guide, but information on them is easy to find.

Boots that cover the ankles are best, not only for ankle support but also for protection against sandflies. New Zealand's weather is capricious, so be prepared for anything; be sure to include a warm pullover, a windbreaker and a light, waterproof covering in your day-pack. Insect repellent (available in New Zealand) is another necessity most of the year.

Fly-fishing

New Zealand is an angler's mecca. Its lakes and rivers teem with trout and salmon, and its beaches are ideal for surf-casters. The North Island's east coast is known worldwide for game fishing. This guide focuses mainly on trout fishing with artificial dry or wet flies in lakes and streams. Trout fishing in New Zealand is entirely for sport. The country has no commercial trout hatcheries, so you never see trout on a menu. You must catch your own, though you may find a restaurant that will cook your catch for you.

Trout were introduced to New Zealand by immigrants from Britain when they found only native eel in the rivers. Brown trout eggs were brought from Australia in 1867, obtained from fish that had been sent there from England. Rainbow trout eggs reached Auckland from the Russian River hatchery in California in 1883. The eggs were rushed to Lake Taupo, where abundant food allowed the fish to grow to sporting size within three years. Lake Taupo and its tributaries have remained a productive fishing spot ever since.

Lake Taupo is generally regarded as one of the world's great trout-fishing lakes. Few anglers leave disappointed.

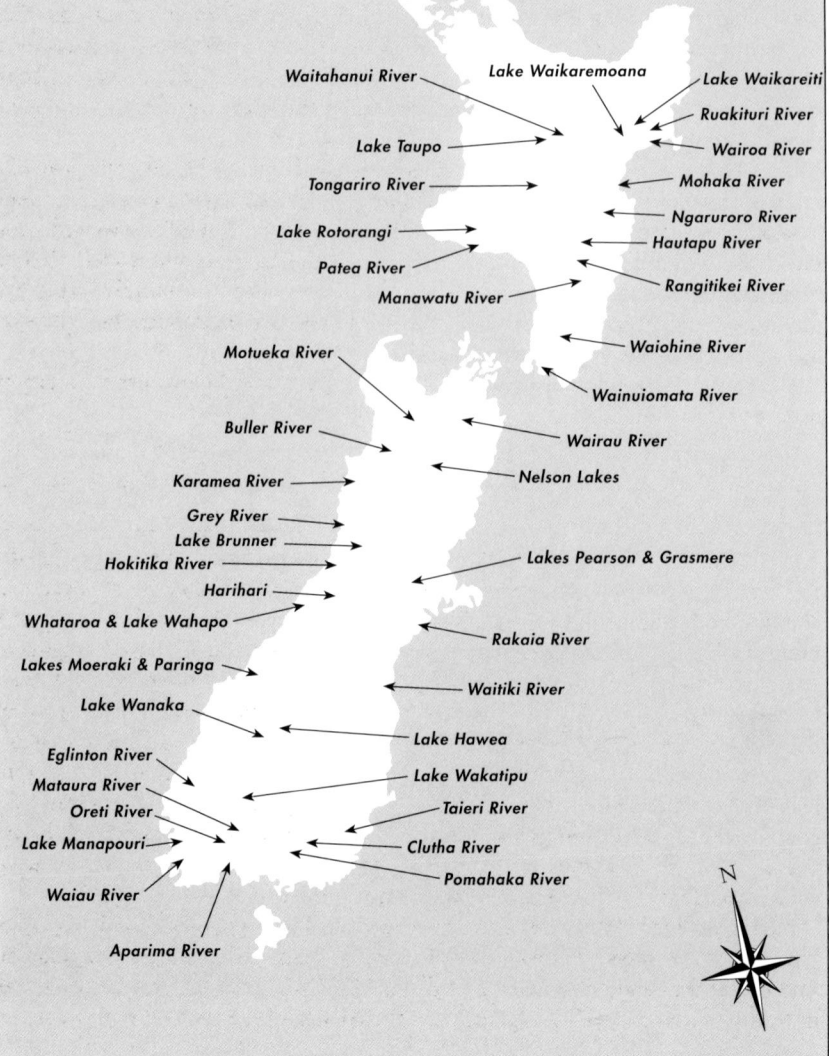

After the introduction of rainbow trout, brown trout were scorned as trash fish. After World War I, efforts to eliminate the browns included shooting them. Mercifully, the fish survived, and today the brown trout is recognized as a top sport fish and an excellent meal.

All anglers must obtain a Fish and Game Licence before fishing. You can buy a licence for the day, week, winter or full season at most sports shops throughout the country. With one exception, just one licence is needed for all 12 regions. The exception is Lake Taupo and the rivers flowing into it; in this area you must get a separate licence from a sports shop or lodging. The fishing season varies from region to region, and also within each region. Many lakes and streams are open year-round, but check first.

If you take a guide, such gear as waders, rods, reels, line, tackle and rain gear will most likely be provided. Rental equipment tends to be expensive and may have had a hard life, so it's best to bring your own rod and tackle. A medium-weight two-piece rod measuring 2.5 to three metres (eight to ten feet) is recommended. Do not bring flies made with chicken feathers, as the import of these is strictly forbidden to protect against the introduction of poultry disease. Use the services of a guide to learn the nuances of local lakes and stream.

If you must cross private property to reach a river, ask the owner's permission to fish off his land.

Golfing

An abundance of uncrowded, well-manicured golf courses set in stunningly beautiful scenery make New Zealand a golfer's paradise. The country boasts over 400 courses, both public and private. That's one for every 9,000 people, the highest number of golf courses per capita in the world. Villages usually have a nine-hole course nearby, with wire strung around the greens to keep out sheep. Mid-sized towns have their own 18-hole courses, and all major cities have at least three of these. The whole country is dotted with interesting courses, some of them real gems, some renowned worldwide. (The map overleaf cites only some of the more exceptional and famous.) You can stop almost anywhere and be assured of a good, friendly game. And you won't have to wait, making three and a half hours the average time for playing 18 holes. Many people take advantage of long summer twilights to enjoy a full round after dinner.

New Zealanders draw a distinction between a golf course and golf links. A links-type course is always situated beside the sea, on sandy soil, taking as its model St Andrews in Scotland, the paradigm of all golf links. Whatever their type, the courses in New Zealand are well designed, well turfed and well endowed with trees.

Bay of Islands Swordfish Club

Golf clubs welcome visitors. Members of overseas clubs are usually accorded guest privileges at private clubs (300 of which are registered in New Zealand), so bring a letter of introduction or handicap card from your home club secretary. Be warned that a green-fee player may have difficulty slipping in on a Saturday or run into ladies' day on a Tuesday or Wednesday morning. Once you are in, the style is friendly and casual. If you need partners, simply go to the pro shop and introduce yourself as a visitor. The pro will gladly set up a game for you. If you stop for a game and find the clubhouse locked, just sign the visitors' book, take a golf card, and put your money through the slit in the box provided. The green fee will be posted. Private-club fees are much cheaper than in the US; public courses are about the same. Golf carts are generally not used, as New Zealanders play for exercise. As one pro said, 'We want our visitors to be happy, but the Americans do long for carts, and the Japanese do long for caddies!' All golf courses supply two-wheeled, hand-pulled trundlers for hire at very cheap rates. Some trundlers have fold-down seats on which you can rest.

Nearly all pro shops can rent you golf clubs in a carrying frame and will let you keep them for a couple of weeks if you leave a deposit. However, many visitors prefer to bring their own clubs and feel it is easier to use a light golf bag than either a frame or trundler. Be sure to bring an ample supply of balls, as good-quality ones are expensive. Bring a few extras as gifts!

Wine-tasting

The size and quality of New Zealand's fast-growing wine industry comes as a surprise to many people. Over 360 commercial wineries (mostly family businesses but also a few big international companies) produce 90 per cent of the wine consumed here and export to more than 30 countries. Around 60 million litres of wine are produced annually, with 20 million litres exported. Though still small in the world market, New Zealand wines attract serious interest from wine writers and from the trade in general.

New Zealand's vineyards actually lie nearer to the equator than those of Bordeaux, France, and the variations of climate here closely resemble those of the major wine-producing areas of Europe. New Zealand is ideal for slow-ripening grapes, and its wines complement, rather than compete with, wines made from the fast-ripening grapes grown in Australia and California. Meanwhile, the country's wide range of latitude means that the North Island can produce wines similar to those of France, while the South Island produces types more typical of Germany and Alsace. Unhampered by tradition, New Zealand vineyards have experimented with many types of vine in the past 25 years, selecting those most suitable to the various soils.

Wine-producing Regions

Waiheke Island
seven small wineries producing world-renowned red wines

Auckland-Kumeu River-Waimauku-Henderson-Mangere
several well-known, family-owned wineries noted for red wines; half of New Zealand's commercial wineries found here

Katikati
Morton Estate, making quality white wines and champagne

Te Kauwhata
two wineries, Botrytised dessert wines a specialty

Gisborne-Matawhero
New Zealand's largest grape-growing district, where many big wineries grow for bottling in Auckland; two interesting independent boutique wineries at Matawhero

Hawkes Bay (Napier-Hastings-Havelock North)
great, long-established wine region, with several renowned wineries making red and white wines

Martinborough
thirty small wineries aiming to produce top-quality French style wines

Nelson (Upper Moutere)
Seifried estate and two small wineries

Marlborough (Blenheim-Renwick)
important wine region since mid-1970s; Montana plus 40 smaller wineries; best known for white wines

Canterbury (Christchurch-Amberley-Waipara-Burnham-Lincoln-Banks Peninsula)
established about 1980 and growing quickly; St. Helena, Geisen and smaller wineries; best known for German-style white wines, but also produces some red

Otago (Queenstown-Arrowtown-Central Wanaka-Alexandra)
New Zealand's newest wine-producing area, with very promising white wines; Alexandra boasts "Southernmost winery in the world"

© Airphoto International Ltd.

The rolling green landscape of the Waipoua District, Northland

James Busby, a Scot, produced New Zealand's first recorded wine around 1835 in Northland. Wine making spread with the farmer-colonists, but was almost halted towards the end of the last century by the vigorous assaults of temperance groups. Luckily, immigrants from Yugoslavia turned to wine making in the Henderson Valley, near Auckland, around 1912, when earnings from the kauri gumfields dried up. Soon after, several wineries around Hawkes Bay on the east coast also began to flourish. Up until the 1960s, New Zealand wines were mostly sweet or fortified, thus suiting only local tastes. But post-war affluence, overseas travel and a new sophistication brought a demand for drier and better wines. In the 1970s, Australian investment in some family companies hastened the transition from American hybrid vines to European varieties. Much experimentation followed, and the recognition the country's wines received at wine competitions was encouraging. New wine areas in the South Island opened up and an important new industry was launched.

New Zealand's elegant white wines, especially Sauvignon Blanc, have been strong international contenders. Prize-winning red wines now come from the Kumeu River region, near Auckland, and from Hawkes Bay. Late entry into competitive wine production has allowed New Zealand's vintners to combine advanced technology with traditional art, as vintners trained the world over start to make their mark here. Wine tasters are warmly welcomed at the cellars of most wineries. Many wineries also have restaurants and some provide accommodation.

Facts for the Traveller

Getting to New Zealand

By Air
Unless you have a great deal of time and money, flying is the only practical way of getting to New Zealand. More than 20 international airlines fly to New Zealand from all parts of the world. Air New Zealand is the national carrier, with flights from Los Angeles, Vancouver, and most Australian capitals. This airline's transpacific flights are routed through many exotic islands—often a free stopover is permitted in such places as Tahiti, Fiji, Tonga or the Cook Islands. Website <www.airnewzealand.com>. Many major European and Asian airlines fly to Auckland; many have code-share agreements that combine their services with Air New Zealand or the Australian carrier Qantas. Round-the-world and Circle-Pacific fares also take advantage of different airlines combining services to make travel to far-flung places like New Zealand less expensive. Combining travel to Australia and New Zealand with one airfare is a good option; the airfare from Europe or North America to either of these countries is similar, so if you're flying down under from, say, London, a ticket to Auckland can easily be made out to include a stop in Sydney. Purchase a return ticket from North America to Sydney with Air New Zealand and you'll get a stopover in Auckland.

New Zealand's major international airport is in Auckland, near the country's northern tip. An increasing number of carriers are also extending their service to Christchurch, on the South Island. At present, direct flights to Wellington, the capital, are possible only from Australia. Between June and September, direct flights are available between Australia and Queenstown. New Zealand's international departure tax is NZ$25, depending on the airport of departure.

By Sea
During the Northern Hemisphere's winter, several cruise lines from England, North America and Hawaii offer voyages to New Zealand (where it is then summer). Amongst these are Norwegian Cruise Line, Carnival Cruise Lines, P&O Cruises, Cunard Line and Princess Cruises.

When to Go
Spring and autumn are the best times to visit New Zealand. (Remember that the seasons are reversed in the Southern Hemisphere; spring is September through November, and autumn is March through May.) The busiest time to visit is from late December until the end of January. This is the high holiday season, when it

seems that every family in New Zealand takes a trip. Roads and trains are jammed, hotels and motels are booked up, and all tourist facilities are crowded. Other times to avoid, if possible, are the two-week school holidays in early April, early July and late September.

Entry Requirements

Australian citizens entering New Zealand need only a valid passport and can stay as long as they desire. Visitors entering New Zealand from all other countries must show a return or onward ticket, evidence of sufficient funds (the equivalent of at least NZ$1,000 per month), and a passport valid for three months beyond the expected time of departure. If these criteria are met, visitors from Great Britain are granted an entry permit valid for six months; those from the US, Canada, the European Community, Scandinavia and Japan, amongst others, receive an entry permit valid for three months. Permits can be extended through the New Zealand Immigration Service if the above criteria continue to be met. Visitors from all other countries must obtain a visa from a New Zealand embassy before arrival. For more information visit the website <www.immigration.govt.nz>.

Customs

There are no restrictions on taking currency into or out of New Zealand. No customs duty is charged on personal effects and reasonable amounts of photographic equipment. Each traveller aged 18 and over can bring in six bottles of wine or beer, 1,125 millilitres (one quart) of liquor (spirits) and either 250 cigarettes, 250 grammes of tobacco or 50 cigars. Golf clubs and fishing rods are permitted, but the import of fishing lures or flies containing chicken feathers is strictly prohibited to protect the poultry industry from imported diseases. (Well-made local flies and lures are available at sports shops in all the fishing areas.) Also forbidden is the importation of any kind of food except sweets, biscuits, tea and coffee. Carefully read the Customs Declaration Card handed out before arrival—items such as hiking boots and tents must be declared for inspection. For more information visit the New Zealand Customs Service website <www.customs.govt.nz>

Money

New Zealand uses banknotes in denominations of 5, 10, 20, 50 and 100 dollars and coins worth 5, 10, 20 and 50 cents and NZ$1 and NZ$2. Travellers' cheques in US dollars and other major currencies can be changed at banks everywhere in New Zealand from Monday to Friday, 9.30 am–4.30 pm. Hotels, restaurants and big shops also change travellers' cheques in major currencies, but at a slightly lower rate. International airports have facilities for changing currency either coming or going. Credit cards are accepted almost everywhere; Visa, Mastercard and American Express are the most common.

Exchange rates vary according to international monetary conditions. In late 2005 NZ$1 was worth around US$0.70 or £0.38.

Tipping has never been an expected practice in New Zealand, but it is now becoming more common in restaurants when the service is good; around ten per cent of the bill is standard.

Health

New Zealand is a very healthy country. You do not need to obtain a vaccination certificate or any shots before you come, and tap water is safe to drink everywhere. Hospitals and doctors are of a high standard and reasonably priced. Dial 111 for an ambulance in cities. Emergency phone numbers are listed in all public phone booths and in the front pages of telephone directories.

Climate and Clothing

The weather in New Zealand is never extreme, though it is often wet and unpredictable. The North Island is the warmer of the two main islands. Auckland's average daily maximum temperature is 24°C (75°F) in midsummer (January) and 15°C (59°F) in midwinter (July). Wellington is about 3°C (5°F) cooler.

The South Island has a variety of climates. The north is sunnier, less windy and a little warmer than Wellington. East of the Southern Alps, on the relatively dry, warm side, Christchurch has an average daily maximum temperature of 22°C (72°F) in midsummer and 12°C (54°F) in midwinter. The mountainous west coast is at least 3°C (5°F) cooler and gets abundant rain (up to 7,500 millimetres annually). The Southern Alps are permanently snowcapped. Queenstown has warm summers, with average highs of 22°C (72°F), and cold winters, with average highs of 8°C (46°F). Dunedin and Invercargill, in the far south, have an average high of around 19°C (68°F) in summer and 9°C (48°F) in winter, with occasional snow to sea level.

Stewart Island is surprisingly mild, and unsurprisingly rainy. For weather conditions across the country check Metservice, website <www.metservice.co.nz>.

While travelling around the country you'll encounter all kinds of weather. The best precaution is to wear light- or medium-weight layers (shirt, sweater, jacket or cardigan, windbreaker) that can be taken off or added as required. Bring a bathing suit, good walking shoes, a rainproof outer covering and sunglasses. New Zealand dress style is casual and comfortable. Shorts are acceptable for both men and women. Men need a jacket and tie and women a dress only for the most upmarket city restaurants or for attending the theatre. Shoppers note: Clothes are expensive in New Zealand.

Electricity

New Zealand current is AC 240 volts, 50 cycles. Most hotels and motels provide AC 110-volt, 20-watt sockets for electric razors only. For other appliances, such as hair dryers or travelling irons, bring a transformer. Power sockets accept only three-pin, flat plugs; for appliances made outside New Zealand you will need an adaptor.

New Zealand's Land Mammals

During New Zealand's long isolation from the rest of the world—about 20 million years—only two species of mammal existed here. In a land of birds, those mammals were, naturally, both bats. The first land mammals deliberately introduced to New Zealand were dogs, brought from East Polynesia by Maori settlers in their canoes. The canoes also held stowaway rats, who were more than happy to colonize the islands. When Captain Cook came, centuries later, he expected to restock his ship's supplies with meat and was surprised to find no large animals at all. He corrected this deficiency on his next voyage by putting pigs ashore to be bred by his Maori friends.

European immigrants who followed brought pigs, goats, horses, cattle and sheep, along with the inevitable mice, rats, cats and dogs. Most of the animals stayed confined to human settlements, but the mice, rats and pigs went wild and multiplied unchecked in the forests. As New Zealand filled with settlers, many mammal species were brought in for food. Others, like deer and rabbit, were imported to provide sport. The Australian possum was imported for its fur. All told, English and Scottish settlers introduced over 50 mammal species to New Zealand. Of these, about 30 became established in the wild. Their numbers increased exponentially and many, like the possum and rabbit, became pests. Weasels and ferrets brought in to control rampaging rabbits found native birds tastier.

After around 1900, the government clamped down on the introduction of new species. Today Fish and Game New Zealand and regional 'acclimatization societies' administer management of the country's mammal populations.

Communications

Post
New Zealand Post is fast and efficient. Domestic mail sent by standard service takes two days for delivery. Fast Post, which offers overnight delivery anywhere in the country, is only slightly more expensive. Mail to Australia takes four to eight days for delivery, while mail to North America, Europe and the rest of the world takes a maximum of 12 days.

On the road to Cape Reinga

Telephone

The public call boxes are efficient, and you'll find phone card, credit card and coin-operated phones on main streets and outside most NZ Post Shops. Phone cards are available at these shops and at some other retail stores, such as dairies. All of New Zealand is on a direct-dial system, and the numbers given in this book all have the internal toll-call prefixes for direct dialling noted in parenthesis—for example, (09) for Auckland, (04) for Wellington and (03) for the South Island. If you are already in the area whose code is thus represented, the prefix must still be dialled. Credit cards can be used to make toll calls from public call boxes. For domestic toll calls, dial 010 and tell the operator your credit card number. For international calls, dial 0170 and give the operator your card number.

Fax and E-mail

Most hotels offer facsimile (fax) services. Connect to the Internet at cybercafes throughout the country and at business-equipped hotels in major cities. To send and receive e-mail on the road, open an account with Hotmail or Yahoo.

Getting Around

By Air

Air New Zealand offers regular flights connecting the major hubs of Auckland, Wellington and Christchurch to all major towns, phone (0800)737-000. A few smaller domestic airlines, such as Soundsair—which flies between Wellington and Picton, saving a sometimes-rough ferry crossing—fill in the gaps, reaching almost every corner of the country. Most airports have charter planes or helicopters available for flight seeing.

By Train

Tranz Scenic runs a daytime service (daily) and an overnight service (Sunday through Friday) between Auckland and Wellington, with stops at major towns in between. On the South Island, the Tranz Coastal, runs between Picton—terminal of the interisland ferries—and Christchurch. The Tranzalpine crosses the Southern Alps daily to connect Christchurch with Greymouth on the west coast. This trip is considered the most scenic in New Zealand. For Tranz Scenic information and reservations phone (04)498-3303 or (0800)802-802, website <www.tranzscenic.co.nz>.

By Ferry

Interislander ferry services cross Cook Strait, connecting the north and south islands. The Lynx is a faster service along this same route. Reservations for both should be made well in advance. Phone (04)498-3302 or (0800)802-802, website <www.interislander.co.nz>. All ferries are modern and have multiple sailings in each direction. A passengers-only ferry links Stewart Island to Bluff, near Invercargill.

By Bus

An excellent network of bus routes covers all of New Zealand. A few major companies operate throughout the country, and many more smaller bus lines serve out of the way places such as national parks and hiking trailheads. Tickets are sold at local information centres, which also often serve as pick-up and drop-off points.

Intercity is the largest long-distance motorcoach company, listing over 1,000 scheduled stops. Comfortable Intercity buses run throughout both islands, often departing from railway stations. Intercity Coach Passes and Flexi Passes are an excellent way to save money. They are valid for three months along a variety of popular routes and can be bought from any information centre or travel agent. These passes also include train and ferry travel. Phone (09)623-1503, website <www.intercitycoach.co.nz>. The next largest network is provided by Newmans, which offers routes over most of the North Island and along the east coast of the South Island. Phone (09)623-6200, website <www.newmanscoach.co.nz>.

In recent years many smaller outfits, known as shuttle buses, have begun competing with the major bus lines. Their service is usually limited to local routes between smaller towns. Local information centres have all the details. Bus drivers on local routes, and those on many long-distance routes as well, like to play tour guide, historian and comedian rolled into one. They'll usually keep up an entertaining and instructive running commentary on the passing scene.

By the time the first Europeans arrived, the moa, a giant ostrich-like bird that ranged across New Zealand, was extinct. Using Maori descriptions and drawings as well as skeletal remains, early artists were able to re-create the moa on paper. This illustration appeared in Walter Rothschild's 1907 book, Extinct Birds.

Local colour in Murchison Township

A number of companies cater primarily to the budget traveller. Magic Travellers Network operates an excellent service, with routes throughout both islands and door-to-door drop-off service at your accommodation. The buses are modern and comfortable and the costs minimal compared to other companies. Phone (09)358-5600, website <www.magicbus.co.nz>. Kiwi Experience offers a similar schedule and a fun-loving style that attracts primarily young travellers. Phone (09)366-9830, website <www.kiwiexperience.com>. Flying Kiwi Wilderness Expeditions is similar to America's Green Tortoise. Phone (03)547-0171, website <www.flyingkiwi.com>.

CAR OR CAMPER RENTAL

As attractive as public transport may be, a rental car or camper is still the best way to see New Zealand. Prices vary considerably with the season; outside the busy summer months of December to February discounts of up to 50 per cent are offered.

Hertz, Avis and Budget have offices in all major towns and tourist spots. These companies charge slightly higher rates in New Zealand than in their North American offices, but they're convenient if you are touring through several regions and want to drop off your car at a distant destination. Rental cars cannot be transported between the islands, but you can arrange for a new one to be waiting for you at the ferry landing. Local car rentals are often cheaper, and you'll have plenty of choice—Auckland alone has over 50 car rental companies. One reliable choice for longer-term rentals is Scotties Rentals, with cars available in Auckland and Christchurch. Phone (09)630-2625 or (0800)736-825, website <www.scotties.co.nz>.

Many companies rent campers with sleeping and limited cooking and bathroom facilities. These vehicles come in various sizes and models accommodating up to eight people (generally, an eight-berth camper is best suited to six people). They can be rented in Auckland, Wellington and Christchurch and some smaller centres. Try Maui Rentals, which offers hundreds of campers of all configurations. The company's main depot is adjacent to Auckland Airport. Phone (09)275-3013 or (0800)651-080, website <www.maui-rentals.com>. Privately owned campgrounds (known in New Zealand as motor camps) are plentiful throughout the country. Almost all have laundry facilities, central toilets and showers, and communal kitchens and dining rooms. Some even have swimming pools and TV.

In the big cities, the Visitor Information Network and the New Zealand Automobile Association (AA) both have full information on car and camper rentals and can help with the arrangements.

A 1930 Buick on display at St. Arnaud

Driving

Traffic keeps to the left, and all cars have right-hand drive. Roads are well surfaced and signposted, with distances given in kilometres (one kilometre = 0.621 miles). Four-lane highways are found only near big cities. Speed limits are generally 50 kilometres per hour in urban areas, 100 kilometres per hour in rural areas. One road rule unique to New Zealand, and very important for visiting drivers to know, is 'Give way to the right'. This rule means that if you want to turn left, any oncoming vehicle turning into that same street (i.e. across your lane) has the right of way.

Petrol is about NZ$1.20 per litre (or about NZ$5 per US gallon). Current driver's licences from the US, Canada, Britain and Australia are valid, as is the international driver's licence.

The AA has offices in every large town. Membership in an affiliated AA overseas entitles the visitor to free maps, comprehensive accommodation guides and tourist information, website <www.aa.co.nz>.

Maps

The AA produces a series of road maps of New Zealand (eight to each island) that are free to its members, or members of affiliated clubs. They are titled by district, which can be confusing to a non-New Zealander.

The AA also produces a variety of route planners and sells a road atlas. Shell and Mobil road maps of New Zealand, available at the respective petrol stations, show distances and driving times. Both are coherent and useful for planning ahead. Another good source of maps is Terralink, website <www.terralink.co.nz>.

Information

Tourist information is abundant and easy to find. The government-run Tourism New Zealand maintains information offices in major cities in the US, Britain, Australia, Canada, Japan, Germany, Hong Kong and Singapore, website <www.newzealand.com>. Within New Zealand, it operates over 80 i-Site visitor information centres (marked with the international "i" sign). These offices supply advice, brochures, maps, timetables, and just about any information you would want about the locality. They also can make bookings for accommodation and onward travel. New Zealand Tourism Online website is <www.tourism.net.nz>.

Most cities and towns, national parks and forest parks have helpful, educational field centres run by the Department of Conservation (DOC), website <www.doc.govt.nz>.

Accommodation

New Zealand is well supplied with hotels, motels, bed and breakfasts, farmstays, lodges, motor camps, campgrounds and backpacker accommodation—ranging from high luxury to unadorned simplicity. A selection of top-end places is listed in this guide (pages 273–284). Many other guides are available to steer you to the type of accommodation you want. The New Zealand Accommodation Guide is the most complete, listing premises inspected by the Automobile Association. Towns are listed alphabetically, accommodation is classified by type, and each listing is supplemented with information supplied by the advertiser. Some listings have photographs. These guides are available at all AA offices; preview their content on the Internet at <www.nz-accommodation.co.nz>. Also available are guides published by Jason's New Zealand, with different editions for motels and motor lodges; bed and breakfasts; campgrounds, holiday parks and backpackers; and for business travelers. These can be useful, but the entries are not rated; some are given in bold type with extensive detail, while others are listed simply by address and phone number in small type. The information in these booklets is online at website <www.jasons.co.nz> Another source of information is Accommodata, an online reservations system, website <www.accommodata.co.nz>.

It is wise to book arrival accommodation from abroad, but from then on independent travellers can do their own planning on the spot. All accommodation can be arranged ahead by phone, and two or three days' notice is sufficient during most of the year. However, during the peak holiday season from mid-December to the end of January, you need to book well in advance, especially for favourite fishing lodges, golf resorts and tourist spots like the Bay of Islands, Rotorua, Mount Cook, Tongariro National Park, Fox Glacier, Franz Josef Glacier and Queenstown.

Hotels and motels in New Zealand run the entire price spectrum. 'Hotels' are licensed establishments, i.e., lodgings permitted to sell liquor in an adjoining pub or restaurant. 'Motels' are unlicensed establishments.

Hotels

Traditionally, the government-owned Tourist Hotel Corporation (THC) provided the top luxury-resort accommodation, especially in areas of special interest and beauty like Mount Cook, Rotorua or Tongariro National Park. But as part of the New Zealand government's thorough, ongoing privatization, the THC lodgings have been sold. Chains such as Flag, International, Mainstay, Quality, Regent, Rydges, Scenic Circle and Sheraton operate in large centres and tourist resorts. Top-end independent hotels are usually clean, comfortable and appealingly smaller and more old-fashioned than the chains. Confusingly, hotels can also be 'pubs', with rooms available above the bar; these rooms are generally basic, and bathroom facilities are often shared. On a positive note, pub rooms are usually inexpensive (from NZ$25 per person) and centrally located. Hotel rooms don't usually have cooking facilities, but most hotels have a restaurant.

A North Island Bike Clubs rally in Cambridge

Motels

New Zealand motels are different from their counterparts in other countries and offer exceptional value. They are nearly all self-catering, i.e., their rooms are complete little apartments, each with a fully equipped kitchen, usually a separate sleeping area, a bathroom with shower, a telephone and television, and laundry facilities nearby. Bella Vista, Best Western, Budget, Flag Choice and Golden Chain motel chains operate throughout the country. Motor lodges and motor inns are like regular motels but their rooms don't have kitchens; usually breakfast is available. Expect to pay from NZ$60 for a motel room in a small town or on the outskirts of a city.

Bed and Breakfast

The European tradition of staying in a bed and breakfasts is now the preferred option for many travellers the world over. The industry has boomed in the last two decades, and New Zealand is no exception. Even mid-sized towns such as Nelson, on the South Island, have over 50 such establishments. Bed and breakfast guesthouses are usually comfortable and reasonably priced, and they're fine places to meet New Zealanders. All are private houses, some built specifically for taking in paying guests, others offering those rooms down the hall that became vacant when the children left home. Some have rooms with private bathrooms, but most have shared showers and toilets. The breakfasts can be sumptuous, and many establishments also provide dinner on request. In most towns, bed and breakfasts can be found for under NZ$50 single, NZ$70 double. The most luxurious places charge over NZ$200 for a double.

Many bed and breakfast places have formed associations. Heritage and Character Inns of New Zealand, for example, is an association whose member inns are all of historic merit, website <www.heritageinns.co.nz>. A great way to plan ahead is with *The New Zealand Bed & Breakfast Book*, compiled by J and J Thomas (Wellington: Moonshine Press), an annual publication describing each house, its owner and its facilities, website <www.bnb.co.nz>. Information centres can often tell you about local availability and make arrangements for you.

FARMSTAYS

Many farm families take guests, either in their home or in separate quarters. Farmstays are similar to bed and breakfasts in that visitors are treated like family members. The main difference is the location. Visitors are given the opportunity to observe a working farm, taking part if they want to or just resting in the country. A stay can range from one night with breakfast to weeks with full board. A number of organizations arrange these visits. Details are available at information centres in New Zealand or through Tourism New Zealand, <www.newzealand.com>. The *New Zealand Bed & Breakfast Book* also lists farmstays.

LODGES

Privately run lodges catering to sportsmen are found in scenic or wilderness settings around the country. Fishing lodges, for example, offer a spectrum of accommodation from simple to luxury, as well as experienced guides (at extra cost) and special facilities for smoking or canning fish. Prices are generally quoted per person and include all meals.

Service is always personal and friendly at the local general store, known in New Zealand as a dairy.

Motor Camps and Camping Grounds

New Zealand's commercial camp ground, known as motor camps, are of the highest standard. Most feature a communal kitchen, barbecues, a laundry and a television-equipped lounge area. In addition to camp sites for tents and campers, most offer a wide variety of other accommodation, such as cabins, on-site caravans (trailers), and tourist (self-contained) flats. Sheets and bedding can be rented if they are not provided. Camp sites are charged on a per person basis—NZ$8–14 is normal. Cabins range from NZ$40–75 while tourist flats start at around NZ$65.

The Department of Conservation oversees camping grounds throughout New Zealand, in national parks, forest parks, and reserves. Facilities are more basic than in commercial motor camps, but fees are reasonable, ranging from free to NZ$10 per person per night. Local DOC offices have all the details.

Backpacker Accommodation

The proliferation of accommodation specifically for budget travellers has made New Zealand affordable for everyone. Traditionally, 'hostels' were operated by the Youth Hostel Association (YHA), now known as Hostelling International. But these are far outnumbered today by independently owned and run hostels, known simply as 'backpackers'. These low-cost lodgings have fully equipped kitchens, laundry facilities, dining areas and lounge areas. Beds in dormitory-style rooms (each room typically holding between four and ten bunks) cost NZ$10–20 per night. Most places also offer single, double and twin rooms for NZ$5–12 extra.

The YHA New Zealand provides clean, comfortable, very inexpensive accommodation usually in prime locations. Guests are required to purchase membership in the organization for a minimal fee; members are afforded many discounts, including 30 per cent off most bus and all rail travel. The YHA Accommodation Guide gives basic information on hostelling along with descriptions and photographs of every affiliated hostel, website <www.yha.org.nz>.

Backpackers outnumber YHA hostels around ten to one, and they range in standard considerably. Some can be overcrowded, noisy, and unfriendly. On the other hand, many are real gems—a labour of love for the owner and a home away from home for the traveller. For example, Peter's Farm Hostel, outside Ranfurly in Otago, offers pick-ups from town, horseback riding, unlimited use of canoes and golf clubs, panning for gold in a local stream, and thousands of acres of hills to explore—all for NZ$20 a night. Budget Backpacker Hostels New Zealand publishes an excellent guide to over 300 properties, each rated by guests. The 'Blue Book', as it's known, is available at hostels and information centres, and you can view it on the Internet at website <www.bbh.co.nz>.

Food and Drink

New Zealand meals are typically hearty and filling. Restaurants throughout the country serve a variety of cuisines, including refined continental. Prices are comparable to those in Western Europe, but more expensive than in North America. Reasonably priced meals are offered in most pubs. As many visitors travel by camper, and most motel rooms have kitchens, self-catering is another inexpensive option.

New Zealand lamb is famous worldwide and the most commonly found meat in homes and restaurants. It's usually roasted with herbs, and it often appears on menus as hogget, meaning one-year-old lamb, which is as tender as baby lamb but more flavourful. Beef is excellent and not too expensive, but as New Zealanders generally prefer it well done, make a point of specifying your preferred style. Domestic venison, often served as cervena, is a speciality worth trying. It is more tender and less gamey than the wild variety. Chicken and duck are everywhere. For something really different, try muttonbird, a Maori delicacy that appears ready-cooked in fish shops in winter. The bird tastes best smoked.

> '*Gee, the beer's crook today.*'
> '*Yeah, I'll be glad when I've had enough.*'
>
> —overheard in a New Zealand pub

Seafood is superb and plentiful year-round. Crayfish (also called lobsters) abound in spring and summer, and all kinds of shellfish are fresh and delicious. The top specialities are succulent Bluff oysters, available in autumn and winter, and green mussels (the colour describes the shell, not the meat). Amongst the best saltwater fish are blue cod, snapper, John Dory, grouper, orange roughy (a type of perch), tarakihi, hoki and kingfish. Whitebait is a much-prized, tiny, transparent fish usually served fried in batter as whitebait fritters. Salmon appears on menus in New Zealand, but never trout. However, if you catch your own trout, some restaurants will cook it for you.

Vegetables are abundant throughout the year. Meat courses are usually served with at least three or four different vegetables. Roadside stands often sell kumara, a type of sweet potato, and fresh fruit. Familiar fruits include apples, pears, peaches, nectarines, apricots and grapes, but try kiwi fruit, feijoa and nashi pears, which are as delicious as they are different. Formally known as the Chinese gooseberry, the kiwi fruit has been a New Zealand marketing success. New strains were developed especially for local conditions and the fruit is now famous around the world. A favourite dessert is pavlova, a sinful concoction of meringue, sliced fruit and whipped cream. All dairy products are of superior quality, with the ice cream being particularly exceptional; try the 'hokey pokey' (butterscotch) flavour. New Zealand also produces a good variety of cheeses, of the English, French and Swiss types.

Tea shops are a fixture in most towns. New Zealanders habitually stop whatever they are doing for a morning and afternoon tea-and-snack break, or coffee, if they prefer. The quality of fare in rural tea shops varies considerably. Some tea shops are gems, serving hot scones with strawberry jam and cream. Others can be terrible; those used by long-distance motorcoaches, who observe the breaks punctually, should be avoided if possible. Small-town bakeries are a delight. Aside from a great range of cakes and pastries (always filled with real cream), there's the ubiquitous pie. 'Pie' in New Zealand means meat pie, made with tender meat and flaky crusts (the factory-made variety can be dismal).

Make sure you try a **hangi**, a Maori-style feast steam-cooked in an underground oven. Rotorua is the place to find them. Though these have become commercialized, they're still enjoyable. The chefs first dig a large hole in the ground, then place hot stones at the bottom. The food to be cooked is placed atop the stones and covered with wet towels. A typical hangi meal includes kumara, which is a Maori staple, along with many other delicious dishes, both familiar and not, served as a buffet.

Beer is the national drink, and New Zealand's two main brewing giants, Carlton & United and Dominion Breweries (DB), produce all the most popular beers, including Lion Red and Export. Drinkers in the South Island tend to be more faithful to their local brewers; look for Monteiths on the west coast and Speights in the far south. A number of small boutique brewers are found in larger cities. Dunedin produces New Zealand's only whisky, but all other hard liquor is imported. Pubs and bars are open 11 am–10 pm (till 11 pm on Saturday), except on Christmas Day and Good Friday. Guests registered in a licensed hotel can be served drinks at any time. Amongst friends it is customary to 'shout' (buy) a round of drinks (as in, 'I'll shout you a drink'). Licensed restaurants serve alcoholic drinks with meals. Unlicensed restaurants almost always invite you to bring your own wine or beer and often display a BYO (bring your own) sign. New Zealand wines—both whites and reds—are excellent, and special space is devoted to them in this guide.

Food and Drink Terms

Most of the terms below originated in Britain, but the list of translations may be useful to American readers.

afters	dessert
aubergine	eggplant
bangers	sausages
biscuits	crackers or cookies

(left) Cape Reinga, the northern tip of the North Island, is reached by travelling along Ninety-Mile Beach on a guided tour.

capsicum	green pepper
chips	french fries
chook	chicken
cuppa	a cup of hot tea (or coffee)
dairy	neighbourhood store selling dairy products, canned goods, fruit, ice cream and newspapers; open every day, early and late
entree	appetizer course, eaten before the main course
greengrocer	fruit and vegetable shop
junket	a thin dessert resembling yoghurt
Marmite or Vegemite	salty, fortified yeast and vegetable extracts that can be spread on bread and butter at breakfast instead of jam; an acquired taste
milk bar	shop selling dairy products, hot snacks and candy, often combined with a neighbourhood dairy
peckish	hungry
pudding	dessert of any kind, eaten at the end of a meal
supper	a snack before going to bed, not the main evening meal
take-away	take-out; fast-food counters are called take-away bars
tea	can mean a cup of hot tea (any time of day), the customary mid-morning or mid-afternoon coffee break of tea and snacks, or a full-fledged evening meal. If you are invited for tea, find out what your host or hostess means before you go.
tomato sauce	ketchup

Shopping

Outstanding New Zealand wool products are sold all over both islands. Wonderful hand-knitted sweaters, weavings, woollen jackets, sheepskin rugs, coats and car-seat covers are not cheap, but are definitely less expensive than elsewhere (except, perhaps, Hong Kong). Prices are often better off the beaten track than in the main tourist centres. Suede clothing and leather goods are also of very high quality. Greenstone is a bargain; it's cheaper than most other kinds of jade and sometimes beautifully worked in Maori designs (look for it in Hokitika). Maori woodwork, finely carved in traditional motifs, makes an interesting souvenir. Good pottery is much used and appreciated in New Zealand. Fine ceramics are most easily found around Nelson, Wellington and Auckland. Bulky or heavy purchases can be mailed home, and most shops are glad to ship them for you. Information on arts and crafts can be found on the Creative New Zealand website <www.creativenz.govt.nz>.

National Holidays

1 January	New Year's Day
6 February	Waitangi (New Zealand) Day
March/April	Good Friday/Easter Monday
25 April	Anzac Day
First Monday in June	Queen's Birthday
Fourth Monday in October	Labour Day
25 December	Christmas Day
26 December	Boxing Day

Local Holidays

22 January	Wellington
29 January	Auckland and Northland
1 February	Nelson
23 March	Dunedin, Otago and Southland
31 March	Taranaki
17 October	Napier and Hawkes Bay
1 November	Marlborough
1 December	Westland
16 December	Christchurch and Canterbury

Annual Events

January
- Auckland — Auckland Cup horse racing, Annual Yachting Regatta, Heineken Open Tennis Tournament, Karaka Thoroughbred Sales, New Zealand Golf Open
- Wellington — National Dragon Boat Championships

February
- Bay of Islands — Treaty of Waitangi Celebrations
International Billfish Tournament
- Napier — Art Deco Weekend (in the city famous for its 1930s' style)

March
- Auckland — Round the Bays Run (famous for its cast of thousands)
- Hamilton — Ngaruawahia Regatta (with Maori canoes)
- Masterton — Golden Shears Championships

Hokitika	Wildfoods Festival (a celebration of west coast cuisine)
Dunedin	Scottish Week

April
Auckland	Royal Easter Show, Auckland Festival

May
Auckland	Great Northern Hurdles and Steeplechase Meeting
Rotorua	Rotorua Marathon

June
Hamilton	National Agricultural Field Days, the best in farm technology and competitions

July
Wellington	Wellington Hurdles and Steeplechase Meeting
Queenstown	Winter Festival

August
Wanaka	World Heli-Challenge

September
Alexandra	Spring Blossom Festival

October
Wanganui	Three-day 'Life Span' triathalon from Mt Ruapehu to the sea
Rotorua	NZ Trout Festival
Kaikoura	Kaikoura Seafest

November
Christchurch	Showtime, Canterbury (quintessential New Zealand); agricultural shows are mounted at various other towns and cities until February
New Plymouth	Taranaki Rhododendron Festival

(top left) Each offering its own charm, even the smallest of museums is worthy of a stop. (top right) Parliament Buildings and the Beehive, Wellington (bottom) A typical rural New Zealand home—compact, neat and well-maintained

North Island

The 115,000-square-kilometre North Island is shaped like a lopsided, elongated diamond. Auckland, on the island's north side, is New Zealand's biggest, most cosmopolitan city and the point of arrival and departure for most international visitors. The setting of this modern metropolis is stunning. The city centre overlooks a natural harbour, which opens to the calm, island-dotted waters of Hauraki Gulf. The climate north of Auckland is warm and dry; here you'll find forests of ancient kauri, magnificent white-sand beaches in the Bay of Islands, and the remote and sparsely populated Far North.

In the middle of the North Island, a volcanic plateau rises from the Bay of Plenty, between the Coromandel Peninsula and the East Cape, to the still-active volcanoes in Tongariro National Park. At the very centre of the island, surrounded on all sides by thermal activity, is Lake Taupo. The easternmost point of the North Island, the East Cape, is a densely forested, sparsely populated region, but farther south, the coast around Hawkes Bay produces abundant fruit and wine. The main population centres in the east are Gisborne and Napier.

The island's richest farmland, the Waikato Basin, lies immediately south of Auckland and is centred around the city of Hamilton. From this point, the wild west coast extends south to the western point of the diamond, formed around a single snowcapped volcano, Mount Taranaki/Egmont.

On the island's southern end is New Zealand's capital, the harbour city of Wellington. A range of rugged green mountains runs north from Wellington to the East Cape, following the same geological fault that created the South Island's mountainous spine.

Almost three-quarters of New Zealand's 4 million people live on the North Island, a large proportion of them in the Auckland metropolitan region (which comprises the cities of Auckland, North Shore, Manukau and Waitakere). Most of the Maori live on the North Island.

The Maori came into New Zealand at the northern tip and spread southward. So did the Europeans many centuries later, after whalers and timber speculators had founded the first trading settlement at Kororareka (now Russell), in the Bay of Islands. Before long, small colonies of European settlers dotted the coast at Wellington, Wanganui and New Plymouth. The Maori life was irrevocably changed with that influx. In 1840, Maori chiefs, who had little concept of European-style land ownership, signed over New Zealand to the British Crown at Waitangi, near Russell. In 1860, tension over land sales erupted into war; a vicious struggle between Maori tribes and colonial troops tore apart the North Island for four years and continued sporadically for two decades. By the end of the century, Europeans occupied all the farmland and were developing the North Island's now-prosperous agricultural industry.

Some of the North Island's most beautiful natural features are preserved in four national parks: the two volcanic regions of Tongariro and Taranaki, the eastern lakes and virgin forests of Te Urewera, and the historic Whanganui River. Tourists usually begin their North Island travels with a quick trip north to the Bay of Islands. Then they return to Auckland before heading down to Wellington by way of Rotorua's thermal springs, the glow-worm caves of Waitomo, Lake Taupo and the volcanoes of Tongariro National Park. They short-change themselves by doing so, because some of the North Island's most exciting and intriguing attractions lie off the beaten track. If time permits, include in your itinerary Cape Reinga (New Zealand's northernmost point), the perfectly symmetrical volcanic cone of Mount Taranaki/Egmont and the wild Wairarapa coastline.

Auckland

New Zealand's principal metropolis, Auckland spreads over an ancient volcanic field on a neck of land only 1.5 km (one mile) wide at its narrowest. Bustling Queen Street, the financial and commercial heart of the city, bisects Auckland before ending abruptly on the shores of Waitemata Harbour. This sparkling body of water opens to the east into Hauraki Gulf, which is dotted with sailboats and islands. The closest of these islands to the city is Rangitoto, the largest of seven small volcanoes visible from Auckland. The symmetrical cone-shaped volcano last erupted just 400 years ago. North of downtown, across the long, eight-lane Auckland Harbour Bridge, are all of the city's best beaches and the trendy waterfront suburb of Devonport. South of downtown, the sprawl of suburbia is broken by Manukau Harbour, spreading as broad tidal flats west towards the Tasman Sea.

Early settlers did not come to Auckland as a well-organized, closely knit colony as they did to Wellington, Christchurch and Dunedin. In 1840, the city was chosen as the site of the new colony's capital mainly for its twin harbours and rich farmlands. The site belonged to the Ngati Whatua, who had been decimated by marauding Ngapuhi from the north and consequently welcomed European settlement on their semi-deserted isthmus. Officials, shopkeepers and labourers straggled south from Russell. The population grew. Auckland's new inhabitants coveted the rich Maori lands to the south and were soon mired in the merciless Land Wars of 1860–64, which resulted in the confiscations of Maori tribal land. The city remained the capital until 1865, when the government moved to the more central city of Wellington. But

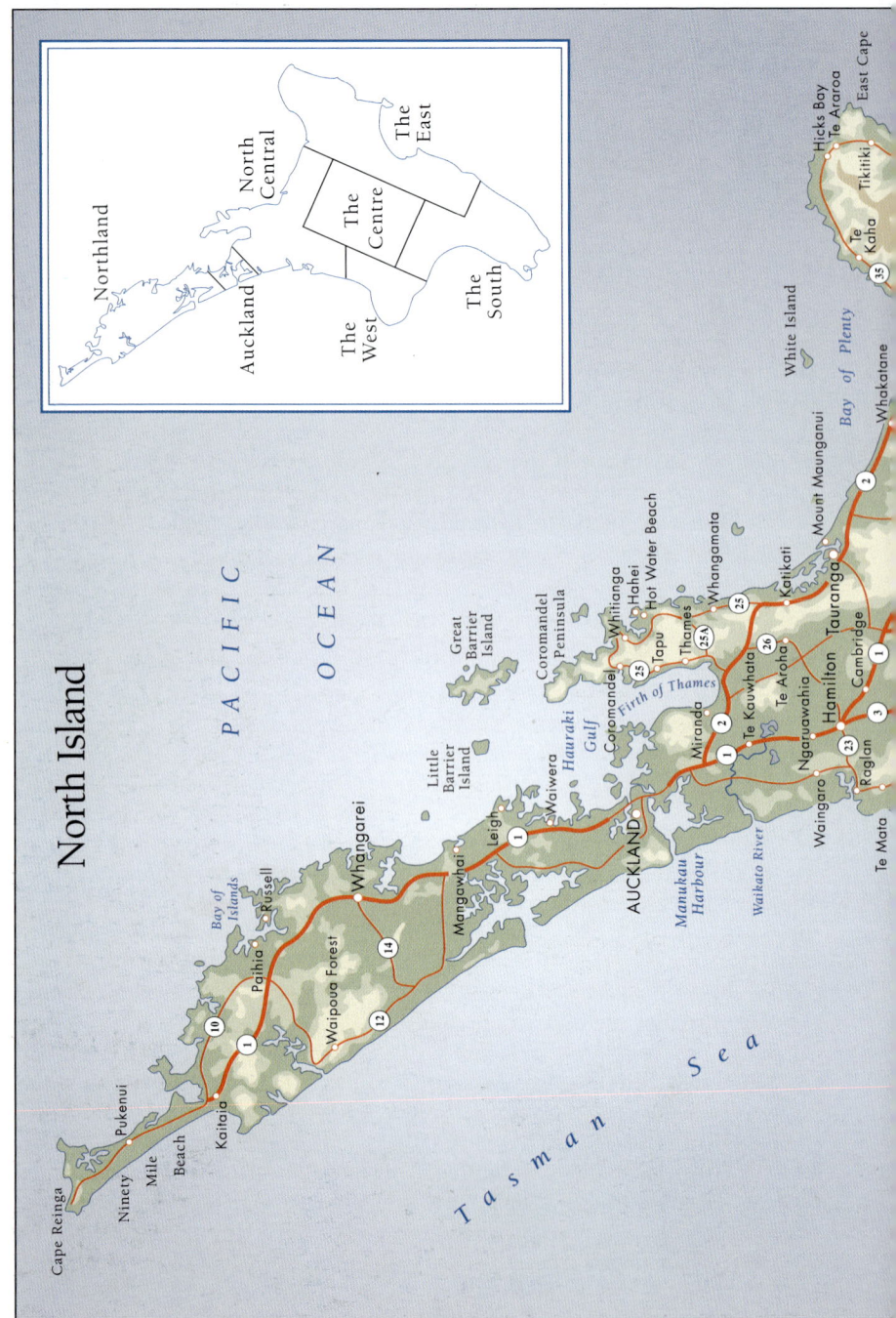

North Island

The growth of Auckland stalled after Wellington was declared the national capital in 1865. But by the turn of the next century, with a goldrush on the nearby Coromandel Peninsula, the city boomed, and many fine buildings, such as the Royal Hotel, were constructed in downtown Auckland.

Auckland kept growing, mainly through commerce developed by the discovery of gold on the nearby Coromandel Peninsula. Today Auckland's population is 1.2 million—almost a third of New Zealand's entire population. The city's promise of opportunity, education and advancement draws people from throughout the rest of the country as well as immigrants from islands all over the Pacific Ocean. Including the indigenous Maori, Pacific peoples now comprise 19 percent of Auckland's population, making it the world's biggest Polynesian city. Migration from Asia is also on the increase, due in part to government incentives offered to skilled migrants.

GETTING THERE

Auckland Airport, New Zealand's international gateway, is 20 kilometres (12 miles) south of the city. The modern international terminal holds a fast and efficient customs and immigration service, an information centre, rental car outlets, currency exchange service, and duty-free shopping. Air New Zealand serves cities throughout the country from an adjacent domestic terminal. The terminals are linked by a shuttle bus. The Super Shuttle offers door-to-door service between terminals and between the airport and all city addresses. Phone (0800)748-885. The Airbus runs between the airport and major downtown hotels every 20 minutes. Phone (09)375-4702.

Some visitors travelling on leisurely schedules and generous budgets arrive on the cruise ships that dock at Prince's Wharf in Waitemata Harbour.

Tranz Scenic provides comfortable trains—the Overlander by day and the Northerner by night—for the 12-hour trip between Auckland and Wellington, with stops at several points in between. Phone (0800)802-802.

Long-distance bus lines Intercity, phone (09)623-1503, and Newmans, phone (09)623-1504, maintain routes all over the North Island, departing from the Sky City Coach Terminal, 102 Hobson Street.

Information and Orientation

Several places in Auckland provide visitors with information, help with travel plans, and make bookings for transportation, tours and accommodation. The **Airport Visitor Centre** at the international terminal is open daily from 5 am until the last flight. Phone (09)275-6467. Downtown, the **Auckland Visitor Centre** in Skycity at the corner of Victoria and Federal Streets is open daily 8 am–5 pm. Phone (09)363 7180. <www.aucklandnz.com>. A smaller information centre operates on Princes Wharf. The **Automobile Association** office is at 99 Albert Street. Phone (09)966-8919. For information on regional parks, local walks and the Gulf Islands visit the **Department of Conservation** office in the Ferry Building on Quay Street. Phone (09)379-6476.

Major national and international car rental companies have offices at the airport and downtown. The Downtown Bus Terminal occupies a full city block immediately east of Queen Elizabeth II Square at the bottom of Queen Street. Routes radiate from the terminal to all suburbs seven days a week. The Explorer Bus operates in a continuous loop from the Ferry Building to 14 major attractions. Phone (0800)439-756. Local rail service is limited to two lines: one running west to Waitakere, the other south to outlying Papakura. Ferries run regularly across Waitemata Harbour to Devonport and out to the populated Gulf Islands. The ferries depart from behind the Ferry Building on Quay Street and are operated by Fullers. Phone (09)367-9111. A helpful telephone information service known as Rideline saves frustration by telling you which bus, train, or ferry to take to your destination and where to board it. Phone (09)366-6400.

Taxis wait in taxi ranks at several corners around downtown and outside major hotels; they also respond to phone calls. The biggest taxi companies are Auckland Taxi Co-op, phone (09)300-3000; CitiCabs, phone (09)379-9199; and Taxi Combined, phone (0800)505-550. Bicycling on the streets of downtown is not recommended, although riding east along waterfront Tamaki Drive is rewarding. Rent bikes from Adventure Cycles on Fort Street. Phone (09)309-5566.

Some Important Events in New Zealand History

c. 800	Possible first settlement by Polynesians after the semi-legendary Kupe had established Aotearoa.
c. 1150	Explorers Chief Toi and his grandson, Whatonga, arrive by canoe from Hawaiki and find inhabitants. One of them may have stayed in New Zealand while the other returned home to tell his people.
c. 1100	Deliberate settlement begins sporadically as the Maori arrive in seagoing canoes. By 1200, Maori settlement is widespread.
1503	French seafarer de Gonneville possibly sights New Zealand's coast.
1521	Portuguese caravel probably stranded off North Island's west coast.
1576	Spanish sea captain Juan Fernandez may have landed.
1642	Dutch explorer Abel Tasman sails up South Island's west coast and anchors in Golden Bay, but is driven away by a hostile Maori tribe. Tasman thinks he has touched Staten Land off the tip of South America.
1769	English explorer James Cook lands at points on North Island's east coast on the first of three voyages. Claims New Zealand for the British Crown.
1790	First European whalers, sealers and kauriwood traders arrive.
1814	First missionaries start converting the Maori.
1838	French captain Jean Langlois provisionally buys land on Banks Peninsula in the hope of establishing a French colony in New Zealand.
1840	Treaty of Waitangi between Queen Victoria and Maori chiefs secures New Zealand for the British Empire, with a guarantee of Maori land rights. Wellington is founded by the New Zealand Company. Auckland is made capital of the new British colony.
1845	First outbreak of fighting as Maori Ngapuhi chief Hone Heke spurns the new British authority at Northland's Russell.
1848	Dunedin is founded as an organized Scottish Presbyterian colony.
1850	Christchurch is founded as an organized Anglican settlement.
1852	First gold strike recorded in Coromandel. The first parliament, with two chambers, is established in Auckland.
1855	Earthquake raises Wellington's coastline.
1860	Land Wars break out in the Taranaki and soon spread to other parts of the North Island. Though the main pitched battles ended in 1865, guerilla bands occasionally raided European settlements for two decades.
1861	Gold rush begins in Otago, on the South Island.
1865	Capital moves from Auckland to Wellington.

1867	Maori given the right to vote. First four Maori members of Parliament are elected.
1870	Economic depression sets in as the gold rush peters out.
1882	First refrigerator ship sails to London in 98 days with cargo of frozen meat. Start of a new economic era for New Zealand.
1893	New Zealand is the first country in the world to give women the vote.
1907	New Zealand, heretofore a colony, becomes a completely self-governing dominion of the British Empire.
1914	New Zealand enters World War I on the Allied side.
1918	End of World War I. New Zealand receives control over mandated territory of Western Samoa.
1919	New Zealand joins the League of Nations.
1931	Earthquake destroys Napier, raises coast and harbour.
1935	Labour Party wins parliamentary majority, introduces the 40-hour work week, and in 13 years of continuous government builds a 'cradle to grave' welfare state.
1939–45	New Zealand fights in World War II on Allied side.
1947	New Zealand becomes an independent, autonomous member of the British Commonwealth of Nations.
1953	New Zealander Sir Edmund Hillary makes the first ascent of Mount Everest.
1973	Britain joins the European Common Market, ending preferential trade with New Zealand. Start of a new, precarious economic era for New Zealand.
1981	Country's biggest-ever civil conflict when the New Zealand Rugby Union invites a still-segregated South African Rugby Team to New Zealand.
1984	Labour Party wins election, initiates legislation to make New Zealand nuclear-free and begins to disassemble the welfare state.
1985	Secret service agents acting on behalf of the French government bomb the Greenpeace ship *Rainbow Warrior* as it sits in Auckland Harbour. The ship sinks and a Greenpeace photographer is killed.
1990	The National Party wins the election in a landslide and continues a programme of privatizing state-owned businesses and dismantling the welfare state. In the following years, the new economic policies become a showpiece for governments around the world.
1995	Mount Ruapehu erupts. New Zealand wins the America's Cup.
1997	Jenny Shipley replaces Tim Bolger as leader of the National Party, and in doing so becomes the country's first female prime minister.
1999	At the end of a decade of political turmoil, the Labour Party, led by Helen Clark, wins the federal election.
2000	New Zealand retained America's Cup (forfeited to Swiss challenger in 2003).
2005	Helen Clark reelected to her third term as Prime Minister
2005	The country continues its starring role in Hollywood, with the releases of 'King Kong' and 'The Chronicles of Narnia: The Lion, the Witch and the Wardrobe', which were both filmed in New Zealand.

Sights

Queen Street, Auckland's main downtown boulevard, runs north–south from the waterfront to suburban Newton along the floor of a natural valley, now transformed into a high-rise canyon. This major commercial artery is lined with big department stores, banks, shopping arcades, cafés, souvenir shops, and the Auckland Visitor Centre. The Downtown Shopping Centre, fronting Queen Elizabeth II Square at Queen Street's bottom end, holds over 70 shops.

Auckland's most distinctive attraction is **Sky Tower** on Victoria Street. Part of the Sky City casino complex, the tower is New Zealand's tallest building, rising 328 metres (1,076 feet) above street level. A glass elevator whisks visitors to the Observation Deck in just 40 seconds. A stunning film, hands-on displays, live weather reports, and glass floor panels combine to make a trip up Sky Tower all the more enjoyable. Phone (09)912-6000.

Down on the waterfront, the **New Zealand National Maritime Museum** catalogues the country's maritime history, from the migration of Polynesians to New Zealand's successful defence of the America's Cup. The Maori war canoe is particularly interesting. The museum is housed in old wharf buildings west of the

This engraving by Sydney Parkinson shows a Maori war canoe. The canoes were carved from a single tree trunk, usually kauri, and extended up to 40 metres (130 feet) in length.

distinctive Ferry Building on Quay Street. Open 9 am–6 pm. Phone (09)373-0800. Some of the historic vessels moored nearby take visitors back in time on harbour cruises. Immediately west of the museum is Viaduct Basin, developed specially for the America's Cup 2000.

On the same side of the city centre, three kilometres (two miles) from Queen Street, is **Victoria Park Market**, a lively, popular marketplace with plenty of bargains on almost anything from fresh fruits and vegetables to books, clothes, pottery and handicrafts. The market is set around a courtyard protected by historic red-brick warehouse buildings. Open daily.

Walk up Queen Street to Wellesley Street, then turn left and walk one block to **Auckland Art Gallery** to one of New Zealand's outstanding art museums. This is the New Gallery, where changing exhibits are featured. Across the road, on the edge of Albert Park, is the Main Gallery, which holds a representative collection of contemporary New Zealand art and a fine collection of international drawings and prints. Open 10 am–5 pm. Phone (09)307-7700.

Auckland Domain (the grandiose word domain simply meaning 'park') is a large green area east of the city centre; get there by walking through the Victorian-style gardens of Albert Park. As well as a fernery, wintergardens, a planetarium and an extensive trail system, the park is home to the fantastic **Auckland Museum**. This museum is the best place in town to gain an introduction to the culture of the Maori and their remarkable art of decorative carving, which records their myths and history. The centrepiece of this section of the museum is a magnificent 25-metre(80-foot)-long war canoe. Other exhibits include a collection of art from neighbouring Pacific islands and displays on New Zealand's natural history—including the reconstructed skeleton of an extinct moa bird. Open 10 am–5 pm. Access by vehicle is from Parnell Road. Phone (09)306-7067.

Auckland's most popular attraction is **Kelly Tarlton's**, developed by one of the world's premier underwater treasure hunters. Six km east of the city centre on Tamaki Drive, it's built under the highway in what were once the city's huge stormwater tanks. The highlight is the Antarctic Encounter. After passing a replica of Scott's 1911 hut, visitors jump aboard a Snow Cat to experience life in the Antarctic by travelling past a penguin colony, an orca whale, and a re-creation of life under the continent's surrounding icecap. The history of Antarctica is also catalogued and a research base of the future rounds off the Antarctica experience. Underwater World is equally intriguing; a moving walkway inside a clear plastic tunnel takes visitors on an eight-minute underwater trip through various marine habitats. Sharks are fed at 2 pm. Open daily 9 am–9 pm. Phone (09)528-0603.

Auckland Zoo, at Western Springs, isn't particularly large but it is pretty, with a stream running through its 18 hectares. Along with lions, tigers and the other animals you'd expect, you'll also see kiwis (in a nocturnal house), rare native birds (in a large walk-in aviary; see *Focus* page 66) and the tuatara—a New Zealand reptile dating back to the dinosaur age and boasting a rudimentary third eye. Open daily 9.30 am–5.30 pm; last admission at 4.15 pm. Phone (09)360-3800.

In the same area, at the edge of Western Springs Reserve, the **Museum of Transportation and Technology** (MOTAT) is an intriguing place to spend half a rainy day. It contains every kind of machine imaginable—from trains and planes to player pianos, computers and a whole fire station, all in perfect working condition. A tramway links MOTAT to the adjacent Sir Keith Park Memorial Site, a replica of a World War II airfield (linked to the rest of MOTAT by tram), complete with authentic and working aircraft, including a massive flying boat. Open 10 am–5 pm. Phone (09)815-5800.

Auckland's main volcanic peaks served the Maoris as fortresses and are now public parks with spectacular views over the city and harbours. **Mount Eden** is the highest point and provides the grandest view. About four kilometres (2.5 miles) south of the city centre, this park can be reached by bus from the downtown bus terminal. **One Tree Hill**, in large Cornwall Park, two kilometres (1.2 miles) further south, can easily be seen from a distance; it's topped by a single pine tree and a tall

obelisk. You can walk or drive to the top—through groves of trees and fields of grazing sheep—for a magnificent view. Auckland Observatory and the StarDome Planetarium are near the Manukau Road entrance. The observatory is open for stargazing Tuesday to Saturday nights while the planetarium features a spectacular audio-visual presentation nightly. Phone (09)624-1246.

The attractive, fashionable suburbs of **Parnell** (east of downtown), **Ponsonby** (to the west) and **Devonport** (to the north) all boast beautifully restored Victorian-era buildings, intriguing boutiques, galleries, gourmet restaurants and trendy cafés. In Parnell, two special attractions are historic, kauri-wood **Ewelme Cottage**, at 14 Ayr Street, off Parnell Road, and the gorgeous **Parnell Rose Gardens**, where you'll find some 4,000 roses in bloom between November and March. Parnell can be reached by bus or by walking across Auckland Domain. Ponsonby's special appeal lies in its narrow, steep streets, working-class cottages (Renall Street, off Ponsonby Road, is particularly well preserved) and picturesque views. But without doubt it is now Auckland's chic urban enclave with a high-class cafe culture (see ponsonbyroad.co.nz). It can be reached by bus or by walking alongside Victoria Park and up College Hill. Devonport is a 12-minute ferry ride across the harbour from the city centre. The Devonport wharf has a restaurant area overlooking the water. Beyond that a street of Victorian- and Edwardian-era

(left) The Auckland Museum sits high above the immaculately groomed grounds of Auckland Domain. (above) Head down to Westhaven Marina anytime, and you'll see why Auckland is known as the 'City of Sails.'

shops stretches up to the foot of Mount Victoria, another of Auckland's pocket-sized green volcanoes.

Offshore from Auckland, **Hauraki Gulf Maritime Park** comprises 47 islands and 13,600 square kilometres of ocean. Fullers runs ferries to three of the islands from the Ferry Building on Quay Street. Phone (09)367-9111. **Rangitoto Island**, ten kilometres (six miles) from downtown, is mostly undeveloped. Visitors can hike to the summit of the volcanic cone or cross a causeway to adjacent Motutapu Island. **Waiheke Island** is much larger and has a permanent population of 6,800. This is the most visited of the Gulf islands and features long, white sandy beaches, pleasant hiking trails and many arts and crafts outlets. Largest and furthest from the mainland is **Great Barrier Island**, home to just over 1,100 residents, all of whom enjoy a relaxed lifestyle far from the bustle of the big city.

Focus

Even though the isthmus upon which Auckland lies is for the most part developed, bird-watching opportunities present themselves along all waterways and the extensive mud flats of **Manukau Harbour**. The oxidation ponds of the Manukau Purification Works, near the airport (on Island Road, off Greenwood Road), are a major habitat for waders, including oystercatchers, New Zealand dotterel and occasionally white heron. The MPW office permits bird-watchers to visit the ponds. Open 8 am–5 pm weekdays. Continue out Island Road to Puketutu Island, where you might see spotted doves in one of their rare breeding areas. Pheasants, finches and various ducks are also common here. On Manukau Harbour's south shore, toward Clarks Beach, the Karaka shell banks attract a good variety of waders, including whimbrel in summer (high tide in the harbour is three hours later than Auckland).

Hauraki Gulf Maritime Park, extending from Waitemata Harbour to Great Barrier Island, protects 47 islands and provides breeding grounds for many bird species, including 13 species of petrel and shearwater. Take a ferry from Auckland's Ferry Building out to Waiheke Island, and keep an eye out for gannet, little blue penguin, reef heron and skua near the shore. To the north, **Tiritiri Matangi Island** is slowly being regenerated from farming land by the Department of Conservation. The island is home to the colourful takahe, once thought to be extinct, as well as North Island saddleback, red crowned parakeet, little spotted kiwi, brown teal and a large population of bellbird. Ferries run out to the island from the Ferry Building and also from Whangaparaoa, north of Auckland. Phone (09)367-9111.

Little Barrier Island lies beside Great Barrier Island on the outer rim of Hauraki Gulf. Access is strictly controlled, but not impossible. Permits to visit must be obtained from the Department of Conservation in Auckland. Phone (09)379-6476. If you're lucky enough to get a permit, you'll also receive a list of boat charter companies leaving from Sandspit near Warkworth, 60 kilometres (37 miles) north of Auckland. Once on the island you may see or hear some of New Zealand's rarest birds, including the kakapo (world's largest parrot), the kokako (New Zealand's finest songbird), the burrowing Cook's petrel, and the last of the black petrels. Other species you might see include brown kiwi, kaka, rifleman, North Island robin, saddleback, and stitchbird.

At **Muriwai Beach**, on the west coast about 40 kilometres (25 miles) northwest of Auckland, a rare onshore colony of Australasian gannets nests between August and February. The gannets occupy a couple of offshore rock stacks and a fenced reserve on the cliff top above Maori Bay. A track leads from the road to a lookout where the birds can be safely viewed.

For those without time to seek rare birds in their wild habitats, **Auckland Zoo** has a large walk-in aviary filled with seldom-seen New Zealand birds like the blue duck, the kaka and the kakariki. The zoo also features a kiwi house.

From downtown, a pleasant **waterfront walk** gives a view of Waitemata Harbour and its famous sailboats. Start at the Ferry Building on the corner of Quay Street and Queen Elizabeth II Square and walk seven kilometres (4.4 miles) east via Tamaki Drive causeway and Takaparawha Regional Park to Mission Bay. Several bus stops line the route. Allow two hours.

The **Coast to Coast Walkway** crosses Auckland's isthmus from Waitemata Harbour on the Pacific Ocean to Manukau Harbour on the Tasman Sea. The walkway is clearly marked and deservedly famous, providing magnificent views of the city and both harbours from gardens and parks along the way. Two of the parks encompass extinct volcanoes. An excellent pamphlet with a detailed map is available from the Auckland Visitor Centre. Start at Queen Elizabeth II Square at the bottom of Queen Street. The route winds through Auckland Domain (the city's largest park), over the city's highest point and through the green oasis of One Tree Hill before emerging at suburban Onehunga Beach, on Manukau Harbour. The whole walk is 13 kilometres (eight miles) long. Allow four hours.

Northwest of Auckland the **Waitakere Ranges**, protected by a series of reserves, provide many hiking opportunities on a 200 kilometre (125 mile) trail system. Start your exploration at the Arataki Visitor Centre on Scenic Road. Phone (09)366-2000.

Between the sparkling waters of Auckland's two harbours lie a dozen golf courses. **Titirangi Golf Club**, at New Lynn in Waitakere City, was designed 50 years ago by Alister McKenzie, the same Scot who helped Bobby Jones design the famous course in Augusta, Georgia, home of the U.S. Masters. The hilly but shortish course is set in a magnificent area of native forest,

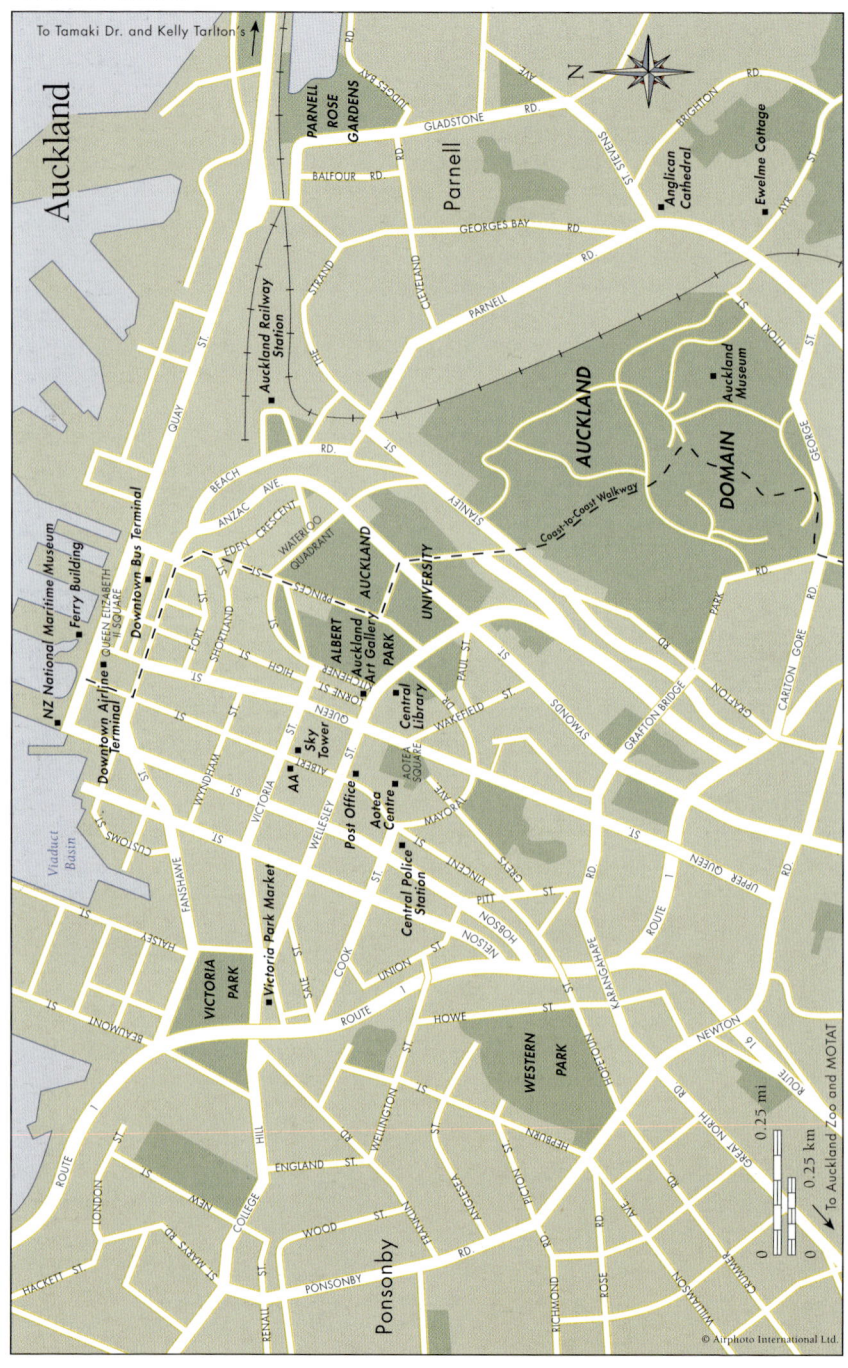

(top) Large ornamental gates open to the industrial waterfront of Auckland's Waitemata Harbour. (bottom left) Many of Auckland's original stone buildings have fared well under the test of time. (bottom right) The Ferry Building stands proudly between the end of Auckland's Queen Street and the busy waters of Waitemata Harbour.

alive with birds. Especially challenging are the par-three holes, including one of 180 metres (198 yards) where the entire carry is over native bush. Views are outstanding. Par 70. Phone (09)827-3967. **Gulf Harbour Country Club**, north of the city on Wangaparoa Peninsula has one of the country's finest courses. It hosted the 1998 World Cup. Ocean views while playing a challenging 6,483 metres (7,130 yards). Par 72. Phone (09)424-0971.

On the south side of the city is **Manukau Golf Club**, just off Highway 1 in the southern suburb of Takanini. Established in 1932, this well-wooded course beside Manukau Harbour resembles both links and inland courses. It is difficult, with numerous doglegs and narrow fairways. Par 71. Phone (09)267-6672. **Chamberlain Park Golf Course** is on Highway 16 in Western Springs near the centre of Auckland. The well-designed public course welcomes all and can be crowded on weekends. Par 70. Phone (09)846-6758.

Another course worth noting is **Muriwai Golf Course**, at Muriwai Beach, about 40 kilometres (25 miles) northwest of Auckland. This recently rebuilt links-style layout spreads across sand dunes overlooking the turbulent Tasman Sea. The sea breeze is almost constant. Some golfers count this one as a must. Par 72. Phone (09)411-8454.

Auckland is the centre of New Zealand's wine industry, though not the country's premier grape-growing area. The giants of the industry—Montana, Babich, Villa Maria and others—mature and bottle their wine here with grapes shipped in from many regions. The Wine Institute of NZ, founded in 1975 to represent all wineries, great and small, and to instil some order in the industry, is also based in Auckland, website <www.nzwine.com>.

Most of the actual vineyards around Auckland's wineries are small or medium-sized and are still run by the families who founded them. The descendants of Yugoslavs from Dalmatia predominate. Described below are some of the vineyards most praised by wine writers and judges. (Montana is not included here. Its vineyards near Blenheim on the South Island are set up for tours and tastings.) All the wineries listed here welcome visitors.

West of the city centre, Waitakere City's **Henderson Valley** is the cradle of New Zealand's wine industry. In recent years, the valley has faced both competition from newer wine-producing areas and loss of land from encroaching motorways and suburbs.

Babich, on Babich Road, Henderson, is one of the best and largest of the family-owned wineries. Most of its grapes now come from the winery's own Hawkes Bay vineyards. The attractive vineyard and modern winery are run by two sons of the founder, a Dalmatian immigrant who turned from gum digging to wine making in 1919. Strengths include a Chardonnay, a Sauvignon Blanc, a fine Pinot Noir and a dry Cabernet, all well-priced. Premium wines are marketed under the Patriarch label. Make two left turns off Swanson Road to Metcalfe, then Babich Road. Phone (09)833-7859, website <www.babichwines.co.nz>.

Collard Brothers, 303 Lincoln Road, Henderson, is a small family winery producing a limited amount of regional varietal wines. The Chardonnay and Chenin Blanc enjoy an excellent reputation but are hard to obtain due to a strong local following and mail-order business. A visit to the winery is the answer. Phone (09)838-8341.

Delegats, at the end of Hepburn Road at Glendene, just east of Henderson, is a family company headed by the son and daughter of its Yugoslav founder. The company first won recognition for its Chardonnay. Top wines are now sold under the Proprietor's Reserve label; try the 1995 Cabernet Sauvignon. Phone (09)836-0129.

A dozen other wineries scattered around Henderson also produce good wines, and all welcome visitors, website <www.delegats.com>.

High land prices around Henderson encouraged the planting of new vineyards northwest of Auckland, along Highway 16 at the villages of Kumeu, Huapai and Waimauku. The area is drier than Henderson, and its red wines are outstanding. Much fruit is brought in from elsewhere for bottling. The wineries are mostly Dalmatian family businesses.

Matua Valley, on Waikoukou Valley Road in Waimauku, is a top boutique winery with an octagonal vineyard. It was founded in 1974 by Ross and Bill Spence, both experienced winemakers. The excellent Pinot Noir is available only at the vineyard. Phone (09)411-8301, website <www.matua.co.nz>.

Coopers Creek, between Huapai and Waimauku, was started in 1982. The small winery uses traditional techniques of maturation in French oak casks. It has a keen local following and growing exports. Phone (09)412-8560.

At New Zealand's second largest wine producer, **Nobilo**, Station Road, Huapai, three Nobilo brothers continue Yugoslav traditions, emphasizing red wines grown entirely at the Huapai vineyard. The top wines are Cabernet Sauvignon, Pinot Noir and Pinotage (a South African cross of Pinot Noir and Cinsault). A fruity Müller-Thurgau blend, marketed internationally as White Cloud, is distinctive for its frosted bottle. Phone (09)412-9148, website <www.cooperscreek.co.nz>.

Kumeu River is on the main road at Kumeu. Winemaker Michael Brajkovich, son of the founder, uses classic French techniques. The 'Kumeu River' premium label continues to win high praise internationally, and the winery's Chardonnay, is consistently voted New Zealand's best under $20. Phone (09)412-8415, website <www.kumeuriver.co.nz>.

Selaks, just outside Kumeu, is another Yugoslav family enterprise, started in 1934. Its white wines are superior. Phone (09)412-8609, website <www.nobilo.co.nz>.

The Treaty of Waitangi

Waitangi is a word visitors to New Zealand hear often. Waitangi Day is New Zealand's national day, a holiday celebrated on 6 February with ceremonies and pageantry, or a day at the beach. Waitangi National Reserve, at the Bay of Islands, is a must on tourists' itineraries. The reserve's Treaty House is a historical shrine, where the Treaty of Waitangi was signed by Queen Victoria's envoys and Maori chiefs in 1840. The treaty sealed an agreement that Britain would take possession of Aotearoa, the Maori's beloved Land of the Long White Cloud, and add it to the British Empire.

For over 155 years, New Zealanders of British descent have prided themselves on the fact that their country was acquired by legal means, rather than by crude conquest.

Great Britain's motives at the time were honourable; in negotiating the treaty, the British government was attempting to resolve increasing tension on the islands. European whalers, sealers, timber cutters and traders had been exploiting the newly founded colony's coastal waters, forests and native people. Speculators, adventurers, mountebanks, and missionaries were also drawn to this wild frontier. The Maori and Europeans were increasingly in conflict, and intertribal battles amongst the Maori es-

calated as well. Those tribes who had traded early in muskets held a deadly advantage and used it, far increasing the carnage over traditional levels. Hongi Hika's Ngapuhi from the far north, and Ngatitoa chief Te Rauparaha further south had begun savage raids far from their traditional territory, and staged great cannibal feasts.

The French, who had formally colonized a number of Pacific islands, were also interested in New Zealand. And English missionaries were putting pressure on Britain to act. England had already annexed Australia; acquiring New Zealand was the next logical step, though one that the Crown was somewhat reluctant to take. Following an ineffectual attempt between 1833 and 1840 to assert British law under a Residency system (the Resident, James Busby, was called 'the Man o' War without guns' for he had no means of asserting his authority). Britain sent Captain William Hobson to take charge as Lieutenant Governor. His instruction was to annex the country with 'the free and intelligent consent of the natives'.

From London this seemed a humane and legal scheme. Hobson, helped by Busby and the missionaries, drafted a treaty whereby the Maori would relinquish their sovereignty to the British Crown in exchange for a guarantee of their customary rights over

The most important event in Maori-Pakeha relations was the 1840 Treaty of Waitangi. Its signing brought together Maori chiefs and representatives of the British government, signalling an end to the Land Wars but the beginning of a land rights controversy that continues to this day. This lithograph, produced by Leonard Cornwall Mitchell, appeared on the cover of the New Zealand Journal of Agriculture, *January 1949.*

(continues on next page)

lands, forests and fisheries—land which could nonetheless be sold to the government. The Maori were also guaranteed the rights and privileges accorded other British subjects. Hobson and some 50 Maori chiefs signed the treaty on Busby's lawn at Waitangi on 6 February 1840. Copies of it were shipped around both islands, and over 500 chiefs finally put their mark to the document. Hobson became the Governor of a new British colony.

But some chiefs did not sign. And the treaty's simple but powerful guarantees of Maori ownership were never formally ratified. For a decade this hardly mattered as the new government did its best to preserve a fair balance between Pakeha (European) and Maori interests. But settlers flooded in. Maori leaders saw the threat to their lands and became reluctant to sell. The Crown increasingly took up the role of prising away Maori land, and simply took by default such relatively undefined assets as fisheries. This process ended in the Land Wars of the 1860s, an uneasy decade of sporadic Maori guerilla attacks.

Large-scale confiscations as a result of the wars, and openly discriminatory legal methods of gaining Maori land left the various Maori tribes with deep-seated historical grievances. They were guaranteed participation in a New Zealand democracy, including their own seats in Parliament, but they had lost much tribal power.

That unsettled state of affairs, with consistent Maori calls and petitions to the British Queen that the treaty be ratified, lasted through to 1975, when a Maori politician succeeded in establishing the Waitangi Tribunal. The tribunal was empowered to investigate Maori land claims, measure them against the guarantees of the treaty, and report to Parliament.

Though it had the power only of recommendation, the Waitangi Tribunal irrevocably changed the balance of Maori/Pakeha power. As a result of its widely publicized reports, many Europeans came to see how unjust past dealings had been. And though the Treaty remained formally unratified, Appeal Court and High Court judgements in the 1980s made clear that its principles were deemed to be operative in New Zealand law. By the 1990s, control of a significant percentage of New Zealand's resources was shifting into Maori hands.

The Treaty has not only become the pragmatic tool of a more genuinely bi-cultural nation, it has been enshrined as a revered founding document. Today its principles are acted upon not only in accordance with the letter of the document, but with its spirit as contemplated by the original signatories.

Villa Maria, on the south side of the city at 5 Kirkbride Road, Mangere, only minutes north of Auckland Airport, is New Zealand's third largest wine company and follows classic Yugoslav traditions. It is still family owned and incorporates two independent wineries in Hawkes Bay. Contract growers supply 98 per cent of its grapes. The winery specializes in premium varietal wines, of which the Reserve Chardonnays are exceptional. (www.villamaria.co.nz), Phone (09)255-0660.

Clevedon is a new grape-growing area south of the city. Here, tucked along a picturesque valley you'll find **Inverness**, on Ness Valley Road. The first Inverness vintage was in 1999 but the winery has quickly gained a reputation for Chardonnay and a Semillon Cabernet Franc blend. The estate includes accommodations and an Andalusian stud, all contained in a delightful setting of surrounding native bush, website <www.inverness.co.nz>.

William Andrew Collins photographed this Maori chief in traditional clothing.

Further south, off Highway 2, the small **de Redcliffe** vineyard is on Lyons Road near Mangatawhiri. Set in natural bush, the complex includes the Hotel du Vin with accommodation and a restaurant. Phone (09)233-6314.

With a climate warmer than the mainland, Waiheke Island has won a world reputation and gold medals in New Zealand and overseas for its red wines. Seven small vineyards are on the island. One of them, **Stonyridge**, website <www.stonyridge.co.nz> in Onetangi, produces a Cabernet blend know as Larose. Phone (09)372-8822. The Waiheke Island ferry leaves regularly from the Ferry Building at the bottom of Queen Street, downtown Auckland.

(top right) St. Stephen's Chapel, Parnell, Auckland; (top left) Sailboats berthed on the calm waters of Kerikeri basin; (bottom) Escape the hustle and bustle of downtown Auckland in the colourful Parnell Rose Gardens, just east of Queen Street.

(right) One of Auckland's oldest and best-preserved suburbs is Devonport, a short ferry ride from downtown.

Northland

The long, ragged finger of land extending north from Auckland for about 450 kilometres (280 miles) is known as Northland—a region of hilly farmland and patches of forest ringed by spectacular shoreline. The subtropical climate here is the gentlest in New Zealand, with warm (but never unpleasantly hot) summers and frostless winters. Foreign visitors often bypass the region in favour of the well-worn tourist track to the south. But the spectacular Bay of Islands, above all, should not be missed, thanks to its compelling scenery and fascinating history.

New Zealand's first European colonists settled at the Bay of Islands in the early 1830s. Their rough, tough town of Russell, also known as 'the hellhole of the Pacific,' was the country's first capital, an honour it relinquished to Auckland in 1840. Until the 19th century, Northland was largely covered with magnificent ancient kauri forests. But then European timber speculators levelled the forests and ravaged the land further in the relentless search for buried kauri gum, a valuable export. The devastation continued until the early 20th century. In the years since, most of Northland has blossomed into rich farmland, while the coasts are a paradise for vacationers, boaters and deep-sea anglers.

Northland's biggest town and main port is Whangarei, on the east coast. Further north, the towns of Paihia and Russell overlook the beautiful Bay of Islands and attract visitors year-round. At the extreme north, the slim Aupouri Peninsula stretches northward from Kaitaia. The peninsula is bounded on the west by unbroken Ninety-Mile Beach (actually 64 miles/103 kilometres long) and ends at Cape Reinga, where the Tasman Sea and Pacific Ocean meet in turbulent waters. Northland's sparsely developed west coast holds the country's last big stand of kauri trees, preserved in the Waipoua Kauri Forest and Trounson Kauri Park. One giant is believed to be 2,000 years old! Dargaville, the largest west coast town, lies at a river mouth on isolated Kaipara Harbour. A hundred years ago, this sleepy dairying settlement was a major port in the brisk trade of kauri gum and timber.

GETTING THERE
Air New Zealand flies from Auckland to Whangarei and the Bay of Islands and Kaitaia. The Bay of Islands airport is inland, at Kerikeri, from where a coach service takes passengers to Paihia. Rental cars are available at all Northland airports.

Intercity coaches run many times daily from Auckland to Whangarei, the Bay of Islands and Kaitaia, with some services connecting the Bay of Islands to the west coast town of Dargaville. Northliner Express operates extensive routes throughout Northland. No public transportation is available north of Kaitaia, although bus tours operate to Cape Reinga, from as far south as Paichia.

Although public transportation runs frequently and is reliable, the best way to visit Northland is by car. Highway 1, the main road, links Auckland and Kaitaia, via Whangarei. Some 50 kilometres (30 miles) before Whangarei, Highway 12 loops around to the west coast, through Dargaville and the kauri forest, rejoining Highway 1 near the Bay of Islands. Highway 10 makes a northern loop by following the east coast from the Bay of Islands to Kaitaia. Thus it is possible to see most of Northland without ever backtracking.

WHANGAREI AND ENVIRONS

Beyond Auckland, Highway 1 passes through a prosperous orchard region known as the **Hibiscus Coast**, where roadside stands sell fresh fruit and vegetables. **Waiwera Infinity Thermal Spa Resort**, 48 kilometres (30 miles) north of Auckland, is an upmarket spa resort with thermal pools ranging in temperature from 33° to 40°C (91° to 104°F). The popular pool area offers kid-friendly waterslides surrounded by adult-friendly lawns. Open 9 am–10 pm. Phone (09)427-8800, website <www.waiwera.co.nz>.

Turn off Highway 1 at Warkworth for **Goat Island Bay**, near Leigh some 70 kilometres (44 miles) north of Auckland. The pretty bay and its island just 150 metres (490 feet) offshore are the centre of a marine reserve where fishing is prohibited and the fish approach snorkellers fearlessly.

Whangarei, Northland's only real city, lies at the head of one of New Zealand's safest deepwater harbours. The Whangarei Visitor Centre on Otaika Road stocks free maps and literature. Phone (09)438-1079. Yachts from around the world are moored at **Quayside**, whose landscaped surroundings, cafés, and cobbled walkways make it a pleasant place to spend a sunny afternoon. Also at the basin is **Clapham Clocks**, worth a visit to see the hundreds of clocks and watches of every type and description, the oldest dating from 1636. Open daily 10 am–5 pm. Phone (09)438-3993. Out front is Australasia's largest sundial. On the city's western edge is the large **Whangarei Museum**, comprising a kiwi house, homestead, and main museum buildings. Through summer, Sundays are busy at the museum, as enthusiasts show off their restored machinery—tractors, steam engines, and all manner of vehicles—to interested visitors. Open daily 10 am–4 pm. Phone (09)438-9630. About six kilometres (four miles) east of the city centre on Ngunguru Road, photogenic **Whangarei Falls** plunges 25 metres (80 feet) over a forested cliff into a deep green pool. Several walkways offer spectacular views.

The **Kawiti Caves**, 50 kilometres north of Whangarei and just one kilometre off Highway 1, are worth a look for their limestone formations and glow-worms. According to Maori legend, the caves were used as a hideaway 300 years ago by a runaway Maori wife named Roku. Maori usually keep away from these underground haunts.

BAY OF ISLANDS

The Bay of Islands received its name from Captain Cook when he first saw the convoluted bay and the 150 islands that rise from its warm, azure waters. **Paihia**, 240 kilometres (150 miles) north of Auckland, is the region's main town. Apart from an aquarium down on the waterfront, Paihia holds little appeal. But it's a good base for exploring the area. Boat trips to the Bay of Islands leave from the waterfront, and plenty of lodgings and restaurants line the main street. Bay of Islands Visitor Centre is on the waterfront. Phone (09)402-7345. Follow the waterfront north from Paihia to the mouth of the Waitangi River, where an historic barque, the *Tui*, is moored. Inside the *Tui* is the **Shipwreck Museum**, which dis-

Pohutukawa, easily recognizable by its clusters of red flowers, thrives in the subtropical climate north of Auckland.

plays jewellery and gold coins amongst the relics of several famous shipwrecks. A fascinating film explains the salvage operations. Open daily 10 am–6 pm. Phone (09)402-7018.

Across the river from Paihia and overlooking the Bay of Islands is **Waitangi National Trust Treaty Grounds**. Here Maori chiefs signed a treaty with the British in 1840 surrendering their country and adding New Zealand to the British Empire. At the main entrance is a visitor centre, where an audio-visual presentation is shown. From the centre, trails radiate through coastal bush to the colonial Treaty House, set in lovely grounds overlooking the bay. Nearby is the Waitangi Whare Runanga, a splendidly decorated Maori meeting house. The carvings are the work of several North Island tribes. The house itself was offered as a gift to the nation on the 100th anniversary of the treaty. Also on the reserve, an open pavilion shelters a great war canoe 35 metres (115 feet) long and carved from kauri trees. The canoe is launched with a Maori crew of 80 during celebrations every February. The reserve also holds an interesting hiking trail (see *Focus*, page 82) and a golf course (see *Focus*, page 83). Phone (09)402-7437.

One of New Zealand's most charming towns is **Russell**, website <www.russellnz.co.nz>, reached by passenger ferry from Paihia or by car ferry

Sandy beaches are a popular attraction on the protected eastern coastline of Northland.

from Opua, just south of Paihia. Old-World Russell retains little hint of its bawdy, brawling, lawless past, but the **Russell Museum** on York Street gives some of that flavour. Open daily 10 am–4 pm. Phone (09)403-7701. A walk along the waterfront passes many historic buildings: a police station dating to 1870, the grand Pompallier House, and the Duke of Marlborough Hotel, which holds New Zealand's oldest liquor licence. A few blocks back from the waterfront is New Zealand's oldest church, built in 1835. Behind town, Flagstaff Hill affords panoramic views back across the bay to Paihia. Russell Mini Tours offers a good one-hour tour of the historic sites. The tour leaves Russell Wharf seven times daily. Phone (09)403-7866.

Several different boat excursions can take you out to see the Bay of Islands from sea level. All major operators have representatives along the Paihia waterfront. Fullers offers a wide variety of excursions. The Supercruise includes the famous **Cream Trip** (with cream tea served, of course) and a stop on an uninhabited island for lunch. Fullers also offers sailing trips aboard the *R Tucker Thompson*, a magnificent schooner, and trips out to **Hole in the Rock**, a massive wave-carved arch that the boats easily pass through. Phone (09)402-7421. A number of high-speed catamarans cruise the bay, including *The Excitor*, operated by Fullers. Yachting, sea kayaking, dolphin swimming, scuba diving and fishing are all vailable from commercial operators in the Bay of Islands.

The Far North

Kaitaia, 324 kilometres (203 miles) north of Auckland, is the main town of the Far North and a good, central base for exploring the region. Tours run regularly from Kaitaia to all the hot spots, including Cape Reinga, at the top of the Aupouri Peninsula. The Far North Visitor Centre, beside Jaycee Park on South Road, Kaitaia, stocks maps of the region and tour schedules. Phone (09)408-0879. The **Far North Regional Museum**, next to the museum, holds excellent displays on ancient Maori culture and the Dalmatian gum diggers who displaced it. Open weekdays 10 am–5 pm. Phone (09)408-1403.

Cape Reinga is the sacred spot from where, according to Maori belief, the spirits of the dead depart across the Pacific to Hawaiki, the Maori mythological homeland. A 116 kilometre (72 mile) unpaved road runs the length of the narrow peninsula from Kaitaia to the cape, giving views of both the Tasman Sea and the Pacific Ocean. A tiny settlement at the cape includes a post office-cum-souvenir shop and a lighthouse. Marvellous views from the headland take in the coast and the clashing seas, where waves reach heights of ten metres (33 feet) in stormy weather. At low tide, the hard sand of **Ninety-Mile Beach** serves as an alternate road up the peninsula's west coast. In Kaitaia, Sand Safaris offers day trips (including a picnic lunch) that go one way via Ninety-Mile Beach and the other way via the road. Phone (09)408-1778. The tours stop en route at various scenic sights, including the intriguing Wagener Museum, at Houhora. Fullers offers similar itineraries from Paihia; these trips involve longer distances and are more commercial.

While the trip to Cape Reinga is touted as the highlight of the Far North, and rightly so, other attractions in the region are worthy of a visit. At Fairburn, east of Kaitaia, the **Nocturnal Park** is one of the best kiwi houses in the country. Night and day are reversed, allowing kiwis to be viewed when they are most active. The park is open until 11 pm, allowing visitors to view glow-worms when they are at their most spectacular. Phone (09)408-4100.

On the wild west side of the Aupouri Peninsula, the small seaside village of **Ahipara** lies nestled behind massive sand dunes at the extreme southern end of Ninety-Mile Beach. Forests of massive kauri trees, which once blanketed the north, caused a gold rush of sorts to Ahipara well after the trees had been harvested by timber cutters in the early 1800s. Gum, which over thousands of years had collected at the base of these giants and become fossilized, was 'mined' by hundreds of Yugoslav gum diggers in the late 1890s. The Ahipara Gum Fields have been protected, and tours leave daily from Kaitaia.

The West Coast

Waipoua Kauri Forest, the oldest and largest remnant of New Zealand's once-great kauri forests, lines unpaved but good Highway 12 for 16 kilometres (ten miles). Two of the primeval giants are awe-inspiring. Tane Mahuta (Lord of the Forest) is over 1,200 years old and the largest known kauri, standing over 51 metres (167 feet) high and measuring 13 metres (43 feet) in girth. It is signposted and reached by a short track from Highway 12. Te Matua Ngahere (Father of the Forest), also signposted, stands at the end of a beautiful forest glade, 15 minutes' walk from the road. This immense tree is believed to be about 2,000 years old. Trounson Kauri Park is a smaller but splendid kauri forest with fine walking paths. To get there follow a five-kilometre (three-mile) detour branching east from Highway 12 south of Waipoua Forest.

Continuing south you'll come to the excellent **Kauri Museum**, which catalogues the tree's natural and human history. Highlights include massive slabs of kauri, a gum collection, a magnificent steam sawmill and a photographic history of the timber cutters. Open daily 9 am–5 pm. Phone (09)431-7417.

Focus

At the mouth of the Waipu River, **Waipu Wildlife Refuge** makes an interesting first stop for northbound bird-watchers. Nesting on the river's sandy banks are New Zealand dotterels (one of the country's rarest waders), Caspian terns, fairy terns and variable oystercatchers. Take Johnsons Point Road through Waipu to access the reserve.

On the south side of **Whangarei Harbour**, mud flats attract pied stilt, godwit, knot and other arctic migrants in summer. The rocky north shore shelters little blue penguin, heron, oystercatcher, tern and other species. The New Zealand dotterel breeds at several points around the harbour.

The **Bay of Islands** offers a fine chance to see pelagic birds by boat. An excellent launch trip is the Cream Trip that leaves Paihia daily, heading far enough out amongst the islands to encounter a wide variety of Pacific sea birds. Urupukapuka Island, where many cruises break for lunch, is home to a colony of pied shags as well as the rare brown teal, introduced to the island after nearing extinction on the mainland.

Rangaunu Harbour in the Far North, 12 kilometres north of Kaitaia, is home to over 40 species of shore birds, migrant waders, crakes, pukeko, harriers and swamp birds. Houhora Harbour, further north, also provides habitat for a variety of waders.

New Zealand's best-known bird, the kiwi, can be viewed at the **Nocturnal Park** near Kaitaia (see page 78) and in more natural surroundings in the remaining kauri forests along the west coast. The owners of Kauri Coast Holiday Park, near the Trounson Kauri Park, lead guided night tours searching out these intriguing birds by torchlight. Phone (09)439-0621.

Inland from the Bay of Islands is Kerikeri and two of New Zealand's oldest buildings—the Stone Store (1832) and Kemp House (1821).

At **Mangawhai Heads**, about 20 kilometres (12 miles) southeast of Waipu (between Wellsford and Whangarei), a five-kilometre (three-mile) coastal walk provides splendid views of the sea as it leads along beach and cliff top, past forest and farmland. Leave Highway 1 at Kaiwaka or Waipu and follow the signs to Mangawhai Heads. The walkway begins on the north side of Mangawhai Harbour, across the water from a wildlife sanctuary on a long sandspit. It follows the beach for a kilometre (0.6 miles) before climbing high cliffs amidst large pohutukawa trees. The path turns inland at a natural amphitheatre known as the Giant's Staircase, which offers pleasant vistas of the surrounding country, and ends where low cliffs approach the Cape Bream Trail. Here a colony of shags occupies a pohutukawa tree. At low tide you could return along the shore, but it's rocky in places. The walkway is closed from July to September for lambing on the farmland. Allow two and a half hours return.

Maori carvings decorate the homes of many New Zealanders, Maori and Pakeha alike. Photographed by Albert Percy Godber.

Within **Waitangi National Reserve**, just north of Paihia, a six-kilometre (four-mile) trail follows the Waitangi River to Haruru Falls. The trail starts 500 metres (0.3 miles) north of the main car park. It leads through a native rainforest and, by boardwalk, through a mangrove swamp full of bird life. The falls are splendid after rain. Allow two and a half hours return.

Cape Reinga, the sparsely populated tip of Northland, is where the spirits of the Maori dead traditionally depart New Zealand for the afterlife. This untamed coast offers good beach walking. Get a map of the walking trails from the Far North Information Centre on South Road in Kaitaia or from the ranger at Waitiki Landing, about 95 kilometres (60 miles) further north. A big map is posted at the Cape Reinga car park. Take drinking water, suntan lotion and insect repellent. The walk (part of a much longer track) starts at the car park or on the path to the lighthouse. From the cliff top you have a fine view of the coast and the turbulence caused by the meeting of the waters of the Pacific

Ocean and Tasman Sea. A steep climb leads down to Te Werahi Beach, which the trail follows to its southern end at Te Werahi Stream. This takes about one hour. From the ridge above Te Werahi Stream, a loop walk to Cape Maria van Diemen is signposted. This detour takes about one and a half hours and brings you to a fine picnic place with spectacular views of the coast and the sea. You can return to the lighthouse by the beach or leave the beach and follow the well-marked track back to the road. The circle takes three hours without the detour.

Northland is the only part of New Zealand without superb fly-fishing. Instead it offers world-famous big-game fishing and surf-casting. Bay of Islands' fishing clubs draw big-game anglers from all corners of the earth. The world's biggest striped marlin are caught here, along with many other species of game fish. The season for marlin runs December to May, and for kingfish (yellowtail), year-round; shark season also runs year-round. The **Bay of Islands Swordfish Club** in Russell charters boats. Phone (09)403-7857. Several deep-sea fishing charter companies in Paihia offer all kinds of amenities. And farther south, the **Whangarei Deep Sea Anglers Club** offers charters from its base at Tutukaka Marina, 30 kilometres (19 miles) east of Whangarei. Phone (09)434-3818. Light-tackle fishing is also popular year-round and is relatively inexpensive. The folks at **Charter** Pier on Paihia's Wharf, do their best to minimize costs for anglers by grouping individuals together on charter trips. Phone (09)402-7127.

Ninety-Mile Beach, on the west coast, is unsurpassed for surf-casting. One of the world's largest surf-casting contests is held here every January, drawing huge crowds of anglers who compete for big cash prizes.

Northland's best-known course is **Waitangi Golf Course**, set on rolling hills that slope gently down to the Bay of Islands. Many holes provide unsurpassed views. As with all coastal courses, wind plays an important role in the degree of challenge offered. Par 70. Phone (09)402-8207. For general information on the island group, contact the Department of Conservation, at 8A Kaka St., Whangarei. Phone (09)430-2133. **Kerikeri Golf Club** provides a long and challenging course of over 6,000 metres (6,600 yards), including five par fives. Par 73. Phone (09)407-8776. The **Whangarei Golf Club** offers a pleasant game across rolling terrain. Par 72. Phone (09)437-0740.

Northland is not renowned for its wineries, although the highway north from Auckland passes through the Henderson Valley (see page 67), one of the country's most important wine-producing regions. New Zealand's northernmost vineyard is the small **Okahu**, on Okahu Road near Kaitaia in the Far North. Chardonnays are the speciality in this often-humid area. Phone (09)408-2066.

The Poor Knights Islands

When captain James Cook sailed along the east coast of Northland in 1769, on his ship "Endeavour", he dropped anchor in front of two islands called Tawhiti Rahi and Aorangi. There, he met a clan of Maori people that belong to a 'hapu' or subtribe named Ngatiwai. Aorangi, the southern island had another 'hapu', named Ngatitoki and was the only possible landing site in calm weather. Tawhiti Rahi, the northern island is surrounded by precipitous cliffs, so that by bad weather canoes could only be lifted by ropes from the sea.

Upon discovering the islands, Cook reported cultivated land and fortified villages. The two islands lay like recumbent effigies of crusaders, heads to the south and feet thrust towards the northern sun. Cook simply named them: the "Poor Knights". A hundred and twenty seven years before him, Dutch explorer Abel Tasman had named the northern most islands of New Zealand: the "Three Kings". South of the Poor Knights, the "Pinnacles" or "High Peak Rocks" and the "Sugar Loaf Rock", were once known as the "Poor Squires".

Cook offered some pigs to chief Tatau, ruler of both islands, which became a treasure of the tribe. These were kept and bred on Aorangi only, and used as barter when dealing with mainland tribes for 'totara' timber, consumed largely by islanders in the building of dwellings, fortifications and canoes.

In year 1808 or about, some natives of the Hikutu tribe of Hokianga, paid a visit to Aorangi and requested some pigs, which were denied to them. They sailed off empty handed and frustrated. A while later, chief Tatau left the island with his warriors, on a fighting expedition to the Hauraki Gulf. Taking advantage of his departure, a slave named Paha, escaped to the mainland in a small canoe. He informed Waikato, chief of the Hikutu tribe of the opportunity to take revenge. Immediately, a raid was organized to secure pigs and slaves. Three large war canoes set out for a 200 miles trip via North Cape to the Poor Knights.

Landing by surprise, the raiders performed overnight a massacre of the defenseless inhabitants and continued so during the following day. Many of those who fled, jumped into the sea from the hair raising cliffs. The Hikutu warriors made off with their bounty, taking along Tatau's wife Oneho and daughter. Back to the mainland, they rested at Whangaroa for a day and were entertained by local people. Tango, the local headman, asking to be shown the slaves, recognized Oneho as a distant relative. During the night, he helped the two women to escape and these were taken by canoe to Rawhiti, in the Bay of Islands. When chief Tatau returned to the Poor Knights, from his fighting expedition in the Hauraki Gulf, he was horrified about what had happened during his absence. At the landing site, he was met by ten of his people, the only survivors of the slaughter of the two islands community. This included the old man Omanoa, who had saved his 5 year old son, by concealing him into a cave. Performing the last rites over the slain, Tatau declared the islands strictly "tapu" (taboo or sacred) and proceeded with his warriors to Rawhiti, 40 miles north, in the Bay of Islands.

Rising 240 metres from the sea, the Poor Knights Islands group is located 12 miles (22 km) from the Tutukaka coast in Northland. Not many specialists agree on the age and origin of the islands, but some estimates date them at about 4 million years old. Volcanic in origin, made of rhyolite acid lava, these islands are thought to be the remains of lava domes that rose from a deep fracture, extending from the Coromandel Peninsula to the east coast of Northland.

The overall outlook of the Poor Knights is cream to golden in colour. Tawhiti rahi, the North Island is 318 acres, while Aorangi, the South Island is 163 acres. Small islets and isolated rocks are scattered around the Knights. As one approaches these mysterious islands by boat, one hour away from Tutukaka harbour, one is struck by the impressive cliffs that turn the Poor Knights into an impregnable fortress. Some of those rock faces plunge to a hundred metres below the surface of the ocean.

During the last ice age, the sea surface was 30 metres below its actual level. Caves and archways are characteristic and numerous in the Poor Knights, many of them being large enough for boats to navigate. Evidences of beaches and cobblestones have been found underwater.

The present vegetation is mainly secondary forest that has regenerated on the seaward slopes, on the inland plateau and in the gullies. On rock outcrops and inland cliffs, the flame red Poor Knights lily is the most beautiful and dominant flower of the landscape.

Seabirds have naturally made a haven of the Poor Knights: 2,5 million Buller shearwaters (rako), 9 species of petrels; large colonies of the graceful Australasian gannets nest on Sugar Loaf and on the Pinnacles. Landbirds such as: bellbirds (korimako), red crowned parakeets (karaiki), fantails (piwakawaka), kingfishers (kotare), pipits (pihoihoi) and harriers (kahu). The dark slated spotless crake (putoto) and the banded rail (mohopereru) have also made their home on the islands. A good size prehistoric reptile, looking like an iguana, the notable Tuatara is endemic to the Poor Knights and practically extinct in New Zealand.

The Poor Knights were bought by Mr. J.S. Pollock in 1845, then sold to the British crown in 1882 to become a lighthouse reserve. Later protected as a scenic reserve, they were made a flora and fauna reserve in 1975. A permit is needed to land as the area is still out-of-bounds for casual visitors. It is the unique underwater life that now attracts visitors and divers, since the Poor Knights were declared a marine reserve in 1980. The islands are bathed by the warm East Auckland current that originates off the north east coast of Australia, flows across the Tasman Sea and down the

continental shelf of Northland. An avenue for tropical fish larvae, which settle in the Poor Knights and live there, when they survive.

A diving experience in the Poor Knights is rather unique, not to be missed and bears little resemblance with diving in the tropics. At least 130 species of fish have been identified in the islands, 20% of the fish are endemic to New Zealand (26 species). The underwater seascape is that of the kelp forest, that grows on a rocky substrate, one metre above the seafloor, and hosts a number of fish species, including stingrays. The volcanic nature of the islands adds to the magic: submerged caves, tunnels, arches, swimthroughs that swarm with fish schools (blue mao mao) and marine life of all sorts and shape. The walls are rich in colour: blue and red sponges, soft corals, white & pink jewel anemones, yellow zooanthids, green bryozoans. An obvious paradise for macro-photographers: nudibranchs abound. Moray eels are found everywhere, on every dive.

The diving is done either on the east coast or the west coast, depending on the swell and the winds. In summer, the sea surface temperatures average a comfortable 22–25°C. However, at the approach of winter, it comes down to a chilly 16°C and even to a frisky stimulating 13°C. Yet local dive masters still want you to believe it is 18–19°C! The visibility is worst in spring time (September/November.), around 10 metres, but this is a good time for nudibranchs. It gets better in the summer (December/April), around 15–30 metres and this is the period for stingrays and tropical pelagics, such as mantas. A good visibility in autumn (April–June), on average 25–40 metres. The best visibility of the year comes in the winter time (June–August), around 30–40 metres. According to Jeroen Jongejans, Director of "Dive Tutukaka", any time is a good time. There is always something special to see in the Poor Knights islands, in any season.

A total of 66 dive sites in the Marine Reserve leave plenty of room for fins and awesome discoveries as well. Great expectations are shared between three major dive areas: the "Poor Knights" (60 sites), the "Pinnacles" (5 sites) and "Sugar Loaf" (1 site). Close to the Tutukaka coast, recent shipwrecks—sunk by Jeroen—lie in less than 30 metres of sea water: that of the "Tui", former hydrographic research ship of the US and NZ Navy—involved in the protesting fleet against the French nuclear tests in Mururoa-, sunk in February 1999 and the "Waikato", a 113 metres long frigate of the Royal New Zealand Navy, sunk in November 2000.

Dive Sites of the Poor Knights

LONG CAVE is located on the east coast of the South Island. A the bottom of the cliff, a canyon leads into a tunnel-like cave, long and dark. Divers need a torch. Red pigfish, mokis, marblefish, northern scorpionfish and Sandagers wrasse at the entrance. Swimthroughs are found on the sides of the canyon. The wall outside the cave is very good for nudibranchs and macro. It leads to another wide cave at 30 metres depth, in the shape of a cathedral. The bread & butter nudibranch is found there. The yellow moray watches from holes in grey sponges.

SUGAR LOAF ROCK is found at the southern end of the Poor Knights Marine Reserve. Sugar Loaf Rock hosts a colony of Australasian gannets, that nest on the island. This isolated rock rises over a hundred metres above sea level, with straight cliffs, that plunge 90 metres below water. A favourite dive site at the southern tip follows the wall

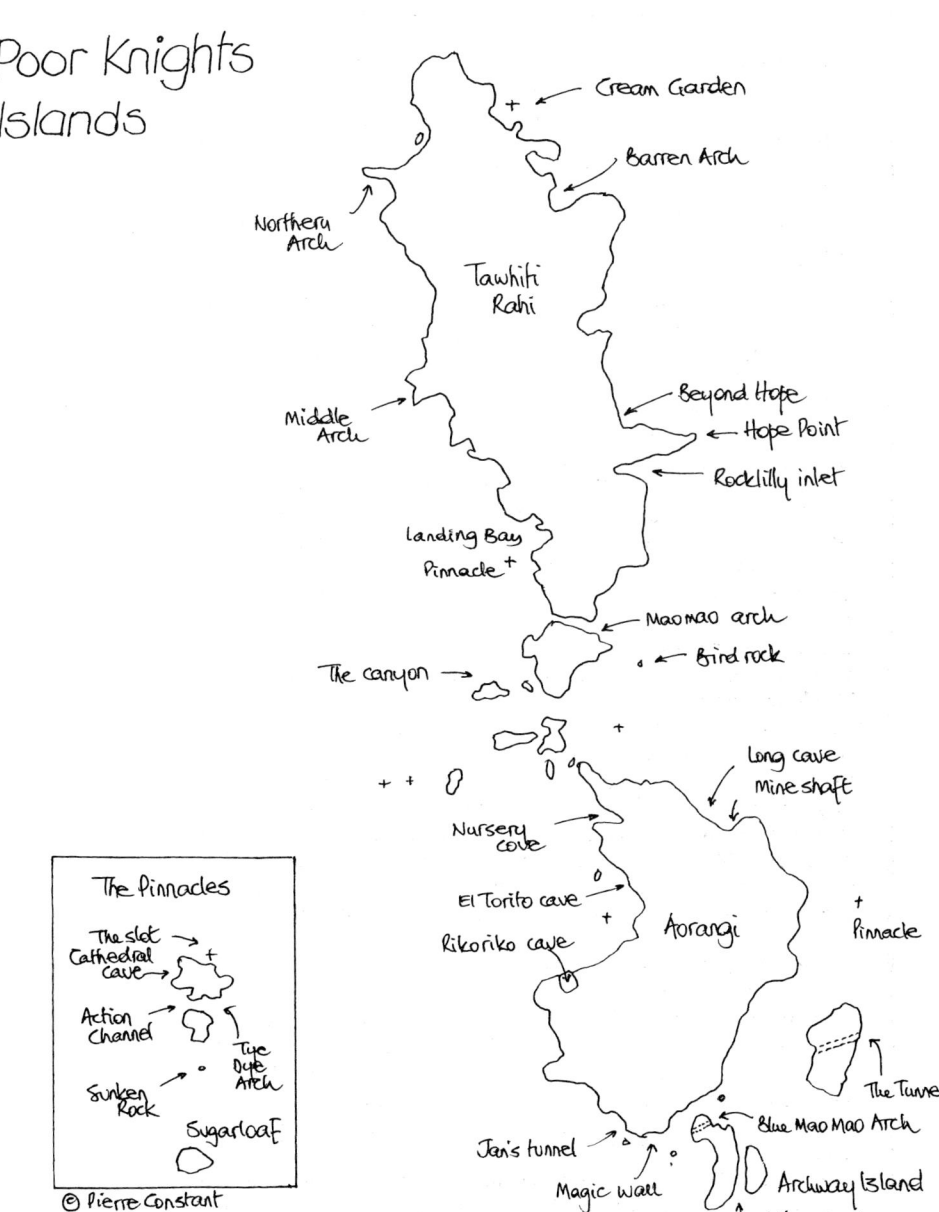

among big boulders covered with kelp, and comes to a ridge going into the deep. Schools of koheru (endemic), knifefish, yellow stripe jacks, kingfish are curious of divers. At depth, below the 36 metres mark, jewel anemones, gorgonians and grey filament sponges, cover and crest the rocks. Yellow morays and grey morays are found on the colourful wall. Sea chubs and blue maomao schools and the endemic butterfish are found in the shallows.

BLUE MAO MAO ARCH WAS made famous by the once upon a time visit of J.Y.Cousteau. This tunnel of 50 metres in length, cuts through the northern tip of Archway Island, south of Aorangi Island. Rather shallow in depth (13m), it is open at both ends. Light comes through an opening of the roof in the middle part. A school of blue mao mao inhabits the arch, flowing in and out, with other fishes like 'demoiselles' (endemic grey damsels with two white spots), red moki, marblefish, dwarf and northern scorpionfish. Lovely red banded blue eyed triplefins (endemic) are found on the walls. Boulders and swimthroughs add to the fascination of 'Blue Mao Mao Arch'. A pod of large bottlenosed dolphins frequents the area. The nearby "Magic Wall" dive site (south Aorangi), is a great place for macro-photography: orange spotted clown nudibranchs, "Ceratosoma amoena" and the variable nudibranch, "Aphelodoris luctuosa" are found here, among others. The wall comes down to 19 metres on sand.

ROCK LILY INLET is a sheltered cove at the bottom of a cliff on the east side of Tawhiti Rahi, the north island. Start the dive under the boat at a depth of 34 metres, among boulders in the kelp forest. Beautiful Sandager's wrasses and red pigfish will come to visit. Yellow and grey morays hide in holes or rest on ledges of the wall. At the far end of the cove, three underwater caves host unsuspected wonders like red spiny lobsters, black rays and the elusive carpetshark, "Cephaloscyllium isabellum" (80cm long), a shy nocturnal predator.

BARREN ARCH is a great dive site on the north east of Tawhiti Rahi. It begins along a wall, then passes over a ridge with kelp swaying in the current, down into a gully that leads into the arch. The bottom is made of boulders, sloping down to 33 metres and beyond, towards the exit. Blue and pink mao mao schools frequent the passage, yellow morays, mados, roughy and bigeyes (both endemic) and spiny lobsters rest under rocks. Encrusting sponges on the walls, jewel anemones, yellow zooanthids, small white gorgonians. A good habitat for nudibranchs. A mystic blue light enters the arch and provides good photographic opportunities for wide angle lenses.

BEYOND HOPE, found north of Hope Point on north island, is a maze of boulders, underwater canyons, swimthroughs, rounded cobblestones in gullies, proving that sea level was much lower than it is now. There are small shallow water inlets to explore. A good wall outside these inlets, is home to the yellow with blue stripes nudibranch,

"Tambja verconis", grazing on green bryozoans. Further down, towards Hope Point, a large underwater cave opens under the rock mass, tantalizing.

NURSERY COVE on the west side of Aorangi island, is a lovely cove with a small cliff crested with trees and vegetation, and a nursing ground for some shark species. Dive under the boat in the shallows. The sea floor of boulders and kelp beds hosts funny conger eels, Sangdager's wrasses and leatherjackets. It slopes down gradually onto white sand, towards the exit of the cove. The water visibility clears up amazingly to about 40 metres. A lone John Dory — silvery brown with a conspicuous black spot on its sides, may hover above the sand. An old anchor lies on the sea floor, covered with green algae. Coming out of the blue, a large school of hundreds of silver trevallies, "Pseudocaranx dentex", circled me into a curious frenzy for a few minutes, and leaves me bedazzled. The hidden shape of a grey ray with small eyes appears under the sediment, stares at me as I approach. With a gesture of the hand, I tried to clear the sand off its eyes. It moved suddenly and the tail emerged, thick like a branch with two dorsal fins and a triangular caudal fin. I realize with awe that this was not a common ray but some sort of angelshark. Cautiously, I disturbed it again with a flip of my fins. It took off over the white seafloor. I was struck by the beauty of its flight. Glenn Edney, a 'kiwi' instructor and photographer to whom I reported the incident, confirmed in fact that I had met with the electric ray, "Torpedo fairchildi". I could have been stunned and knocked unconscious by a jolt of more than 200 volts! As I returned to the mooring site, over a ridge covered with kelp, I saw a school of pink mao mao shining with electric splendour hovering over the white sand and glittering in the afternoon sunlight. This magnificent vision of the Poor Knights will remain in my memory, an out-of-this-world experience, to be repeated some day when I return for more.

The Poor Knights Islands, a Marine Reserve since 1980, was declared a total Reserve on 1 October 1998. Its boundary extends 800 metres (0.435 nautical miles) around the islands, including the "Pinnacles" and "Sugar Loaf Rocks". No fishing or landing is allowed. Commercial fishing is prohibited except for long lining within 3 nautical miles of the islands. No commercial fishing (all methods) is allowed within a radius of one nautical mile (1852m).

Pierre Constant
(www.calaolife.com)

FURTHER READING
Coastal Fishes of New Zealand—an identification guide by Malcolm Francis, Reed Books, Auckland 1996
Discover the Poor Knights Wonderland—identification guide to 65 species of fish + 50 species of invertebrates by Glenn Edney, ed. Seatech, Auckland (October 2001)

For general information on the island group, please contact **The Department of Conservation**, at 8A Kaka St., Whangarei. Phone: (09)430-2133.

To dive the Poor Knights islands area, contact **Dive Tutukaka**—Jeroen Jongejans, Poor Knights Dive Centre, Marina Road, Tutukaka, RD.3, Whangarei, Tel: 64-9-4343-867. Website <www.diving.co.nz>

North Central

The North Central region of the North Island, south of Auckland, encompasses the Coromandel Peninsula, the Bay of Plenty and the rolling farmland of the Waikato. Its population centre is Hamilton, New Zealand's eighth largest city.

Today the prosperous Waikato region is bucolic and peaceful, but it wasn't always so. The Waikato was once the homeland of the Tainui tribes, who resisted the tide of European settlement. At first they had tolerated the settlers, willingly trading with them and accepting their Christian religion. But many Tainui leaders felt tribal sovereignty was being threatened by land sales and the erosion of traditional culture. In an effort to withstand the foreign onslaught, the Waikato's Maori started the King Movement. Potatau I, a respected Waikato chief, was named a Maori king and ruled complete with flag, council of state, and law-making powers over a number of tribes. He was installed by his followers at Ngaruawahia, near Hamilton, in 1858. After war broke out in 1862 between British troops and Taranaki Maori over land purchases, the British government prepared to push into the Waikato too—partly in pursuit of Maori aggressors in the Taranaki war, but partly in response to the Waikato-based King Movement and its opposition to sale of Waikato land. The British offensive resulted in the bloody Waikato wars of 1863–64. The Waikato tribes were defeated and the Maori king was driven into exile in the neighbouring bushclad hill-country, since then known as 'The King Country'. The British then confiscated much of the Waikato from the rebel tribes, or took it later by stealthier, pseudo-legal means.

The sparsely populated Coromandel Peninsula was one of the first parts of New Zealand to attract European settlers, who came first for the kauri trees and later for gold. Today this narrow finger of land attracts artisans and vacationing city folk.

The beautiful **Bay of Plenty**, as it was appreciatively named by Captain Cook, stretches from the Coromandel Peninsula to the East Cape. White Island, 50 kilometres (31 miles) offshore, belches steam and ash from its cone, marking the northeastern end of New Zealand's volcanic zone. The bay itself is lined with golden beaches and backed by fertile land supporting fruit and dairy farms. At the bay's western end, the twin seaside resort towns of Tauranga and Mount Maunganui are renowned centers for surf-casting and deep-sea fishing. At the bay's eastern end lies the smaller and quieter Whakatane, a popular holiday spot for sun and sea.

Hamilton, New Zealand's largest inland city, lies in the Waikato Plain, a fertile green expanse full of dairy farms, orchards, and market gardens. Mineral springs support an Edwardian-style spa at Te Ahora. And around Cambridge, stud farms breed and train thoroughbred racehorses on the lush pastureland.

The Waitomo Caves, one of New Zealand's greatest attractions, lie south of Hamilton off Highway 3. Kilometres of subterranean limestone caverns, many still unexplored, are illuminated by thousands of glow-worms that twinkle in the darkness like stars. The caves are also the centre of adventure-tourism, with abseiling and blackwater rafting the most popular activities.

COROMANDEL PENINSULA

Dominated by a rugged spine of mountains, this 100-kilometre (62-mile)-long finger of land separates the Firth of Thames from the Bay of Plenty. The mountains descend steeply to the Firth on the west and slope more gently down to magnificent stretches of white-sand beaches on the east. The undeveloped mountains and lovely coasts, a couple of hours' drive from Auckland, are favourite haunts for nature- and sun-loving New Zealanders but are not well known to outsiders.

The Coromandel has a chequered history. Its kauri forests were ruthlessly plundered for timber and gum, and a gold rush in 1867 brought short-lived prosperity, swelling the peninsula's population for a decade before giving out. Today the untamed scenery and calm isolation attract many craftspeople as residents.

GETTING THERE

Intercity buses run regularly between Auckland and Thames. From there, Murphy buses continue north to Coromandel and over the Coromandel Range to Whitianga. Shuttle buses run north to Fletcher Bay and south from Whitianga to Hahei and Hot Water Beach. Air Coromandel provides a link between Auckland and Whitianga.

SIGHTS

Thames, at the base of the Coromandel's west coast, is the peninsula's largest town. Thames Information Centre, at 206 Pollen Street, is a good source of information on the whole peninsula and is the main bus depot. Phone (07)868-7284. The town's main attractions revolve around its gold-mining past. Visit the **Thames Gold Mining Complex** for a tour of an underground mine and the chance to see a stamper battery in use. Phone (07)868-7448. Through the original gold rush, mining skills were taught at the **Thames School of Mines**, now a museum displaying a large collection of minerals on Cochrane Street. Phone (07)868-6227.

The coast north of Thames to Tapu is a delight of rocky headlands and picturesque sandy coves. The main road runs right alongside the Firth of Thames to the picturesque town of **Coromandel**. This stretch of coast is known as the Pohutukawa Coast, for the trees that bloom a distinctive red colour through summer. Like Thames, Coromandel has a stamper-battery display and a small mining museum, but the highlight is **Driving Creek Railway**. Built by a local potter to transport clay from high on a hillside to his studio, the railway also transports passengers, taking them through tunnels, around switchbacks, and over a couple of high trestles. Phone (07)866-8703.

The Giant Kauri

The kauri (*Agathis australis*) is the king of New Zealand's magnificent forests. In the same league as California's giant redwood, the tree grows to an enormous size and a staggering old age. One towering monarch still standing in the Waipoua Kauri Sanctuary is thought to be 2,000 years old. The kauri forests once stretched through Northland to beyond Auckland and across the Coromandel Peninsula. Sadly, today few of the trees remain.

The kauri's silver-grey trunk soars skyward in a perfectly straight shaft toward a canopy of thick, leathery leaves. This results in startling beauty, but also invited destruction at the hands of New Zealand's early shipbuilding industry. Young kauris made excellent masts, while the straight-grained hardwood of the mature trees was ripped into clean, wide planks for building the rest of the ship.

The Royal Navy and shipbuilders of all kinds set up operations in Kaipara and Hokianga Harbours in the mid-1800s. Sawmill settlements dotted Northland's west coast and later the Waitakere Ranges west of Auckland. The timber boom could not last because the kauris grew too slowly to replace themselves; the trees need 80 to 100 years to become commercially millable and 800 years to reach full maturity. By 1860 the big forests were gone.

Tane Mahuta, 'Lord of the Forest,' is New Zealand's largest kauri tree. It stands 52 metres tall, 13 metres in diameter and is estimated to be well over 1,000 years old.

But there was still money to be made off the kauri. Dead trees left deposits of resinous sap as hardened gum in the soil. Beds of the petrified gum lay underground where prehistoric forests had once stood. The Maori chewed the fresh gum, burned it as fuel, and used its soot for tattooing. The gum commanded a high price abroad as a base for varnish and linoleum, and a 'poor man's gold rush' gathered steam. By 1880, some 2,000 gum-diggers had swarmed to the gum fields, most of them coming from Dalmatia to escape conscription into the Austrian army. The gum trade peaked around 1890, and when the gum fields were exhausted the Dalmatians moved south to the area around Auckland to plant vineyards, inaugurating New Zealand's wine industry.

The devastation of the kauris left behind infertile land, for the big trees over centuries had leached the soil, which gum-diggers then reduced to potholes. Fertilizers and much hard effort have finally created farmland. In 1952, public pressure saved the last of the kauris when Waipoua and Omahuta were proclaimed forest sanctuaries. The Matakohe Kauri Museum, at Matakohe, records the whole kauri saga in exhaustive, fascinating detail.

This cave provides access to a pleasant stretch of beach at Cathedral Cove.

Two roads lead from Thames across the peninsula's mountainous spine to the east coast. Highway 25 passes many protected coves and beaches along a round-about route to Whitianga, while the unsealed 309 Road passes a kauri grove, pretty **Waiau Falls**, and two gardens open to the public.

Whitianga, the main town on the east coast, has a sheltered harbour famed for big-game fishing and a long beach lined with palm trees. A passenger ferry runs across Whitianga Harbour to Ferry Landing, from where a short walk leads to a lookout offering views across the entire sweep of Mercury Bay. Nearby **Hahei** is worth visiting for **Cathedral Cove**, where a massive cavern has been eroded into coastal cliffs. The coast around Hahei and the offshore islands are protected as a marine reserve, which means fishing is prohibited and marine life is abundant; divers can have a great time exploring the underwater world. To the south at **Hot Water Beach**, underground thermal waters lie just below the sand. Scoop at the sand a couple of hours either side of low tide to enjoy a hot soak. Still further south, the beach at **Whangamata** is well known to surfers for its waves.

Inland, **Goldfields Railway** follows a historic route between Waihi and Waikino three times daily. Phone (07)863-8640.

BAY OF PLENTY

The Bay of Plenty is indeed a delightful area of plenty. It is famous for kiwi fruit, the premium product of New Zealand's fruit and vegetables sector and the country's fourth largest export earner (after meat, dairy and forest products). Highway 2 runs along much of the Bay of Plenty shore. Air New Zealand serves Tauranga and Whakatane from Auckland and Wellington. Intercity and Newmans link the area with all parts of the North Island, although neither offers direct service between Tauranga and Whakatane.

Tauranga is the region's main city and port, through which passes export timber cut from pine forests around Rotorua. The city's gentle climate and white, sandy beaches make it a favourite retirement area and a centre for holidays and sports, especially big-game fishing. The Tauranga Visitor Information Centre is on Willow Street. The bus depot is around the corner at 80 Dive Crescent. Phone (07)578-8103. A downtown beautification programme has transformed **The Strand**, the town's main street. Cobbled roads, Old World-style street lamps and a selection of outdoor cafés make for a pleasant stroll. Follow The Strand north along the harbourfront, passing lovely gardens, to the city's well-preserved historical area dating from the early 1800s. It is still called the 'Camp', after the original military settlement overlooking the bay. The first mission house, **The Elms**, built between 1838 and 1847 and containing some original furnishings, is one of the oldest homes in New Zealand. It's open Saturday, Sunday, and Wednesday 2–4 pm. The fine garden, laid out in the same period, is open to the public 9 am–5 pm. Phone (07)577-9772.

Mount Maunganui, across the harbour, stands 232 metres (761 feet) high. Once an island, the 'Mount' is now joined to the mainland by the slim isthmus on which the town of Mount Maunganui sits. A track leads to the wooded peak of the Mount, which offers superb views on all sides. (Allow one and a half hours return.) Rare hot saltwater pools at the base of the Mount offer soothing relaxation. The surf and golden sand of magnificent Ocean Beach stretch for 15 kilometres (nine miles) along the bay and can be reached from Marine Parade, on the eastern side of the Mount. A summer-only ferry service departs regularly from the end of Wharf Street, Tauranga, for Mount Maunganui.

Lying 40 kilometres (25 miles) off the coast is **Tuhua (Mayor) Island**. The remnant of an ancient volcano, this island makes a delightful destination for a day trip, with forests of pohutukawa trees, two lakes, and a rugged shoreline lapped by clear waters. Scheduled ferry services run out to the island in January only. Phone (07)575-4165.

Whakatane, the main town of the eastern end of the Bay of Plenty, is smaller than Tauranga and full of flowers in summer. It also offers splendid surf and sand at Ohope Beach, six kilometres (four miles) east of the town. Whakatane is one of the best places to swim with dolphins. Dolphins Down Under supplies the boat ride and wet suits for this unique experience. Phone (0800)354-7737. **White Island** is another local attraction. This still-active volcano, which belches ash many hundreds of metres skyward, lies 50 kilometres (31 miles) north of Whakatane. It can be reached by boat or helicopter. Tours to see the island, as well as big-game fishing excursions and jet-boat trips on the Rangitaiki River, are easily arranged at the Whakatane Visitor Centre, Quay Street. Phone (07)308-6058.

HAMILTON AND ENVIRONS

A military post established in 1864, Hamilton has grown into a thriving industrial, farming and agricultural-research centre with a population of 124,000. It is nicknamed the 'Fountain City,' but its pleasant parks and gardens bordering Hamilton Lake and the Waikato River—which meanders leisurely through town centre—could earn it other equally poetic names.

GETTING THERE

Air New Zealand connects Hamilton with Auckland and Wellington. The Airport Shuttle meets all planes, providing bus service to the city. Hamilton is on Tranz Rail's main trunk line; trains run daily to Wellington and Auckland. The station is off Queens Avenue. Intercity and Newmans operate from the Transport Centre at the corner of Ward and Anglesea Streets, joining Hamilton with towns in all directions. Highway 1 connects Hamilton with Auckland, some 129 kilometres (80 miles) to the north, and with Wellington, 532 kilometres (330 miles) to the south.

INFORMATION

Hamilton Visitor Centre is in the Transport Centre at the corner of Bryce and Anglesea Streets. It is open weekdays 9 am–5 pm and weekends 10 am–2 pm. Phone (07)839-3580.

SIGHTS

Hamilton is not a tourist centre, but it is nevertheless a pleasant city with interesting sights and makes a good base for visiting the surrounding areas. The modern and spacious **Waikato Museum**, on Grantham Street, holds an excellent collection of historic and contemporary Maori art centred around a superb war canoe built in the 1830s. The painting exhibits are often outstanding. The building also offers a restaurant and outstanding river views from the upper levels. Open 10 am–4.30 pm. Phone (07)838-6606. **Founders Memorial Theatre**, on the corner of London and Tristram Streets, is the city's cultural centre. The wonderful Centennial Fountain is nearby. Other pleasant fountains are found in parks and gardens throughout the city, especially Garden Place, on Victoria Street. Upstream from downtown, accessible from Cobham Drive or by a pleasant riverfront walk, are **Hamilton Gardens**, the largest garden complex in the Southern Hemisphere. Cruises on the Waikato River aboard the historic MV *Waipa Delta*, a paddleboat with on-board restaurant, depart Memorial Park Jetty on Memorial Drive daily for lunch and dinner. Phone (07)854-7813.

Cambridge, 24 kilometres (15 miles) southeast of Hamilton on Highway 1, is also on the banks of the Waikato River. It is a quiet, pretty town with tree-lined avenues, English-style gardens and a village green where men in white play cricket. Church bells peal, transporting the visitor back to the uncomplicated England of another era. Along the highway from Hamilton, racehorses graze in the emerald fields of stud stables.

Ngaruawahia, 19 kilometres (12 miles) northwest of Hamilton on Highway 1, is on the confluence of the Waikato and Waipa Rivers. It was the original site of the Maori King Movement and is still the official residence of the Maori queen, Te Arikinui Dame Te-Ata-i-Rangi-Kaahu. The **Turangawaewae Marae**, where she resides, is open to the public on occasional weekends; obtain the schedule at the information centre in Hamilton. The marae contains a splendid meeting house, much fine wood carving and the queen's residence, which has a five-sided tower on one corner. In mid-March, on the Saturday nearest St. Patrick's Day, the Ngaruawahia Regatta is held at the Point, the confluence of the two rivers. Events at this unique carnival include traditional Maori canoe races, horse swimming, tribal dance competitions and a parade of great war canoes, with a spectacular salute to the Maori queen and her guests.

Te Aroha, 53 kilometres (33 miles) northeast of Hamilton on Highway 26, was a gold-mining town and fashionable spa at the turn of the century. Its Te Aroha Domain retains the atmosphere of the Edwardian era with 20 hectares of gardens, walks, and manicured lawns, dotted with Edwardian gazebos and pavilions. Behind the bathhouse complex, a boiling soda-water geyser, reputedly one of the few in the world, shoots skyward approximately every 30 minutes. The **Te Aroha Mineral Pools**, a modern complex of private pools, is open daily 10 am–10 pm. Phone (07)884-8717. Approximately the same distance from Hamilton but to the northwest is another hot springs, **Waingaro**, which enjoys sulphur-free waters. Phone (07)825-4761.

Raglan, 48 kilometres (30 miles) west of Hamilton on Highway 23, lies at the mouth of picturesque, many-armed Raglan Harbour. The black-sand beaches at this seaside resort don't have the appeal of the golden beaches on the east coast, but this is immaterial to surfers, who come from around the world to ride the perfectly formed waves of nearby Whale Bay and Manu Bay. Downtown Raglan is compact but picturesque. The main street is lined with date palms and ends on the harbourfront, from where a narrow footbridge crosses the water to a large grassy reserve.

Near **Te Mata**, 21 kilometres (13 miles) south of Raglan on the inland road to Kawhia, a track is signposted to **Bridal Veil Falls**. A ten-minute walk through dense forest leads to a waterfall that plummets 60 metres (197 feet) down sheer cliffs to a deep pool below. A further ten-minute climb down a steep path brings you to an even more dramatic vantage point at the foot of the falls. Beyond the falls is strange **Lake Disappear**, which occupies an elevated valley in wet weather but disappears completely through cracks in the rocks during dry spells.

Kawhia Harbour, at the end of the road, is a remote corner of the North Island, forgotten by time. This is the best natural harbour on the west coast and was once a major trading centre, but when Europeans fled the King Country in the 1860s, history passed it by. Railways and main roads went elsewhere, and the area remains a time capsule of an earlier New Zealand. At **Te Puia Hot Water Beach**, beyond the tiny township of Kawhia, hot springs seep up through the sand, like those at Hot Water Beach on the Coromandel Peninsula. At low tide you can relax in a hot soaking pool scooped out of the sand with your own hands.

Glow-worms

Glow-worms are one of the few living creatures that create their own light. They occur throughout New Zealand, thriving in dark, damp environments, but are especially prolific in Waitomo's Glow-worm Cave. The glow-worm is a stage in the life of the fungus gnat, a small creature similar in appearance to a mosquito. At the larval stage, the fungus gnat grows as a wormlike creature, hanging from a wall or overhang. It feeds continuously, catching in a sticky mass of thread insects attracted to its light. At maturity, usually six to nine months, the thread becomes a cocoon and the larva evolves into an adult gnat. Eleven months after hatching, the gnat bursts from the cocoon. Within days it mates, lays about 50 eggs, then dies.

WAITOMO CAVES

The remarkable Waitomo Caves lie beneath rugged hills 74 kilometres (46 miles) south of Hamilton, west of Highway 3. Two of the six main caves are open to the public. Some offer easy exploration on foot, while others require skilled caving techniques. The introduction of a wide range of adventure activities in the caves has seen Waitomo grow into a premier visitor attraction.

Intercity offers day tours to Waitomo from Rotorua and Auckland, but these tours are rushed. The nearest stop on Intercity's scheduled route is Otorohanga, from where the Waitomo Shuttle makes the short run to the caves. Taxis are also available in Otorohanga. The attractions of Waitomo are spread out over one kilometre (0.6 miles) either side of small Waitomo village, which exists only to serve visitors. Although accommodation in the village is limited, it extends the full price spectrum—from camping, through budget to the luxury Waitomo Caves Hotel.

The focal point of the village is the **Waitomo Museum of Caves**, which holds the official information centre. As well as advising on the range of available activities in the area, the centre operates the post office, exchanges foreign currency and makes adventure bookings. The museum itself houses excellent information about the caves, including displays, fossils and an audio-visual presentation. Open 8 am–5 pm, until 8 pm in summer. Phone (07)878-7640.

The most visited attraction at Waitomo is **Glow-worm Cave**, 500 metres (1,640 feet) west of the museum. Groups of up to 50 are taken on a 45-minute guided tour of the cave. A well-constructed walkway leads through awe-inspiring limestone formations, but the high point is a boat ride in a flat-bottomed punt into a vaulted cavern twinkling with the blue-green lights of thousands of tiny glow-worms. The tour of this cave is not cheap and is very commercial, but this is the most spectacular of Waitomo's caves. Two kilometres (1.2 miles) further west is **Aranui Cave**. Smallest and prettiest of the caves, Aranui holds delicately fluted stalactites and stalagmites. Tickets are sold at the entrance to Glow-worm Cave and at the information centre.

    Black Water rafting is a unique Waitomo experience that since the mid-1980s has grown to become one of New Zealand's most popular commercial adventures. First you're decked out in a wet suit and a helmet with a light, and given a flotation tube. Then experienced guides lead you underground for a three-hour trip, part walking, part floating—including a jump over a small waterfall. At the final stages of the journey, you'll float down a river through caverns festooned with glow-worms. Hot showers and a bowl of soup are provided afterwards. A second six-hour blackwater adventure includes a 35-metre (115-foot) abseil into Ruakuri Cave and a flying-fox journey to glow-worms. No previous caving experience needed. These adventures operate from the Black Water Café, two kilometres

The prehistoric-looking tuatara is found only on New Zealand's offshore islands. Experts estimate this reptile, which predates the dinosaur, evolved into its current form 250 million years ago.

(1.2 miles) east of Waitomo Village. Phone (07)878-6219. Lost World is a much longer adventure, taking a day and a half. The first half-day is spent learning to abseil, then a full day is spent on an incredible journey, beginning with a 100-metre (328-foot) abseil into the 'Lost World.' This underground wonderland features glow-worms by the thousand, fossils, rock formations and waterfalls, viewed as you wade, walk or swim through the kind of places rarely seen except by speleologists. For those with less time, the same company offer the Haggis Honking Holes, a half-day combination of abseiling, caving and toobing. Book through the information centre or phone Waitomo Adventures at (07)878-7788.

Not all the action at Waitomo is underground. Waitomo Caves Horse Treks offers rides ranging from one hour to a full day, as well as overnight treks. Phone (07)878-5065. Ohaki Maori Village, on the road to Waitomo, is worth a stop. A reconstructed pa, or fortified village, it is open for inspection, and you can take an instructive walk through the forest to Opapaka Pa (see *Focus*, page 101). Open daily 10 am–4.30 pm.

Watch for three natural wonders during a half-hour drive along Te Anga Road, which leads west from Waitomo Village. Mangapohue Natural Bridge is signposted 26 kilometres (16 miles) along the road. A 15-minute walk leads to the remarkable limestone arch—the eroded remnant of an ancient, collapsed cave—standing 15 metres (50 feet) high in a forested gorge. Piripiri Cave, signposted 30 kilometres (19 miles) along Te Anga Road, is a small cavern containing giant fossil oysters around 30 million years old. A flashlight and good footwear are needed. A further two kilometres (1.2 miles) west, at Marokopa Falls, the Marokopa River bounds down a series of steps before plunging a spectacular 36 metres (118 feet) down a forested cliff. A ten-minute walk on a good track leads to the base of the falls. At the end of the road, at the small fishing village of Marokopa, it's possible to walk 800 metres (one-half mile) along the bank of the Marokopa River to a wide black-sand beach lashed by the wild waters of the Tasman Sea.

FOCUS

The **Firth of Thames**, between Auckland and the Coromandel Peninsula, has extensive tidal mud flats and shell banks perfect for migratory waders. The best bird-watching sites are near the village of Miranda, which is about 70 kilometres (44 miles) southeast of Auckland. Up to 60 species annually are recorded along this stretch of coast, with godwits, knots and South Island pied oystercatchers most common in summer. Other migrants include sandpipers, turnstones, shovelers and red-necked stints. Large numbers of wrybills overwinter. The Miranda Shorebird Centre on East Coast Road, near Miranda, is an information centre that also offers basic overnight accommodation. Phone (09)232-2781.

In the forested **Coromandel Range**, kiwi, bellbird and tui are all common. Kaka and the North Island kokako are present but seldom seen.

At the north end of **Tauranga Harbour**, in the Bay of Plenty, pied oystercatcher and godwit gather on tidal flats. Further south on the harbour, wrybill can be seen January to August. At Tauranga itself, the Waikareao Estuary supports wrybill, godwit, pied stilt and Caspian tern. Blue penguins occasionally come ashore at Mount Maunganui. A large lagoon at **Matata** provides habitat for over a dozen bird species, including black swan and a variety of shags and ducks. At the lagoon's outlet, banded and New Zealand dotterel feed on exposed mud flats.

Since the arrival of Europeans, areas of wetland in the **Waikato** have decreased over 90 per cent as swampland has been reclaimed for dairy farming. The most significant remaining area is the **Whangamarino Wetlands**, reached by leaving Highway 1 at Meremere. Resident bird life here includes New Zealand's largest breeding population of bittern, as well as heron, egret, shag, spotless crake, kingfisher, pukeko, shining cuckoo and many other species. Amongst the waterfowl on the Whangamarino River are a few brown teal, New Zealand's rarest indigenous duck. To the south is Waikato's largest lake, **Waikare**, where you'll find kingfisher, shag and Caspian tern. West of Hamilton, reef heron nest in the limestone cliffs of **Raglan Harbour**.

At **Otorohanga**, 46 kilometres (29 miles) south of Hamilton near the Waitomo Caves, the Kiwi House is a famous breeding centre. The first artificially incubated kiwi eggs were successfully hatched here in 1977. In the Kiwi House night and day are reversed, with the kiwis foraging through the day by artificial moonlight. Outdoor cages and enclosures and a walk-through aviary hold an assortment of native birds. Open 9.00 am–4.30 pm. Phone (07)873-7391.

Coromandel Forest Park, protecting the interior of the Coromandel Peninsula, offers a great variety of walking opportunities. Start by visiting the Department of Conservation field centre in the Kauaeranga Valley, east of Thames. Phone (07)867-9080. The best views are from the summit of Castle Rock, east of Coromandel. The stone pinnacle rises 520 metres (1,700 feet) above sea level. Allow two hours each way.

A walking trail leads up the slope of oceanfront **Mount Maunganui**, east of Tauranga, while another circles this ancient volcano.

At **Waitomo Caves**, the interesting five-kilometre (one-way) Waitomo Walkway begins at the Museum of Caves. The walkway leads through a narrow gorge and along Waitomo Stream to the Ruakuri Scenic Reserve and a natural limestone bridge. When the river is low you can climb down inside the arch and look for fossils. Allow three hours return. West from Waitomo are trailheads for a variety of short walks to waterfalls, through old growth forests, and to other natural bridges.

Ohaki Maori Village is the starting point for a lovely little walk to Opapaka Pa, the hilltop site of an old fortified village. A gravelled path leads steadily upward through a fine forest in which many Maori medicinal plants are labelled and described. Allow about 45 minutes return.

The town of **Whitianga**, on the east coast of the Coromandel Peninsula, is only a little less famous than the Bay of Islands in the world of big-game fishing. The season runs from 26 December to the end of April, with February and March considered the best months. Boat charters can be arranged at the Whitianga Information Centre at 66 Albert Street. Phone (07)866-5555. Bookings should be made well in advance.

All the rivers in the **Waikato** area around Hamilton have fish in them, but this densely populated area is less rewarding than the nearby Taupo area.

The Bay of Plenty holds a trio of lovely courses. The **Tauranga Golf Club** at Gate Pa meets the high standards of the many keen golfers in the area. Flowering shrubs and trees line the fairway making it especially beautiful. Par 71. Phone (07)578-5433. In the general vicinity, **Mount Maunganui Golf Club**, on Fairway Avenue, is an excellent links course offering a fine test of skill. Par 72. Phone (07)575-3889. **Whakatane Golf Club**, at the eastern end of the bay, is also a good links course, with wide undulating fairways. Par 70. Phone (07)308-8117.

Hamilton has two very fine golf courses. The well-manicured **Hamilton Golf Club**, at St. Andrews just north of the city, occupies a picturesque, undulating site beside the Waikato River. Par 72. Phone (07) 843-6898. **Lochiel Golf Club** is a nearly flat, tree-lined course near the airport at Rukuhia, about ten kilometres (six miles) south of the city. Par 72. Phone (07)843-6281.

Vineyards are comparatively rare in the North Central region, and most wineries here import grapes. Founded in 1979, **Morton**, on Highway 2 near Katikati, 30 kilometres (19 miles) from Tauranga, combines wine-making skill with high technology. Vintner Evan Ward has built a high reputation for his Chardonnay, Sauvignon Blanc and méthode champenoise. Phone (07)552-0795, website <www.mortonstatewines.co.nz>.

In the Waikato, Te Kauwhata, reached by turnoff from Highway 1, 70 kilometres (44 miles) south of Auckland, was formerly a distinguished vineyard region that boasted the Te Kauwhata Viticultural Research Station, a government-funded wine-research centre that operated for over 90 years. The facility was closed down in

1991, victim to a policy of government withdrawal from the marketplace. Research from the station has benefited private vineyards in the area. Tom van Dam and Dr. Rainer Eschenbruch, both former research-station employees, established **Rongopai** in 1986. In 1995, they moved their small operation into the still-standing research station buildings on Te Kauwhata Road. The winery specializes in sweet wines made with botrytized grapes. The botrytis fungus grows naturally in the Te Kauwhata area. Vintners like it because it absorbs moisture from the grape and so concentrates the natural sweetness. Rongopai's botrytized Riesling and Chardonnay are both highly unusual dessert wines, naturally sweet, and pricey too. But the winery also produces a range of dry whites and reds and a smooth tawny port. Phone (07)826-3113, website <www.rongopaiwines.co.nz>. **Quarry Road** is the new name for Aspen Ridge, started in the mid-1960s by a former director of the research station. Although its Chardonnay seems to have the most potential, this winery is still best known for its Aspen Ridge grape juice. Phone (07)826-3595.

Land's end at Cape Regina, New Zealand's northern tip

The Centre

The centre of the North Island is a volcanic plateau where hot springs bubble, geysers erupt, and steam seeps unexpectedly from cracks in forested mountainsides. In the middle of the plateau lies Lake Taupo, teeming now with rainbow trout but testament to the awesome volcanic power of the region. It is one of the world's largest volcanic craters. The volcano's first eruption, an estimated 300,000 years ago, blew out 1,000 cubic kilometres (35 million cubic feet) of tephra in one of the mightiest eruptions ever known. Another Taupo explosion in AD 186, though only a tenth that size, caused such a darkening of the world's atmosphere that Roman historians noted stars shining during the daytime. South of the lake in Tongariro National Park, three volcanoes rise abruptly from the plateau. Tongariro, the oldest, smoulders. Young Ngauruhoe still periodically erupts. The third, Ruapehu, erupted spectacularly in 1995. Ruapehu is the North Island's highest mountain, and its snowclad slopes draw skiers and climbers from all over the world. The city of Rotorua, the North Island's foremost tourist resort, lies north of Lake Taupo, in the centre of spectacular volcanic scenery complete with geothermal activity and a string of lakes.

ROTORUA

Rotorua with a population of 60,000 is at the centre of a geothermal wonderland, halfway along a volcanic fault stretching from fuming White Island in the north to Mount Ruapehu, in Tongariro National Park, in the south. The city hugs the shore of Lake Rotorua, the largest of a dozen lakes strung across the northern volcanic plateau. To the east looms Mount Tarawera, a ravaged volcano that split asunder during a violent eruption in 1886. In Rotorua the sulphurous smell in the air and the unexpected sight of steam rising from cracks in the ground never let you forget that the earth has a molten core.

For hundreds of years before European settlers arrived, the Whanau Maori lived at Ohinemutu (now part of Rotorua city), drawing benefit from the curative mineral springs and natural hot water. After the Land Wars of the 1860s and the subsequent fight against the rebel Te Kooti, the region became safe for visitors. In the 1870s, ever-growing numbers of tourists marvelled at the famous Pink and White Terraces—natural crystalline silica steps that descended like stairs on Tarawera's southwestern side. The terraces were destroyed by the mountain's violent 1886 eruption, which also buried three villages and claimed more than 150 lives. By the turn of the century, Rotorua was a fashionable spa in the European mould, with a bath house and sanatoriums. It never lost its popularity and today offers modern tourists an appealing array of sights, activities and events. The Maori are now integrated into Western life, but have kept traditional culture alive. At Rotorua, arts and crafts centres display traditional Maori weaving and carving. And at many of the hotels, Maori performers present the fierce haka war dance and sweeter songs of love and legend.

GETTING THERE

Air New Zealand serves Rotorua from most North Island cities, and both offer direct flights to Christchurch. Intercity and Newmans run buses to all major towns, including Auckland, a four-hour ride to the north. The bus terminal is at 67 Fenton Street. Intercity also offers (long) day tours of Rotorua sights from Auckland. Continuing south through the central plateau, the two main bus lines are joined by numerous shuttle services to Taupo and the communities around Tongariro National Park. Highway 5 joins the city with Hamilton, Taupo and Napier while smaller highways link Rotorua to Tauranga to the north and Waitomo Caves to the west.

SIGHTS

The earth's crust is thin here. You'll see steam billowing from roadside vents, and you'll smell the distinctive hydrogen sulphide gas that gives Rotorua its distinctive odour. Most of Rotorua's wonders are commercially packaged. The most popular attractions focus on geothermal phenomena or Maori culture. They cost money, but you are paying, usually, for the distinctly awesome. Visitors on a budget can wander through pretty Government Gardens and see its boiling springs, or explore Kuirau Park, Whakarewarewa Forest Park, or Okere Falls and the Hillside Herb Garden—all of which are free. Tourism Rotorua, at 67 Fenton Street, provides information, maps and bookings of all sorts. Phone (07)348-5179 or (0800)768-678. Within the complex are a café, foreign currency exchange and souvenir shop, while out front is the main departure point for long-distance coaches.

Determined that Rotorua could be the Southern Hemisphere's greatest spa, an enthusiastic government built the **Government Gardens** in 1908. The gardens originally enclosed a series of hot pools and treatment rooms, but corrosive hydrogen sulphide gases made it a maintenance nightmare. The pools were shut in the 1960s. Today the site is a lovely, uncommercialized park of flower gardens interspersed with thermal hot spots; white-clad residents play bowls or croquet on the manicured lawns. The park is only a short walk from the information centre and is easily recognized by a grand Tudor edifice. The gardens' history is encapsulated in the **Rotorua Museum of Art and History**, which occupies the park's original Bath House. This is one of the best little museums in the country. Open daily 9.30 am–5 pm and until 6 pm in summer. Phone (07)349-4350. Also within Government Gardens is the **Orchid Garden**, which displays in two thermally heated greenhouses hundreds of tropical and native orchid varieties amidst streams and waterfalls. A 'water organ' fountain gurgles delicately or gushes aggressively according to the mood of booming classical music—quite a treat. Phone (07)347-6699. On the southern edge of Government Gardens, on Hinemoa Street, is the **Polynesian Spa**, a complex of hot mineral springs and

> *Now and then some small boy or girl falls into a boiling hole, and the parents are relieved of further trouble with them.*
>
> —*Oceania: or England and Her Colonies,*
> 1886, on Rotorua

public and private pools on the site of the 19th-century spa. A recent addition here is the Lake Spa: four 'rock-pools' right on the lake with full bar service and many touches you'd normally expect only from a four-star hotel. The complex is open daily 6.30 am–11 pm. Phone (07)348-1328.

Whakarewarewa, commonly known as 'Whaka', is the closest of the commercial thermal areas to downtown. It brings together the two best elements of Rotorua, highlighting Maori culture within the confines of a dramatic thermal reserve. The entrance, at the extreme south end of Fenton Street, is through a replica of Rotowhio Pa, a fortified Maori village. Maori guides are available to accompany visitors and are a real bonus for their knowledge and insight into Maori lore. The walkways through Whaka Thermal Reserve pass pools of bubbling mud, steaming silica terraces and (if you are lucky) geysers. The geysers lost some of their pizzazz in the 1970s and '80s as thermal energy was poached for home use, but they're restored now after an ordinance closed many domestic bores. The tour ends at Rahui Maori Village, where Maori women show how food is cooked in thermal water and explain other Maori customs adapted to the volcanic environment. If you keep your ticket stub you can

The Tudor-style Bath House, in Rotorua's Government Gardens, has been restored and now houses a museum.

Champagne Pool, Waiotapu Thermal Wonderland

Maori Carving

Of the various traditional Maori arts, wood carving, or *whakairo rakau*, was the most important and remains the most vigorous today. Objects made from jadelike greenstone and bone were also skillfully carved.

In pre-European times, the Maori master carvers were of noble rank, as the sacred act of re-creating and perpetuating the ancestral myths through carving was of deepest significance to the tribe. Trained in the art from early childhood, a great carver enjoyed as much status and renown as any mighty warrior. Carvers were always men; women were not even permitted to watch the process, just as they were banned from viewing other tribal rites.

The blades of adzes and gouges were made of chipped rock. Chisels for making fine details were made of greenstone, which could be honed to a surprisingly sharp, long-lasting edge. Tall native trees offered excellent, straight-grained wood for carving, and their size allowed carvers the freedom to work on a grand scale. Totara was the favoured wood, followed by kauri.

Highly symbolic, curvilinear carved designs embellished almost every object the Maori used. But carving reached its highest form in the elaborate decoration of buildings, especially food-storage houses and meeting houses. The all-important meeting house still serves as the focal point and spiritual centre of every Maori community. It is conceived as a living being. The head is represented by a central mask below a standing figure atop the gable. The arms are the ornamental boards covering the edge of the roof, often completed with fingers at the lower ends. The ridgepole is its spine, the rafters its rib cage, and the interior its belly. The carvings and paintings on different parts depict the ancestors, gods and mythological events most intimately connected with the life of the tribe. They constitute a visual history that,

Maori carvings

together with storytelling, relates and perpetuates the soul and culture of a tribe.

A distorted human figure, male or female, is the most common subject in Maori carving. The head is magnified because it is the container of *mauri ora*, the life spirit. Slanted eyes and three-fingered hands are thought to be superimposed bird features. Also common is the beaked *manaia*, a half-bird, half-human deity. The *marakihau*, half-fish, half-human, has a tubelike tongue capable of sucking up whole canoes. The *pakake* is a whale, and the *moko* a great lizard. *Tiki*, the term for any carved human figure, is applied now to the well-known greenstone charms (*hei-tiki*), whose original purpose and meaning have been lost.

The greatest examples of Maori carving are found in the major museums. The Maori themselves have never looked on a work of art as an object but rather as a living treasure with a soul. Such treasures belong to their tribe of origin forever and are only held in trust by museums. Meanwhile, young carvers are once again learning the traditional art from masters at Rotorua's Arts and Crafts Institute and other places, and a few contemporary Maori sculptors are exploring new ways of expressing ancient beliefs.

wander back the way you came instead of exiting here. Opposite the main entrance is the **New Zealand Maori Arts and Crafts Institute**, a government-assisted training school aimed at keeping the standard of Maori arts and crafts at a high level. On weekdays, Maori boys work under master carvers, and women demonstrate flax weaving. Open daily 8.30 am–5 pm. Phone (07)349-3463.

Waimangu Volcanic Valley, about 25 kilometres (15 miles) southeast of Rotorua, was created along with Lake Rotomahana by the devastating Mount Tarawera eruption of 1886. A three-kilometre (two-mile) walk offers stunning views of craters, cauldrons, steaming red cliffs and a boiling lake. Minibuses give free lifts back up the hill. Open daily 8.30 am–5 pm. Phone (07)366-6137.

Wai-O-Tapu Thermal Wonderland, noted for its many-coloured phenomena, is about 30 kilometres (19 miles) south of Rotorua, signposted off Highway 5. Easy pathways lead past variegated craters and silica terraces to a waterfall that changes colour after rainstorms and to the fizzing, multicoloured Champagne Pool. At 10.15 every morning Lady Knox Geyser shoots a mass of water and steam 21 metres (69 feet) skyward to the delight of gathered visitors. Open daily 8.30 am–5 pm. Phone (07)366-6333.

The smallest but most active of the commercial thermal areas is **Hell's Gate**, 16 kilometres (10 miles) northeast of Rotorua. The highlight here is Kahahi Falls, a thermal waterfall. Open daily 9 am–5 pm. Phone (07)345-3151.

Maori concerts, with dances and traditional games, are given in costume at the New Zealand Maori Arts and Crafts Institute and at Ohinemutu. Several big hotels offer

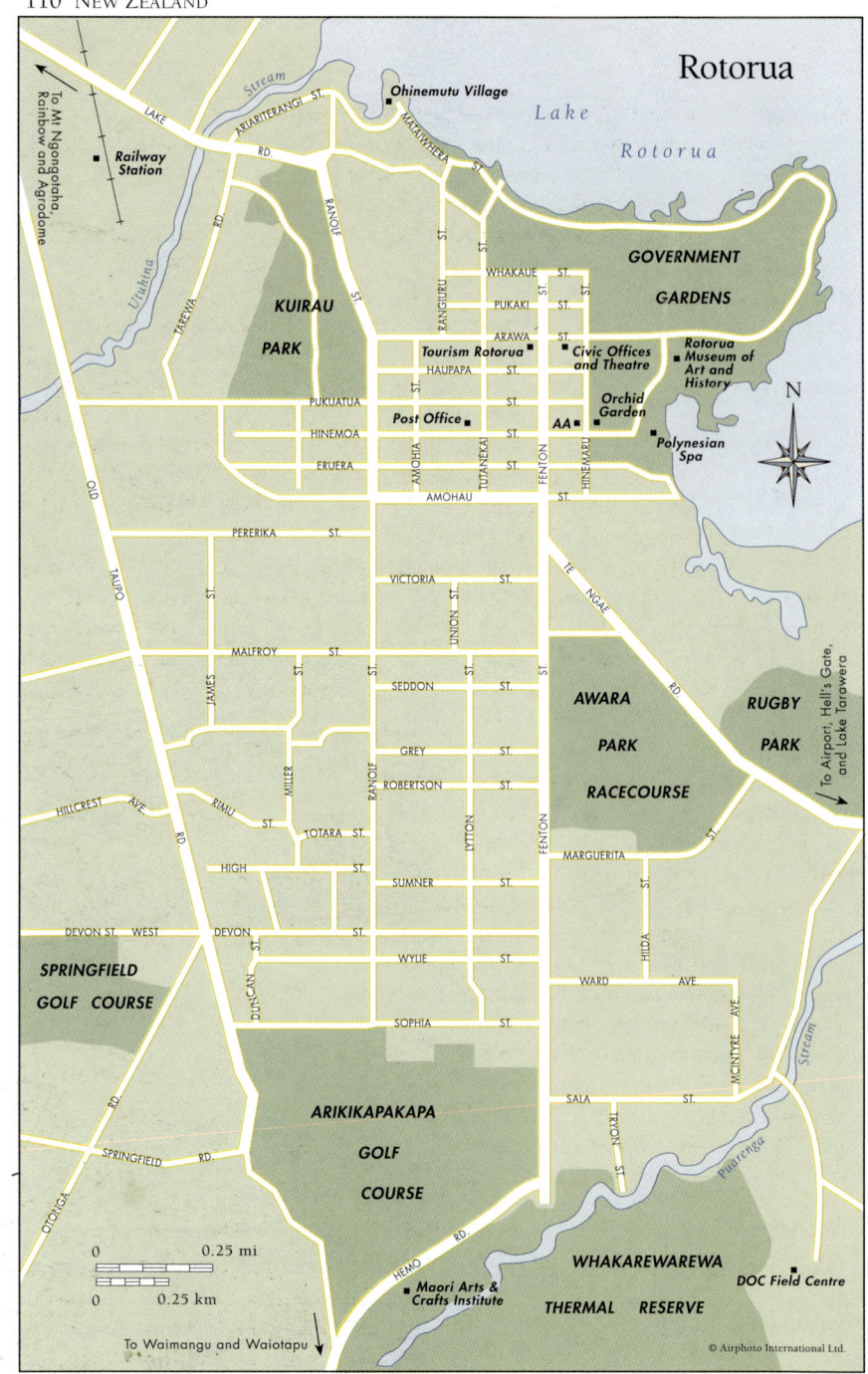

concerts in the evening along with a hangi, or traditional Maori feast, steam-cooked underground. The hangi offers authentic Maori dishes along with familiar fare. The Rakaeio and Paruahanui Maraes close to town also serve hangis. Contact Tourism Rotorua for details. Reservations are essential.

Ohinemutu Village was the original Maori village around which Rotorua grew. Its modern Maori inhabitants now live in Western-style houses, making full use of the thermal activity for cooking, washing and heating. But they cling to their Maori customs and lifestyle. The marae, or communal compound, has a splendidly ornate meeting house; some of the interior carvings are 200 years old. The compound is used for meetings, community affairs and the nightly magic of the maori, a concert which includes the traditional Poi dance and a haka (at 8 pm). Phone (07)349-3949 for reservations. St Faith's Anglican Church, opposite the meeting house, interprets the Christian faith through Maori art in a beautiful synthesis. An etched window depicts Christ in a chief's kiwi-feather cloak, apparently walking on the water of Lake Rotorua.

The **Buried Village**, 14 kilometres (nine miles) from Rotorua on Tarawera Road, is the partly excavated ruins of Te Wairoa, a part-European, part-Maori village buried by the 1886 eruption under two and a half metres (eight feet) of mud and ash. This tranquil place, away from the active hot spots, is full of strange stories and interesting relics. Open daily 9 am–4.30 pm. Phone (07)362-8287. Continue along Tarawera Road to reach Lake Tarawera, where a small launch cruises across the lake to a hot-water beach.

Mount Ngongotaha, 12 kilometres (7.5 miles) north of the city beside Highway 5, offers a fine panoramic view over the whole area. You can drive to the top or ride up by gondola to a restaurant high on the mountain's slopes. At the top you'll find a chairlift, luge rides and mini-golf. Next door, at **Rainbow Springs Nature Park**, crystal-clear waterfalls, pools and streams are set amongst ferns and forest. The wild trout here, protected from anglers, grow to an enormous size. Phone (07)350-0440. Further north along Highway 5, the **Agrodome** offers an hour-long show featuring well-trained sheep, fabled New Zealand sheepdogs and skilled shearers who can shear off

Fishing is foremost at Lake Taupo.

> *But why, I wonder, in a country so full of pleasant things are they so proud of Rotorua? As you alight from the train a great whiff of sulphur greets you and remains with you until you depart. Nevertheless I decline to rave about the disorderly manifestations of Nature which constitute a 'Thermal Region'; indeed, were I New Zealand I should keep it dark. It is though one took a visitor into one's bathroom, showed him the taps running and the bath leaking and said, 'The drains don't work, and at any moment the pipes may explode. Isn't it capital?'*
>
> —'Mr. Punch Goes A-Roving,'
> Punch 169, 1925

a whole fleece in less than two minutes. Shows are held three times daily. Phone (07)357-1050.

Other activities offered in Rotorua include: NZONE skydiving which offers the extreme thrill of a 15,000 feet jump, with a full 60 seconds free falling at 200kph! (see www.nzone.biz) ; flightseeing excursions by floatplane from the lakefront jetty or by helicopter or plane from the airport (an exciting way to see Mount Tarawera's gaping crater); four-wheel-drive tours up Mount Tarawera; raft trips down the Kaituna River, which include a seven-metre (23-foot) freefall over the world's highest commercially rafted waterfall; a variety of lake tours; horseback rides; and tandem-skydiving adventures. See the information centre about the various possibilities and costs.

Lake Taupo

At 600 square kilometres (232 square miles), Taupo is the largest lake in New Zealand. It lies bright blue and clear in its prehistoric crater, surrounded by white pumice beaches, colourful cliffs and hot springs—all reminders that the lake lies along a great volcanic fault.

Taupo, 84 kilometres (52 miles) south of Rotorua on Highway 5, is a pleasant, low-key town at the northeast end of the lake, with a wonderful view across the water to the volcanoes in Tongariro National Park. It attracts visitors year-round for what is regarded as the country's best trout fishing (see *Focus*, page 119). Golf, hiking and water sports are also popular activities. Maps and information about local attractions are available from the Taupo Visitor Centre, near the lake end of Tongariro Street. Phone (07)376-0027. All Taupo's main attractions are north of town within **Wairakei Park**, which extends along the Waikato River for five kilometres (three miles). All are accessible by road, or take the Taupo Walkway (see *Focus*, page 115) along the river. The park's best-known feature is **Huka Falls**, where water from the Waikato River is forced through a narrow chasm and over a thunderous waterfall 11 metres (36 feet) high. A bridge over the river allows views from different angles. Cross back over Highway 5 to reach **Craters of the Moon**, a large area of thermal activity. Everything has been left in its natural state, with bubbling pools of mud and vents belching steam high into the air. Best of all, admission is free. The **Volcanic Activity Centre**, on Huka Falls Road, is a research centre that monitors volcanic activity throughout the region. At an area set aside for interested visitors, a video explains the most-recent eruptions. Open daily 10 am–4 pm. Phone (07)374-8375. Huka Falls Road ends on the riverfront, where the Huka Jet departs for a high-speed trip up and down the **Waikato River**. At **Wairakei Geo-thermal Power Station**, about ten kilometres (six miles) north of Taupo, the power of the steam is harnessed to produce around five per cent of New Zealand's electricity. A road leads through the station past a massive complex of steaming vents and pipes. Adjacent to the power station is Taupo's only commercial thermal attraction, **Wairakei Natural Thermal Valley**, where visitors are greeted by a great variety of farm animals. Open daily 9 am–5 pm. Phone (07)374-8004. Hot pools for soothing those aching muscles can be found at the A.C. Baths in downtown Taupo and at Taupo Hot Springs south toward Napier.

Turangi, on the Tongariro River at the south end of the lake, is a much smaller town, devoted mainly to trout fishing and the management of the Tongariro Power Development Project. The Turangi Visitor Centre at Ngawaka Place has information about the town and the surrounding area. Phone (07)386-8999.

TONGARIRO NATIONAL PARK

This vast tract of land south of Lake Taupo was New Zealand's first national park and one of the first national parks in the world. It forms the southern anchor of the volcanic plateau. The whole beautiful area, rich in Maori legends, was presented as a gift to the nation in 1887 by wise Maori chief Horonuku Te Heuheu Tukino. The chief foresaw the danger of partitioning by land-hungry settlers and bestowed the gift with the words, 'It shall be a sacred place of the Crown and a gift forever from me and my people.'

The park gained worldwide notoriety in September 1995 when the North Island's highest mountain (and the only one with glaciers), 2,797-metre (9,176-foot) **Mount Ruapehu**, blew its top. Rocks and ash were thrown 18 kilometres (11 miles) into the air, and major belches occurred every few hours for many days. Ash fell on surrounding communities and closed local ski areas. It was the largest eruption in 50 years. Since the last eruptions in June 1996 the mountain has remained

Few anglers leave Lake Taupo without catching their limit.

relatively dormant, and ice-rimmed Crater Lake is slowly returning to an aqua-green colour. To the north, **Mount Ngauruhoe** (2,291 metres/7,516 feet) looks the way a volcano should, with a perfectly symmetrical cone and a plume of steam rising from its crater. It smoulders constantly and once in a while puts on a display, belching out showers of ash and lava. **Mount Tongariro** (1,968 metres/6,457 feet), which gives its name to the park, is the most northerly, lowest and oldest of the park's three volcanoes. Although Tongariro has not erupted in recent times, its truncated peaks contain several small craters, some of which vent steam or gas. On the windy, rain-shadowed eastern side of the mountains, the Rangipo Desert presents a desolate, gravel-strewn landscape. By contrast, the hills and valleys on the park's western side are covered with forest, heather and rich vegetation.

The park is bounded east and west by Highways 1 and 4, respectively, and north and south by Highways 47 and 49. Tranz Rail's trunk line runs along the park's western boundary, stopping at the small village of National Park and further south at Ohakune. Intercity buses also make stops at these two places. National Park has an airstrip from where sightseeing planes can take you on an unforgettable flight over the park.

Highway 48, the only road to enter the park, leads to **Whakapapa Village** and the elegant Grand Chateau. Within the village is the Whakapapa Visitor Centre, which provides information and features a small ski museum. Phone (07)892-3729. A number of short walks on good tracks start near the village. You can drive from Whakapapa Village up Bruce Road to the 'Top o' the Bruce' for panoramic views and incredible sunsets.

On the opposite, southwest flank of the mountain, the other main gateway to the park is the township of **Ohakune**, off Highway 49 (turn off from Waiouru on Highway 1). Through town is the Department of Conservation's Ohakune Field Centre, which offers information, maps and brochures of other lovely walks, many including views and waterfalls. Phone (06)385-0010.

FOCUS

If Rotorua's relentless tourist hype starts to get to you, take a walk along the lakefront between Government Gardens and the Polynesian Spa in one of the town's few uncommercialized spots. At the wildlife sanctuary you may see a number of birds, including black-billed and red-billed gulls, which seem to thrive in the harsh thermal environment. A nesting colony occupies a low island at **Sulphur Point** from September to January. The lovely redwood forest near the headquarters of **Whakarewarewa State Forest Park** (just beyond the famous Whaka thermal area) is renowned for its numerous finches.

Northeast of Rotorua, **Lake Rotoiti** is home to shags, black swans and a variety of ducks. Viewing is good from Highway 30, which skirts the lake's southern shore. At Lake Rotoehu, also on Highway 30, **Rotoehu State Forest** is home to a great variety of forest birds including kaka, tui and North Island kokako. In dry weather the trails may be closed to protect against forest fires, so inquire first at the Rotorua Department of Conservation; phone (07)346-1155 between 8 am and 4.30 pm.

Around **Lake Taupo**'s southern outlet, a reed-fringed delta is home to 40 species including spotless and marsh crake, fernbird, bittern, dabchick and many varieties of duck. On the lake's west side, Pureora Forest Park holds healthy populations of kaka and bush parrots.

In **Tongariro National Park** look for pipit, skylark and banded dotterel in the open country on the dry eastern side. On the forested western side, the bird life is much richer. The two-hour forest walk around virgin **Lake Rotopounamu** is higly recommended for its prolific combination of water birds and bush birds, including New Zealand pigeon, bellbird, rifleman, grey warbler, North Island tomtit and fantail.

Hikers can head to the bird-watching areas recommended above, or find fine walking at **Whakarewarewa State Forest Park**, just beyond the Whaka thermal area. The forest was planted after the devastating eruption of Mt Tarawera in 1886 and has flourished for over a century. Stop first at the visitor centre on Long Mile Road for information and maps. Eight well-marked walks through the forest range in duration from one and a half to four hours. The shortest one, in a grove of California redwoods, is also one of the most beautiful.

At Taupo, the ten kilometre (six mile)-long **Taupo Walkway** features two great spectacles: Huka Falls and Aratiatia Rapids. The track begins at the end of Spa Road and can be hiked in sections. The first section crosses a hot-water stream, then follows the bank of the Waikato River to the thunderous 11-metre (36-foot)-high waterfall. Allow two hours up and back. The trail continues near the river for seven kilometres (four miles) with views of waterfalls, rapids and the Wairakei Geothermal Power Station. The walk ends at Lake Aratiatia, near the power station's spillway. The amazing Aratiatia Rapids, downstream of the spillway, flow only when the gates of the power station are opened, releasing a mighty torrent of water. Normally this takes place between noon and 2 pm; sirens warn of the impending release. The rapids are most spectacular when the water first surges through, so the times given above should be verified at the Taupo Visitor Centre. The walk from Huka Falls takes two hours. The whole walk from Taupo takes three hours one-way.

In Turangi, a very peaceful walk around **Lake Rotopounamu**, near the edge of Tongariro National Park, is also recommended for bird-watchers. From Turangi turn west on Highway 41. After four kilometres (2.5 miles) turn left on to Highway 47. Drive about seven kilometres (four miles) over Te Ponanga saddle to the start of the track, which is signposted on the left. Parking is on the right. After an easy 20-minute climb through fern-filled native bush, the path branches down to the unspoiled forest-clad lake. The flat round-the-lake walk through native flora takes one and a half to two hours.

(left) New Zealand's quiet rural roads are perfect for horseback riding.

Tongariro National Park offers so many good short walks (ranging from 20 minutes to two and a half hours) on such a variety of terrain that it is best to get a set of brochures, maps and advice from the visitor centres at Whakapapa or Ohakune. Anyone of a reasonable level of fitness should consider walking the **Tongariro Crossing**, regarded as the finest one-day walk in New Zealand. The track traverses a great variety of terrain, and on a clear day the views are unsurpassed. The track takes eight to ten hours one-way, with most hikers using the services of shuttle buses for the return trip; inquire at the Whakapapa Visitor Centre. Most hikers begin from the south, at the end of Mangatepopo Road. From this point the track climbs steadily through lava flows of differing ages past the colourful Soda Springs to the head of the valley at a high saddle. From this point, between Mount Ngauruhoe and Mount Tongariro, the track winds through South Crater to Emerald and then Blue Lakes before descending to Ketetahi Hot Springs, where you will find boiling mud, hot springs, small geysers, blowholes and steam vents. Keep left at the track junction to reach the Ketetahi Hut. Do not stray from the marked track in this area because the ground is treacherous. If the steam thickens and blocks your view, wait for it to clear before walking further. The warm stream below the thermal area has some good bathing spots, but no facilities are available for changing, so wear a bathing suit under your clothes and bring a towel. Drinking water is available at the Ketetahi Hut up the mountain above the springs. The track continues, marked with poles, across tussock grass, then descends below the timberline through a delightful region of upland forest to the northern trailhead, accessed from Highway 47A.

Huge **Lake Taupo**, in the middle of the North Island, is the fishing mecca of New Zealand. Anglers enjoy year-round trout fishing from boats, from the shore of the lake or from the lower reaches of the rivers flowing into the lake. Local guides claim a 97 per cent success rate for their fishing expeditions. The trout consider Lake Taupo an inland sea and go up its adjacent rivers to spawn. Before the area was so well known, four- to five-kilogramme (ten-pound) catches were fairly common. The average now is 1.5 to two kilogrammes (three to four pounds) for rainbow trout and two to 2.5 kilogrammes (four to five pounds) for brown trout. Bigger fish often lurk where streams enter the lake. The limit is three trout per person per day, and you need a separate fishing licence for the Taupo and Rotorua areas (inquire in any sports shop, hotel or information centre). To fish at some of the lakes in this area—Rotoaira, for instance—you'll have to pay a special levy imposed by Maori owners.

The township of Taupo draws great numbers of fishing enthusiasts. It offers easy access to the east-shore river mouths, along with amenities for the fishing community such as smoking and freezing facilities. From late afternoon to sunset it seems the whole population of the town goes out to fish! Taupo is also the best place to get out into the middle of the lake, with charter boats filling the downtown marina. Richard Staines, the lake's most experienced guide, takes up to three people out on his boat, *Whitestriker IV*, for a reasonable hourly rate, including all the equipment you'll need for downrigging. He'll even deliver your catch to the local restaurant of your choice. Phone (03)539-4339 or (0800)235-628.

The village of **Waitahanui**, about ten kilometres (six miles) south of Taupo on Highway 1, is a fishing centre at the mouth of the Waitahanui River, where three to 3.5-kilogramme (six- to eight-pound) catches are not unusual. Local wits claim that the anglers lined up at sunset across the river mouth form a 'picket fence.' In any case, you will need thigh or chest waders. The village has three motels that cater specially to fisherfolk. Parking is available on both sides of the main bridge.

The lower reaches of surrounding rivers seem to attract the largest rainbow and brown trout. **Turangi**, which proclaims itself the trout capital of the world, sits astride the famous Tongariro River. Turangi is much smaller and quieter than Taupo, but its lodges and motels offer all the facilities necessary for cleaning, smoking, freezing and vacuum packing your catch. Any restaurant in town will cook your trout for you. You'll find good fishing within walking distance of town, and fishing guides can take you in vehicles to more remote spots. Inquire at the Turangi Visitor Centre at Ngawaka Place. Phone (07)386-8999.

Also interesting is the **Tongariro National Trout Centre**, three kilometres (two miles) south of Turangi on Highway 1. The hatchery has an underwater viewing chamber and a good information centre. Open daily 9 am–4 pm. Phone (07)386-8085.

The village of **Tokaanu** lies right at the mouth of the Tongariro River and is much favoured by fisherfolk. The historic settlement has the added attraction of being in a thermal area with public and private hot pools.

Knowledgeable guides abound in all of the fishing centres. They can be hired by the day or half-day (minimum three or four hours), and their fees include tackle, equipment, and often food and drink. Unless you are a real pro, you have a better chance of success with a guide than on your own.

Some golfers put the Taupo-Rotorua area at the very top of their list. The 85-year-old Arikikapakapa course at **Rotorua Golf Club** offers a unique golfing experience amidst astounding scenery. The short, exciting course, opposite the Whakarewarewa thermal area at the south end of Fenton Street, is sprinkled with extinct mud pools and occasional active steam vents. In some spots the ground is hot. A very explicit score card suggests a strategy for each hole. Par 69. Phone (07)347-1575. Nearby, the club's entertaining (and easier) nine-hole course (opposite the Thermal Motor Camp on Old Taupo Road) has natural hazards that include bubbling mud, boiling pools and steam vents. The third course at Rotorua is **Springfield Golf Course**, a pleasant, rolling, tree-lined course right in town at the western end of Devon Street. Par 72. Phone (07)348-2748.

Recently restored to its former glory, **Wairakei International Golf Course**, six kilometres (four miles) north of Taupo, is rated by some as the top course in the country. It is open to visitors and is a very long, well-designed course with three sets of tees for each hole. The course features numerous water hazards, bunkers and trees. The 14th hole, nicknamed the 'Rogue' after past volcanic activity, is especially memorable. This course is a must on any golfer's list. Par 72. Phone (07)374-8152. Nearby, the Wairakei Resort operates a nine-hole course. Another unique golfing experience presents itself down on Taupo's lakeshore, but this one is purely for novelty value. From a tee box on the edge of the lake, golfers (and many non-golfers) attempt to land a golf ball on a deceptively small floating green 120 metres (135 yards) into the lake. Prizes are given for landing the ball in various sized holes. Good luck.

 The central volcanic plateau is the only region of the North Island where no vineyards exist. But the area is well supplied with good hotels and restaurants where you can sample the whole range of New Zealand wines.

The East

When Captain Cook first reached New Zealand, it was on the east coast of the North Island, near modern-day Gisborne, that he made his first landfall. Met with unfriendly Maori tribes and failing to get the supplies he needed, Cook named his landing place Poverty Bay. The name stuck, but it has proved a complete misnomer; the east is now one of the North Island's richest farming and fruit-growing regions.

East Cape, which separates the Bay of Plenty from the Pacific Ocean, marks the north end of the region. Steep, forested mountains cut the cape off from the rest of the North Island, leaving its population, which is heavily Maori, thinly spread around the coast.

At the south end of the East Cape is Gisborne, which, lying close to the International Date Line, prides itself on being the first city in the world to see the rising sun each day. Indeed, the sun often shines on the fertile vegetable farms, orchards and vineyards around the city. The balmy climate, beaches perfect for swimming, surfing and fishing, and the easy-going pace of life bring New Zealand vacationers thronging to Gisborne. Yet the city is frequently missed by overseas visitors.

The pleasant town of Wairoa straddles both banks of the Wairoa River at the north end of Hawke Bay. Nearby, Te Urewera National Park preserves a huge expanse of virgin forest covering a remote mountain range between Wairoa and Rotorua. Park headquarters is on the Wairoa side of the range, on the banks of bright blue, star-shaped Lake Waikaremoana.

Hawke Bay (the surrounding mainland region is, confusingly, known as Hawkes Bay) scoops a large bite out of the east coast. The biggest city here is Napier, known for its many fine examples of art deco architecture. A devastating earthquake nearly destroyed Napier along with nearby Hastings in 1931, killing hundreds of people. It raised new land and changed the configuration of the coastline, but looking at the rebuilt cities today it's hard to imagine the catastrophe. Havelock North completes the triangle of towns that anchor the southern end of Hawke Bay.

GETTING THERE

Air New Zealand flies daily from Auckland and Wellington to both Gisborne and Napier. Both airports have shuttle buses that meet all flights. Tranz Scenic runs daily train service between Napier and Wellington. Intercity coaches run from Auckland to Gisborne (via Rotorua and Whakatane) and to Napier (via Taupo). Southbound from Gisborne, buses run around Hawke Bay to Napier and on to Wellington. Contact local information centres for shuttle services running around the East Cape.

If you are travelling by car, you'll have a choice of two routes between the Bay of Plenty and the east coast. Highway 35 winds picturesquely around the coast of the

Jet-boating is popular on many New Zealand rivers.

Voyager Kupe and Captain Cook

Two great explorers came to the shores of New Zealand from opposite ends of the earth, over eight centuries apart, and both are revered by their people for discovering a 'virgin' land they could make their own.

The first was Kupe, a Polynesian explorer whose voyage became legendary, passed down in story and song. He came by canoe from a Polynesian island, remembered only by the name of Hawaiki, but probably located close to Tahiti. Without compass or sextant, he set his course across the vast Pacific, navigating by the stars, by wind direction, and cloud shape. He is said to have landed in the far north some time before AD 800 and to have named the North Island Aotearoa, meaning 'Land of the Long White Cloud.' Kupe is said to have visited both islands, which he found uninhabited. Then he made his way back to Hawaiki. Two centuries later, Chief Toi and his grandson Watonga are said to have repeated the voyage, returning home to verify Kupe's story. Curiously, though, tradition says this time they found people living in Aotearoa.

Authorities disagree as to when the first settlement took place; some say AD 800, others argue for AD 1100. Radiocarbon dating has established that the Polynesian population was widespread in both islands by AD 1200. Colonization was deliberate, and the canoes that brought the early Polynesian settlers were by legend big and double-hulled. They are still remembered. Tribal groups like Tainui take their name from their founding canoe.

The first European to discover New Zealand was Dutch explorer Abel Tasman. In December 1642, he recorded 'a large land, uplifted high'. He dropped anchor in the South Island's Golden Bay, but his attempts to woo the local Maori by waving linen goods from his two ships ended tragically. Ngati Tumatakokiri warriors rammed a Dutch rowboat, killing four of its crew. A horrified Tasman hurried on up the western coast, without attempting to land, and returned to Batavia (Jakarta). Theorists of the time thought he had sighted the Great Southern Continent, thought necessary to counterbalance the land masses of the Northern Hemisphere. His find was given the name Nieuw Zeeland, after a province of Holland.

More than a century later, in 1769, James Cook landed near the North Island's East Cape and claimed New Zealand for Britain. This brilliant Yorkshireman, trained as a seaman on coal ships in the wild North Sea, served in the Royal Navy in time of war, his skills attracting the attention of his superiors. When he was chosen to head an expedition that included a search for Tasman's Great Southern Continent, Cook requested a coal ship, a humble vessel in the eyes of some, but stable under sail and provided with a huge hold for supplies. He carried on board the converted *Endeavour* a team of scientists who recorded every detail of the voyage, and by his experiment of combining every known dietary theory for the prevention of scurvy—from fresh vegetables to lemon juice and sauerkraut—and enforcing the diet with rigid discipline, he significantly curbed the killer disease for the first time on long voyages.

Though Cook's first encounter with the Maori was as hostile as Tasman's, he persevered. He mapped the entire coast of New Zealand and befriended other Maori tribes. On his second voyage of 1772 he visited New Zealand again, probed southern latitudes, and circled Antarctica, proving that the great fertile southern continent envisioned by armchair theorists in Europe did not exist. His three separate voyages into the Pacific established a new map of the world. His reports of the beautiful New Zealand, rich in fish and timber, soon brought European sealers, whalers and lumberjacks to gather up its wealth—and missionaries to gather up the souls of what Cook called its Indians. European settlers followed.

Nathaniel Dance Holland's engraving of Captain James Cook, c. 1779

East Cape from Opotiki to Gisborne. Highway 2, the main road, cuts across the base of the cape by a less interesting route. The roads meet again in Gisborne, and Highway 2 continues south along the east coast to Napier and Hastings. Two roads run inland across the largely unpopulated mountains to the main tourist areas. Small Highway 38 leads from Rotorua through Te Urewera National Park to Wairoa. The more-direct Highway 5 follows an old Maori track from Taupo to Napier.

THE EAST CAPE

Ruggedly magnificent Highway 35 stretches 334 kilometres (209 miles) around the cape coast from Opotiki to Gisborne. The drive takes six hours without stops, but there are many reasons to stop and make it a full-day trip. Groves of ancient pohutukawa trees burst into flame-red flower in summer beside rocky coves and deserted beaches. Villages along the way are worth exploring. And a few roads penetrate into the mountains and gorges of the wild interior Raukumara Range.

Opotiki, where the west end of Highway 35 branches off Highway 2, is 60 kilometres (37 miles) east of Whakatane on the Bay of Plenty. The little port town is surrounded by pleasant beaches and sits at the edge of Hukutaia Domain, home to an extensive collection of native plants including a 2,000-year-old puriri tree. The Hiona St. Stephen the Anglican Church, on Church Street, displays a glass case with blood-stained relics of a gruesome incident that took place here in 1865; an attack on the church by Hauhau fanatics during the Land Wars led to the particularly grisly murder of the church's resident German missionary.

Te Kaha, 69 kilometres (43 miles) to the northeast, is a picturesque old whaling port from which open-boat whaling continued into the 1930s. The intricate Maori carvings on the triangular meeting house are some of the best in the region.

Hicks Bay, 84 kilometres (52 miles) beyond Te Kaha on the north coast, also boasts an outstanding meeting house with century-old interior carvings. The rafter designs glorifying the death of warriors in battle are unique to the East Cape.

Te Araroa, beneath the tall cliffs of a narrow bay 23 kilometres (14 miles) further on, boasts the largest pohutukawa tree in New Zealand. Estimated at 600 years old, the tree has a girth of 20 metres (66 feet). A 42-kilometre (26-mile) detour leads

This wool-products shop in Tirau is hard to miss on the drive between Hamilton and Rotorua.

A young New Zealander near Cambridge.

to the East Cape lighthouse, perched on the high cliffs of the North Island's most easterly point.

Tikitiki, 150 kilometres (93 miles) from Gisborne on the east coast, lies inland along the Waiapu River. Its marvellously ornate Anglican Church is a memorial to soldiers of the Ngati Porou tribe who died in World War I. The carved panels and rafters and stained-glass windows recount the history of the Ngati Porou, the principal Maori tribe on the East Cape.

Ruatoria, to the south and a slight detour from Highway 35, offers the first clear sight of Hikurangi (1,752 metres/5,748 feet), sacred mountain of the Ngati Porou. Ownership of the mountain was returned to the tribe in 1990. As New Zealand mountains go it is not particularly high, but it dominates the local landscape. Its peak is said to be the first point on earth to see the sunrise each day (going by Greenwich Mean Time).

Te Puia Springs, 103 kilometres (64 miles) north of Gisborne, is the site of relaxing hot pools. A short walk to the source of the springs ends with a good view over the surrounding countryside.

Tokomaru Bay, 92 kilometres (57 miles) from Gisborne, is the first point at which the road touches the east-coast shoreline. Once a busy commercial port for freezing works, which are now abandoned, the town has a well-carved, modern meeting house near the wharf.

Anaura Bay, 23 kilometres (14 miles) further south, lies behind a beach flanked by rocky headlands. It is worth the 16-kilometre (10-mile) detour to reach its unspoiled stretch of golden sand and its scenic walkway (see *Focus*, page 131).

Tolaga Bay, 54 kilometres (34 miles) from Gisborne, is a pretty inlet where the road again touches the shore. Captain Cook spent a week here, replenishing his supplies.

Gisborne

The attractive little city of Gisborne (population 34,000) perches at the north end of Poverty Bay, at the junction of two rivers and in easy reach of beautiful white-sand beaches. Gladstone Road, the main street, is adorned by an impressive clock tower and two tall masts holding aloft models of Captain Cook's ship, the *Endeavour*. The Gisborne Visitor Centre is at 209 Grey Street. Phone (06)868-6139. Next to the centre a small park surrounds a fine totem pole, a gift from Canada in 1969 in commemoration of Captain Cook's landing 200 years earlier.

The southern point of Poverty Bay is a headland of white cliffs named **Young Nick's Head**. Sailing south from Tahiti, Captain Cook offered to award a gallon of rum to—and name a coastal feature after—the first crew member who sighted land. The winner was 12-year-old Nicholas Young, dubbed Young Nick. Other crew members, whose names are long forgotten, no doubt helped the lad dispose of the rum, but Young Nick's name lives on at this prominent landmark.

Kaiti Hill Lookout provides spectacular views of Gisborne, its two rivers, the surrounding countryside, the harbour and all of Poverty Bay. Cross the Gladstone Bridge and look for signposts on the right. At the foot of Kaiti Hill, on Kaiti Beach Road by the river mouth (the beach is good for windsurfing, not swimming), the **Cook Landing Site National Historic Reserve** marks the place where the Englishman first landed. Across the road, a short track leads up to Cook Bicentenary Plaza. The observatory at the plaza offers three telescopes for public use. At the foot of Kaiti Hill, at Queens Drive and Ranfurly Road, the **Poho-o-Rawiri Meeting House** is one of the largest decorated Maori meeting halls in New Zealand. The carvings—some dating to the early 1800s—and woven reed-work were executed by the Arawa tribe in Rotorua. If the main door is closed, use the side door or ask the caretaker (who lives in the adjacent building) for permission to enter.

Tairawhiti Museum, on Stout Street by the Taruheru River, traces east-coast history with a collection of Maori and colonial artifacts, including a whaling boat used at Te Kaha on the East Cape. On the grounds is the 1872 Wyllie Cottage, Gisborne's oldest house. Part of the museum is devoted to the *Star of Canada* **Maritime Museum**. The *Star of Canada* was wrecked on a Gisborne beach in 1912. Various parts of the ship were salvaged and now form the centrepiece of an exhibition cataloguing the maritime history of Hawke Bay. Open Monday to Friday 10 am–4 pm and weekends 1.30–4 pm. Phone (06)867-3832.

WAIROA AND ENVIRONS

This is the only sizeable town at the north end of Hawke Bay. It lies slightly inland on both banks of the broad Wairoa River. A solid kauri lighthouse dating from 1877 stands incongruously by the palm-lined river bank near the bridge; this old light was saved after a newer one replaced it on Portland Island in 1958. The incandescent light, once visible for 39 kilometres (24 miles), enlivens the river every evening. The Wairoa Bridge was washed away by the rampaging, debris-filled river in March 1988, when Cyclone Bola came howling through, dumping 915 millimetres (36 inches) of rain on the Gisborne area in 30 hours and causing immeasurable damage. The bridge was rebuilt, but throughout the Gisborne area the name of the once-in-a-lifetime cyclone still evokes tales of destruction.

Two roads connect Wairoa and Gisborne. Highway 2 follows the spectacular coastline of white sand, sparkling water and pohutukawa trees. Cutting behind the sparsely populated Mahia Peninsula at the northern extremity of Hawke Bay, it passes through **Morere**, 40 kilometres (25 miles) from Wairoa, a delightful green oasis of native bush with hot springs. Eight pools of varying temperatures are open daily from 10 am. Phone (06)837-8856. The Tiniroto road follows a lovely, less-travelled route inland through the hills, passing many small settlements. The Maori village of **Te Reinga**, beside Te Reinga Falls, stands at the junction of the Ruakituri and Wairoa Rivers. Its simple, unpretentious marae (communal compound) offers a welcome to travellers.

Katherine Mansfield summed up perfectly the mist-enshrouded landscape of **Te Urewera National Park** when she wrote that 'It is all so gigantic and tragic—and even in the bright sunlight it is so passionately secret.' The park protects the North Island's largest virgin forest and is the habitat for New Zealand's only two native land mammals, both species of bats. The park is dominated by massive **Lake Waikaremoana**, formed when an ancient landslide blocked a river. Highway 38, connecting Wairoa and Rotorua, a distance of 222 kilometres (138 miles), traverses the park and the Huiarau Mountains by a beautiful, winding route that follows the lakeshore for 30 kilometres (19 miles). The visitor centre is by the lake, 62 kilometres (39 miles) from Wairoa. Phone (07)838-3803. It is the most convenient spot from which to start fishing or exploring the park's virgin forest on foot (see *Focus*, page 131). The village of **Ruatahuna**, close to the park on the Rotorua side, is the traditional home of the Tuhoe people. From here, a small detour of four kilometres (2.5 miles) leads to **Mataatua**, where the truly magnificent Te Whai-a-te-Motu Meeting House was completed in 1888. Amongst the splendid interior carvings, those at the base of the centre poles show two of the Tuhoe ancestors wearing European neckties—a measure of the impact made by Western culture on sacred Maori traditions.

Napier

Napier is 'Art Deco City', a charming 1930s period piece born from a cataclysm. On 3 February 1931, a devastating two-and-a-half minute earthquake measuring 7.9 on the Richter scale struck the Hawkes Bay area without warning, killing 256 people, flattening much of Napier and starting fires that swept through what remained. High cliffs crumbled, and the bed of Napier's inner harbour rose above sea level, creating 3,343 hectares (8,260 acres) of new land. Large swamps and a lagoon vanished at the spot where Napier Airport stands. The city was rebuilt in art deco, the architectural style that at the time had captured the imagination of young architects.

Marine Parade, the waterfront avenue, was built over the rubble of the collapsed city. The long, attractive esplanade is bordered by Norfolk pines and faced on the west by low buildings from the 1930s. The sea side of the Parade is dotted with attractions for visitors, including the Napier Visitor Centre. Phone (06)834-1911. The centre has information on all the best the region has to offer as well as a deck with beautiful views across the ocean. It's also the main bus stop for long-distance services and the place to book tours to Cape Kidnappers gannet colony, one of the region's most popular attractions.

Walking north from the information centre, you pass the Colonnade, where a market is held on weekends. The **Hawkes Bay Museum**, at 65 Marine Parade, has a fine collection of ancient Maori and moa-hunter artifacts, a fine art deco collection, a horrifying audio-visual presentation of the 1931 earthquake and the photographic story of Napier's reconstruction. Open daily 10 am–4.30 pm. Phone (06)835-7781. A climb or drive up to **Bluff Hill Lookout**, signposted from Lighthouse Road, gives an excellent cliff-top view over the city, harbour and coast. Stop at **Centennial Gardens** on the way up. (Take a city map.)

South of the information centre, **Marineland** presents shows at 10.30 am and 2 pm, in which dolphins, seals and sea lions perform acrobatic and swimming stunts. Visitors are also invited to visit injured penguins at the recovery

> *In a very short time they return'd again and one of the fishing boat[s] came along side and offer'd us some more fish, the Indian Boy Tiata, Tupia's servant being over the side, they seized hold of him, pulled him into the boat and endeavoured to carry him off, this obliged us to fire upon them which gave the Boy an opportunity to jump over board and we brought the Ship too, lower'd a boat into the Water and took him up unhurt. Two or Three paid for this daring attempt with the loss of their lives and many more would have suffered had it [not] been for fear of killing the boy. This affair occasion'd my giveing this point of Land the name Cape Kidnappers.*
>
> —from the journal of Captain James Cook, on the naming of Cape Kidnappers, 15 October 1769

Parapenting is among the many adventure sports possible in New Zealand.

centre and even swim with the dolphins. Nearby, **Hawkes Bay Aquarium**, one of the best in the Southern Hemisphere, is excellently designed, offering three floors of display tanks around a huge oceanarium. A diver feeds the fish at 3.15 pm. Both attractions are open daily 10 am–5 pm. Ocean Spa, 42 Marine Parade, is an oceanfront complex of swimming and spa pools. Phone (06)835-8553.

Hastings, 21 kilometres (13 miles) south of Napier, produces the fruit, food and farm products that are exported from the port of Napier. The two cities are rivals, each one believing itself to be the true centre of Hawkes Bay. The 1931 earthquake damaged Hastings severely, but the town was beautifully rebuilt with many Spanish Mission-style buildings. It's a pretty place, full of parks and gardens and surrounded by vineyards and orchards.

Havelock North, five kilometres (three miles) southeast of Hastings' commercial centre, is a quiet, mostly residential, tree-filled town that has kept its rural qualities. **Te Mata Peak**, rising south of the town, offers a magnificent view over all of Hawkes Bay, from Cape Kidnappers to Mahia Peninsula. You'll see the orderly streets of Hastings nestled amongst lush orchards and market gardens; Napier sprawling back from the Bluff Hill headland; and the fertile plain stretching away to the rugged Kaimanawa Mountains. A six-kilometre (four-mile) road leads to the summit, signposted off Te Mata Road. The 2.2-kilometre (1.4-mile) Peak Trail over the last stretch offers a 45-minute alternate route for the energetic.

Focus

East Cape, north of Gisborne as far as Tokomaru Bay, is the best place on the North Island to see wekas, which are tough, inquisitive, flightless rails. Wekas had virtually disappeared from the North Island by 1930, probably due to disease, but a few survivors continued breeding on the East Cape. The birds have made a remarkable and widespread comeback over the last 30 years. The Gisborne Botanical Gardens, on the banks of the Taruheru River, shelter a rare species of weka that is still found only on the East Cape. The paradise shelduck is another East Cape denizen that has recently increased in great numbers; these birds are nearly always seen in pairs, the male and female being very different in colouration.

Lake Waikaremoana and **Lake Waikareiti**, in Te Urewera National Park, comprise a rich avian habitat. Shags, swans, various ducks, scaups, shovellers and dabchicks stay near the water. Blue duck can be found on fast-running streams. Amongst the abundant forest birds are kiwis, robins, tuis, moreporks, falcons, pied tits, bellbirds, long-tailed and shining cuckoos, kakas and riflemen. In the park's remote Otamatuna area, rats and possums have been eliminated, boosting the recovery of rare birds such as the kokako. The best bird-viewing area in the park is Aniwaniwa Valley, accessible by road from Highway 38.

Hawkes Bay's great attraction is the gannet sanctuary at **Cape Kidnappers**, about 30 kilometres (19 miles) south of Napier. It's one of the birds' only large mainland nesting sites in the world. Three colonies, numbering about 9,000 pairs, offer an unforgettable sight (and smell, so stay upwind). The sanctuary is open from late October to June (the last birds leave in April); it is closed for nesting and mating from July to October. To get there, you can walk from Clifton along the beach below the cliffs when the tide is out (about five hours return); see *Focus* page 134. Gannet Safaris operates small coaches overland to the colony. Phone (06)875-0888. Gannet Beach Adventures takes passengers along the beach route in a tractor-pulled trailer. Phone (06)875-0898. Book all tours and check tides at Napier Visitor Information Centre.

Black-fronted dotterel, an Australian wader first recorded nesting near Napier in 1954, is a species to watch for. It is now firmly established around Hawkes Bay and is starting to appear in South Island riverbeds.

The East Cape boasts two spectacular coastal walks north of Gisborne at bays where Captain Cook landed in 1769. **Cook's Cove** is about 53 kilometres (33 miles) north of Gisborne, just south of Tolaga Bay. Turn seaward off Highway 35 onto Wharf Road, about two kilometres (a mile) south of Tolaga Bay township, and go left at the end of the road to a car park. The walkway, across from the car park, climbs to a splendid cliff-top lookout over Tolaga Bay, then follows a farm track to a fine lookout over Cook's Cove. An easy path to the shore passes the famous 'Hole in the Wall,' a natural arch that astonished Captain Cook's crew. The walkway crosses private property and is closed in August and September for lambing. Take your own drinking water. Toilets are at the wharf near the car park. Allow two and a half hours for the five-kilometre (three-mile) return trip. **Anaura Bay Walkway**, about 85 kilometres (53 miles) north of Gisborne, is a bit shorter. Turn seaward off Highway 35 onto Anaura Road. The walkway starts at the north end of the beach, 500 metres (a third of a mile) beyond the Recreation Reserve campground, by a tin haybarn. The walk offers magnificent views of the coast, crosses part of Waipare Forest and follows Waipare Stream through the native bush of Anaura Bay Scenic Reserve. The track emerges on Anaura Road about a kilometre (0.6 miles) south of the starting point. The 3.5-kilometre (two-mile) walk takes about two hours.

Te Urewera National Park, New Zealand's third largest national park, holds dozens of good forest tracks, including five short walks to waterfalls. The visitor centre at Aniwaniwa, on an eastern arm of Lake Waikaremoana (62 kilometres/39 miles northwest of Wairoa), is a good starting place. Be sure to take plenty of insect repellent. The **Lake Waikareiti** trail starts 200 metres (220 yards) from the visitor centre and climbs through fern-filled beech forest to picturesque

(following pages) Lyttleton Harbour

Lake Waikareiti, dotted with forest-covered islands. Rowboats stored here can be hired from the park headquarters before setting out. The popular 3.5-kilometre (two-mile) walk takes one and a quarter hours to the lake, or two hours return. The track to **Lake Ruapani** starts at the same place, 200 metres (220 yards) from the visitor centre. After an hour it reaches Waipai Swamp, known for its orchids, sundews and other carnivorous plants. A further hour's walking through red and silver beech forest brings you to little Lake Ruapani. Allow two hours from the park headquarters to the lake, or four hours return. For an excellent full-day's walk, make a circle by taking the connecting track from Lake Ruapani to Lake Waikareiti. This three-hour link trail passes a delightful series of forest ponds and skirts the western shore of Lake Waikareiti before ending at the day hut. The downhill track back to Aniwaniwa takes less than an hour. Allow six hours for the 17-kilometre (ten-mile) circle.

The Napier Visitor Information Centre offers a **Napier Art Deco Walk** self-guided tour brochure for a small fee. The brochure will lead you past the best of Napier's 1930s-style architecture on a pleasant one-hour stroll through the pedestrian-oriented, easy-paced city. A guided walk leaves the Art-Deco shop on Tennyson Street daily at 2 pm; an audio-visual presentation is included in the small fee. Phone (06)835-0022.

Cape Kidnappers, named for an incident on Captain Cook's first voyage when his translator was temporarily captured by local Maori, is the destination of a fine coastal walk. Between late October and April, the activities of the large, yellow-headed gannets on the tip of the cape provide an added attraction. The walk stretches eight kilometres (five miles) each way and can be accomplished only by leaving the trailhead three hours before low tide. Tide times are available at the information centre in Napier or Hastings. From the parking lot beyond Clifton, 21 kilometres (13 miles) south of Napier, walk down the sandy beach beneath towering cliffs of stratified rock to Black Reef, where a rest hut provides water and toilets. (Don't walk directly under the cliffs; there are occasional rock falls.) A path leads up from Black Reef to the plateau for a close look at the gannets. Start your return journey along the beach no later than one and a half hours after low tide. Allow five hours for the whole trip.

Te Urewera National Park spreads across the least-populated region of the North Island. Its rivers and lakes all offer excellent rainbow and brown trout fishing, but the sparkling waters of 55 square–kilometre (21 square–mile) **Lake Waikaremoana**, set in primeval forest, are the most renowned. Of the many streams flowing east from Te Urewera National Park to join the Wairoa River, the favourite of several knowledgeable anglers (and one they would prefer to keep secret) is the **Ruakituri River**. A small road follows the river upstream from its junction with the Wairoa River at Te Reinga. Near the river's source the road loops south to join Highway 38 about 15 kilometres (nine miles) from the park. Fishing anywhere in the park requires a Rotorua District licence.

Depending on the time of year, **Hawkes Bay**, around Napier, may have some good fishing. For information on local rivers and fishing conditions, consult the Napier Visitor Information Centre, 100 Marine Parade. Phone (06)834-1911, website <www.hawkesbaynz.com>.

Gisborne offers two very nice courses. **Gisborne Park Golf Club**, south of the city on Cochrane Street in the Park Domain, is a pleasant, fairly flat, well-treed course with springy turf. If you tee off first in the morning, you'll be the first in the world to golf on that day. Phone (06)867-9849. Poverty Bay Golf Club's **Awapuni Links**, near the airport on Awapuni Road, is a well-cushioned links course with a fine view over the bay. The last six holes are difficult par fours, so golfers must build a good score early. Phone (06)868-6113.

Hawkes Bay is another strong golfing centre. **Cape Kidnappers Golf Course** is, quite simply, absolutely stunning. Opened in 2004 and already rated one of the world's best courses, it occupies a lofty position along an ocean peninsula. Par 71. Phone (06)875-1900. **Napier Golf Club**, at Waiohiki (south of Taradale), is ranked in New Zealand's top five courses while also being one of the country's oldest. It's a shortish course, with rolling fairways, lots of green-side bunkers and several doglegs. Par 72. Phone (06)844-7913. Four kilometres (2.5 miles) west of Hastings is **Hastings Golf Club**, at Bridge Pa, a flat, lush, windy course with challenging fast greens. Par 72. Phone (06)879-7217. **Hawkes Bay Golf Club**, on Valentine Road in suburban Flaxmere, west of Hastings, has a tranquil setting and abundant wildlife. Par 73. Phone (06)879-8890.

Gisborne is the centre of the largest commercial wine-producing region in New Zealand. Grapes, mainly Müller-Thurgau, are grown here in volume by major wine companies such as Montana and Villa Maria. The region's yield is almost double other New Zealand wine-producing areas. Most grapes are either trucked to Auckland fresh or are processed by crushing and fermenting plants in Gisborne.

Matawhero, on Riverpoint Road south of Gisborne, produces a popular Gewürtztraminer, as well as Pinot Noir and Syrah. Phone (06)868-8366.

Millton, on Papatu Road in Manutuke, 16 kilometres (ten miles) south of Gisborne off Highway 2, was New Zealand's first organic vineyard. The winery produces a variety of interesting dry white wines using viognier grapes, from France's Rhone Valley, that create a distinctive spicy after taste. The winery is closed from July to October, but will open by appointment. Phone (06) 862-8680.

An interesting local wine enterprise, selling from 24 Banks Street in Gisborne, is **Smash Palace Bar**. They sell two dry, flinty champagne-style wines, along with a light red and ports from inside a unique complex, complete with a full-size DC3 on the roof. Phone (06)867-7769.

Hawkes Bay is New Zealand's most important and longest established wine region. The climate here is drier than Gisborne's, similar to Bordeaux's. Fruit and vegetables thrive here. The area's wine reputation rests on top-quality Sauvignon Blanc, Chardonnay and Cabernet Sauvignon, but many other excellent wines are now produced. A series of takeovers by large wine companies seems to have slowed. As an old vine-worker remarked, 'Those small, family-run boutique wineries—it's a way of life, not a means of living. They'll never sell out. Good thing.' The 40-odd Hawkes Bay wineries are all within 50 kilometres (30 miles) of one another. Many offer free wine-tasting and some operate free tours. A brochure titled *A Guide to Hawkes Bay Wineries* is available at the information centres and hotels throughout the region. It provides cellar hours and sales data and includes a good map. Afternoon wine tours by minibus are run from Bay Tours, phone (06)843-6953, and Vicky's Wine Tours, phone (06)843-9991.

Mission, on Church Road in Taradale, Napier's southwestern suburb, is the region's oldest winery. Dating from the 19th century, it was managed until recently by monks of St Mary's Seminary. Its strengths are Chardonnay and Cabernet Sauvignon, but a great variety of other wines are produced. An historic seminary building has been transformed into a restaurant, which serves lunch and dinner daily. Phone (06)844-2559, website <www.missonestate.co.nz>.

Brookfields is on Brookfields Road at Meeanee, about four kilometres (2.5 miles) east of Taradale. Small and dedicated to quality, its strengths are Cabernet Sauvignon and Chardonnay. The restaurant is open for lunch daily and for dinner Wednesday to Saturday. Phone (06)834-4615, website <www.brookfieldsvineyards.co.nz>.

Sacred Hill is on Dartmoor Road in Puketapu, about six kilometres (four miles) west of Taradale. Its specialty is Fumé Blanc, but the winery produces a wide variety of styles in all price ranges. This is one of the region's most improved wineries. Phone (06)879-8760, website <www.sacredhill.com>.

In Dartmoor Valley, just downriver from Sacred Hill, watch for **Riverside**, whose vineyard fans out over 16 hectares of alluvial river flat. This is a new winery, but it's establishing a reputation for a peachy Chardonnay, a mellow Cabernet/Merlot and red wine blends. Phone (06)844-4942, website <www.riversidewines.co.nz>.

Driving from Taradale to Hastings on Highway 50, you'll pass **C J Pask**, a small yet modern and innovative winery best known for its red wines. It's on Omahu Road, north of Fernhill and

Spot this giant salmon, and you're in Rakaia, the heart of salmon-fishing territory.

about ten kilometres (six miles) south of Taradale. Chris Pask has expanded his vineyards to 60 hectares and now produces some of Hawkes Bay's most underrated wines marketed on three tiers, including award-winning Merlots and Sauvignon Blanc. Phone (06)879-7906, website <www.cjpaskwinery.co.nz>.

The oldest winery in Hastings, dating from 1905, is **Vidal**, at 913 St Aubyn Street East. The winery, owned by Auckland's Villa Maria, also features an attractive restaurant and wine bar. Only the more expensive Reserve labels—including a popular Cabernet Sauvignon—are made from Hawkes Bay grapes. Bottle-fermented Vidal Brut ranks with New Zealand's best méthode champenoise wines. Phone (06)876-9662, website <www.vidal.co.nz>.

Ngatarawa, on Ngatarawa Road near Bridge Pa, six kilometres (four miles) west of Hastings, was founded in the early 1980s. Alwyn Corban, of Auckland's celebrated Corban wine family, is the winery's highly skilled owner and vintner. Strengths are Cabernets marketed under the international Glazebrook label, but Ngatarawa also produces New Zealand's most expensive wine, the Alwyn Noble Harvest, a sweet dessert wine from reisling grapes. Phone (06)879-7603.

At Havelock North, **Te Mata** is one of New Zealand's best-known wineries. Started in 1892 with vines supplied by mission monks, the company has since grown into a massive operation with a modern winery on Te Mata Road. Grapes are brought in from vineyards throughout the region. Te Mata's two best wines, both Cabernet/Merlot blends, are named after its two separate vineyards: Coleraine and Awatea, while the Estate Rosé is the perfect accompaniment to a summer picnic. Phone (06)877-4399, website <www.temata.co.nz>.

Lombardi, also on Te Mata Road, has a delightfully scenic location and an outdoor amphitheatre for concerts. The Cabernet Sauvignon is a highlight. Phone (06)877-7985.

At Eskdale, north of Napier towards Taupo on Highway 5, **Eskdale** is Hawkes Bay's smallest vineyard. Its highly individual Chardonnay, Gewürztraminer and Cabernet Sauvignon are aged in oak and worth a visit to obtain. Phone (06)836-6302. One kilometre (0.6 miles) nearer to Napier at Bay View, on Highway 2, is **Esk Valley**, owned by the Villa Maria Group. Its strengths are Merlot blends, Chardonnay and Sauvignon Blanc. Phone (06)836-6411, website <www.eskvalley.co.nz>. Nearby **Crab Farm**, at 511 Main Road North in Bay View, opened in 1987 on land reclaimed by Mother Nature in the 1931 earthquake. The winery produces a mid-priced Cabernet Sauvignon and Chardonnay and also has a restaurant open daily for lunch. Phone (06)836-6678, website <www.crabfarmwinery.co.nz>.

The West

The western portion of the North Island, immediately south of the Waikato, is known as Taranaki and is dominated by Mount Taranaki/Egmont, a central snowcapped volcano. Solitary and symmetrical, the volcano rises high above a flat landscape of dairy farms, where well-fed cows graze in the fields. Local Maori tribes named the sacred volcano (and themselves) Taranaki. Their myths link the mountain closely to the three volcanoes on the horizon in Tongariro National Park, but Mount Taranaki/Egmont is less active, having last erupted around 1755. Captain Cook sailed along the coast in 1770, naming the volcano Mount Egmont after England's first lord of the admiralty. Today both the Maori name and Captain Cook's name are recognized in the official name: Mount Taranaki/Egmont. On the lower slopes of the mountain, **Egmont National Park** protects the last of the region's native forest.

When European settlers arrived in the 1840s they found the land around the volcano deserted, the Taranaki Maori having been driven southward during the Taranaki war two decades previously. As the Maori slowly returned to find their land farmed by the settlers, war broke out again and lasted until 1870. The Europeans had settled mainly on the north of Cape Egmont, the site of New Plymouth, which today is Taranaki's main port and only city. From New Plymouth, Highway 45 follows the coast around the cape, joining Highway 3, the main west-coast road, at Hawera.

The long Whanganui River runs southwest from Tongariro National Park into the South Taranaki Bight, forming the unofficial boundary of the western lands. Whanganui National Park was created in the mid-1980s to preserve the historical sites and natural beauty of this navigable waterway, which long served as the only route into the interior. At its mouth stands the comfortable, attractive port city of Wanganui, one of New Zealand's oldest towns. Rather confusingly, the town is not spelled the same way as the river or the park.

NEW PLYMOUTH

New Plymouth (population 70,000), Taranaki's only city, is the export centre for the region's agricultural produce and the management centre for onshore and offshore natural gas fields. Port Taranaki, the largest port on New Zealand's west coast, handles 5 million tonnes of freight annually. Apart from the blight of an industrial foreshore, New Plymouth is a charming, hilly city with many parks and gardens, good beaches to the north and south and always the spectacular backdrop of Mount Taranaki/Egmont.

GETTING THERE

New Plymouth is served by Air New Zealand with daily direct flights north to Auckland and south to Wellington. From the airport 11 kilometres (seven miles) northeast of the city, Wither's Coachlines provide door-to-door service for passengers. Intercity and Newmans buses offer regular service from Wellington via Wanganui and from Auckland via Hamilton. All buses arrive and depart from the Travel Centre on Queen Street. For those driving, New Plymouth is equidistant from Auckland and Wellington, which are 360 kilometres (225 miles) to the north and south, respectively.

INFORMATION
You can get a city map, brochures about all the region's sights and other travel information and assistance from the excellent New Plymouth Information Centre in Puke Ariki on Ariki Streets. The information and displays here on contingency plans should Mount Taranaki/Egmont ever erupt again are interesting but hopefully unnecessary. Open weekdays 9 am–6 pm and weekends and public holidays 9 am–5 pm. Phone (06)759-6060.

SIGHTS
Puke Ariki, on Ariki Street, is a modern complex that combines New Plymouth's main museum with the visitor centre and a library. Overlooking the ocean, it showcases a splendid collection of early Taranaki Maori art in stone and wood and exhibits on colonial and natural history. Open weekdays 9 am–6 pm and weekends 9 am–5 pm. Phone (06)759-6060. The **Govett-Brewster Art Gallery**, on Queen Street, is the scene of contemporary and changing exhibits. Open weekdays 10.30am–5 pm. Phone (06)758-5149.

Pukekura Park is widely considered to be New Zealand's finest city park. Its attractions include mossy avenues, fernery and begonia display houses, waterways with black swans and other waterfowl and an illuminated fountain. The park is at the upper end of Liardet Street, a ten-minute walk from the information centre. The adjacent **Brooklands Park** was once the home of an early settler. It's worth visiting to see a puriri tree estimated to be 2,000 years old. **Pukeiti**, 20 kilometres (12 miles) southwest of New Plymouth on Carrington Road, is a beautiful botanic garden internationally famous for holding 500 of the world's 800 rhododendron species. Open daily 10 am–5 pm. Phone (06)752-4141. **Pouakai Zoo Park**, at 1296 Carrington Road, has a walk-through aviary, several kinds of animals (mostly of the hoofed variety) and lakeside walks where you can see a variety of exotic birds. Open daily. Phone (06)753-3788.

Lying close to the coast off New Plymouth are the **Sugar Loaf Islands**,

Carved Boxes.

Intricately carved wooden boxes.

eroded remnants of an ancient volcano that now support large populations of bird life. New Zealand fur seals breed on three of the islands. The islands have a long human history; evidence of early Maori habitation remains, and Moturoa Island supported a whaling station in the early 1800s. The best land-based vantage point is Paritutu Centennial Park, along Centennial Drive. For a bird's-eye view, climb the adjacent Paritutu Rock, a steep-sided spire of the same volcanic origin as the islands. Ask at the Information Centre for boat and diving operators who visit the islands.

EGMONT NATIONAL PARK

The map of Taranaki is a study in concentric circles. In the centre is the symmetrical snowcapped cone of **Mount Taranaki/Egmont**, which rises 2,518 metres (7,554 feet) above sea level. Girdling the mountain is circular Egmont National Park, around which lies a flat plain of dairy farms that thrive on the rich, volcanic soil.

Three roads climb from the surrounding plain through dense native bush into the park's lower elevations. One comes from Egmont Village to the north (the nearest to New Plymouth), one from Stratford to the east, and one from Eltham to the southeast. The roads are not linked; each dead-ends within the park. All three end well below the summit. The North Egmont Visitor Centre, at the end of the road leading up from Egmont Village, is open daily 9 am–5 pm (except on Tuesdays during the winter) and offers maps, information, and exhibits. At East Egmont, terminus of the road from Stratford, the Stratford Mountain House provides maps and accommodation. This access road climbs above the treeline from where a short trail leads to Manganui Skifield, open for a short winter season. The road from the southeast ends at Dawson Falls Lodge, where a small display centre is open daily 9 am–5 pm. The park is best-known for its high rainfall, around 7,000 millimetres annually, but most-loved for its hiking (see *Focus*, page 147).

In many ways the best views of Mount Taranaki/Egmont are from afar. The 179-kilometre (111-mile) drive around the mountain affords fantastic panoramas of the peak, with ever-changing angles. South of New Plymouth on Highway 3 is **Stratford**, named after the birthplace of William Shakespeare. Each street in the town is named for a Shakespearian character.

The small town of **Eltham**, 11 kilometres (seven miles) south of Stratford, lies at the heart of some of the country's most productive dairy land and is the self-proclaimed cheese capital of New Zealand. The New Zealand Rennet Company makes a dozen excellent French cheeses from Raclette to Bleu de Bresse to Pyrenees, with production supervised by French and Swiss cheesemakers. The factory has a retail outlet at the town's main crossroads. Open weekdays only. Phone (06)764-8008.

Hawera, the main town of South Taranaki, was home to New Zealand's best comic novelist, Ronald Hugh Morrieson, who died in 1972. To honour Morrieson's place in the New Zealand literary pantheon, some residents wanted to preserve his house in memorium. But in 1992, just like a comic plot from a Morrieson novel, the fast-food chain Kentucky Fried Chicken unwittingly bought the site of his house for a fast-food outlet.

Aside from its wonderfully illuminated water tower, Hawera has three other main points of interest. **Tawhiti Museum**, on Ohangai Road near the Ohangai-Tawhiti crossroads, is a marvellously imaginative re-creation of Taranaki history. The private brainchild of Nigel and Teresa Ogle, it's open 10 am–4 pm, Friday to Monday most of the year, Sunday only from June to August. Don't miss it! Phone (06)278-6837. Two kilometres (1.2 miles) north is **Turuturu-mokai Pa**, a pre-European Maori fortress with earthworks cunningly designed for hand-to-hand tribal warfare. A similar distance east is **Dairyland**, on Whareroa Road at the entrance to the world's largest dairy-products manufacturing site, operated by Kiwi Co-operative Dairies. Milk is collected from over 700,000 cows on 4,000 farms, brought by tanker to the plant and processed into a number of products, including powdered milk. At Dairyland, audio-visual and interactive displays describe the whole operation. Within Dairyland, a café serves up excellent banana milkshakes. The centre is open daily 9 am–5 pm. Phone (06)278-4537.

From Hawera, Highway 3 continues southeast to Wanganui, while Highway 45 leads northwest along the coast back to New Plymouth. Along the latter route, near Pungarehu, 40 kilometres (25 miles) south of New Plymouth, a five-kilometre (three-mile) detour leads to the lighthouse on **Cape Egmont**, the most westerly point in Taranaki. Curious conical mounds remain from lahars (mudslides) let loose during periods of volcanic activity.

WANGANUI

One of the North Island's most pleasant cities, Wanganui spreads through a valley on the west bank of the Whanganui River estuary. In its early days, the port handled international shipping and served as a gateway to the interior for canoes and river boats. It saw bloody battles over European settlement during the 1840s but was largely unaffected by the Land Wars of the 1860s; on one occasion the local Maori even saved the settlement from attack. Although Wanganui has mellowed into a friendly city of big trees, old houses and comfortable gardens, tensions still exist, with recent Maori demonstrations making worldwide news.

GETTING THERE

Air New Zealand flies three times daily from Wanganui to Auckland and Wellington. Intercity and Newmans buses serve the major cities south and north of Wanganui. Intercity also runs north to Ohakune and National Park. For those travelling by car, Highway 3 runs through Wanganui from New Plymouth in the north and Palmerston North in the south. Highway 4 runs south from Tongariro National Park and intersects with Highway 3 at Wanganui.

Maoritanga

Maoritanga means 'the Maori way of doing things'—the daily exercise of a unique Polynesian culture that was nearly lost forever. A hundred years ago, reeling under the impact of European civilization, the Maori faced the tragic prospect of dying out as a people. Today their numbers are increasing and their birthrate is almost twice that of the Pakehas (New Zealanders of European ancestry). It is hard to count the Maori, as intermarriage has left few, if any, full-blooded Maori. The best estimate places the Maori population at 12–15 per cent of the New Zealand total, or roughly 400,000 individuals. What is certain is that Maoritanga is enjoying a renaissance, and New Zealand is consciously moulding a bi-cultural society, trying hard to set right some of the wrongs of the past.

The Maori's rich heritage was passed down through stories and songs, which were reinforced by the symbolic carvings that stood in for a written language. In the beginning, Maori myths say, all was primeval darkness, in which Ranginui, the sky father, and Papa-tua-nuku, the earth mother, were locked in an eternal embrace. Their children, the gods, longed for light and struggled to separate their parents. The god of war would have killed them, but the eldest brother, Tane, god of the forest, pried them apart, creating night and day. Ranginui wept so copiously for his wife that his tears, falling from the sky, formed the oceans. After many battles amongst the gods, peace descended and Tane created a woman out of clay. Through his daughter, the dawn maiden, Tane became the father of mankind.

Later, the myths recount, there was born the human hero Maui, a character common to the mythology of all Polynesians. Maui was so small and weak he was tossed into the sea. The gods rescued the infant, and Ranginui nursed him to maturity. Maui returned to his family blessed with magic powers, which he used to benefit his people. He slowed the sun on its journey across the sky to make more daylight for gathering food. He unlocked the secrets of fire. He set out in his canoe and formed new lands by fishing up out of the ocean the islands of Polynesia. He created Aotearoa—the Land of the Long White Cloud, as the Maori know New Zealand—by fashioning the South Island from his canoe, Stewart Island from its stone anchor, and the North Island from a great fish. Finally, Maui tried to win immortality for mankind but failed in this last quest and perished, as all men must.

Most Maori can trace their ancestry to the chiefs of Hawaiki (an unidentified island probably near Tahiti), who migrated southward by canoe four centuries after the great explorer Kupe discovered Aotearoa. An archaic Maori settlement of Aotearoa was begun probably by AD 800, but most tribes today trace their names and identities from the seven or more ocean-going canoes said to have carried Polynesian colonists across the Pacific Ocean between AD 1200 and 1350.

Each subtribe had a hereditary chief whose mana (a god-given quality of prestige and honour) was drawn from his ancestors. A tohunga, or specialist, had priestly functions. His powers were derived from his special skill, such as carving, and his special knowledge of rituals, sacred lore, tribal history and the secrets of the gods, which had been passed down from older tohunga. In Aotearoa, the Maori brought stone-age technology to a high point, using sharpened nephrite, the hardest of jades, to work beautiful carvings, and building pa (forts) that were bigger and more complex than any stone age equivalent in Europe.

The Maori settlers had brought with them the kumara, the Polynesian sweet potato that has remained their staple food. When the kumara-growing season was over, the Maori engaged zestfully in tribal warfare, a perennial struggle based on the principles of mana and utu (retribution); an insult to one man's mana was an insult to his whole subtribe, and utu inevitably followed. In war season, people left their temporary farming settlements and gathered in the strategically located pa, which was fortified with palisades, ramparts and trenches. Inside were dwellings, decorated storehouses and a finely carved meeting house facing a marae (ceremonial courtyard). The rules of warfare were well understood. Warriors gained fame for valour and cunning, while dances and elegantly carved weapons added lustre to the fray.

The Maori way of life was distorted by European colonization. Muskets, introduced by the first traders, brought havoc to the ritual tribal warfare and threatened the Maori with self-inflicted genocide. Missionaries brought new hope but hastened the crumbling of traditional life. Much of the land that provided each

Woodcarving is one of the most distinctive forms of Maori art. Carvings adorn meeting houses throughout the country, including this one in Te Kaha, captured by photographer John Dobree Pascoe.

(continues on next page)

Elaborate Maori carving from the Tamatekapua meeting house in Ohinemutu, Rotorua. The carving replaces work that was transferred to another meeting house.

tribe's identity and mana was confiscated after the wars of the 1860s or by suspect purchase, and broken up into farms. By 1900, the devastation of the Maori was nearly complete. Numbers had dwindled to 40,000, and they were generally regarded as a dying race.

Several factors brought a turnabout. Against all odds, many surviving Maori clung to their cultural roots. Distinguished Maori political and religious leaders arose to give their people pride and hope. Their influence in the 20th century has helped to bring about more enlightened government policies towards the Maori minority.

Maori communities live by their old traditions and are run on democratic principles evolved from strict, traditional codes of behaviour. The meeting house represents the human form. It is named for an ancestor and carved with symbols recalling tribal myth, thus unifying the group. The marae (the open ground in front of the meeting house) remains the focus of community life—the venue for social, political and ceremonial events. The marae symbolizes the ancient lands of the tribe and its mana.

Multitribal marae, adapted to modern circumstances, function as community centres in the cities where Maori workers have migrated. Many urban Maori have become political activists, fighting poverty and discrimination and refusing to allow their culture to be debased as a mere lure for tourists or entertainment for visiting royalty. That spirit of protest has been backed even by the High Court, which has insisted that the Treaty of Waitangi principles, though unratified by any New Zealand Parliament, are an organic part of New Zealand law (see the Special Topic, 'The Treaty of Waitangi,' pages 68-70).

In the 1970s, Britain joined the European Common Market, ending its favourable trade relationship with its former colony. This caused an economic crisis and also one of identity. Severed from British apron strings, all New Zealanders looked with renewed interest at Maori culture as something the country could claim as its own.

Students of both races started studying the Maori language, and many adults formed bi-racial groups to learn Maoritanga. Teaching of Maori language began in New Zealand schools, and a dramatic Maori initiative sparked the creation of over 400 kohanga reo,

The waves at Raglan, west of Hamilton, attract surfers from around the world.

> kindergartens where Maori language, customs and values can be passed on to preschool children before the Maori elders are all gone. Nightly news programmes in Maori are now broadcast on television, and regular commentators set a good example to the nation by pronouncing Maori place names correctly, instead of using the customary Anglicized abbreviations. Maoritanga is becoming the birthright of all New Zealanders.

SIGHTS

Wanganui is a good city to explore on foot (see *Focus*, page 147). Maps, brochures and information on nearby Whanganui National Park are available at the Wanganui Information Centre at the corner of Guyton and St Hill streets. Phone (06)349-0508.

Victoria Avenue, the city's main street, is extensively restored, even down to gaslamps. **Queen's Park**, a block away, is the cultural heart of town. It occupies a high, grassy knoll, site of an early military stockade, and includes the stately War Memorial Hall, a modern public library, the domed Sarjeant Art Gallery and, at its foot, the famous **Whanganui Regional Museum**, one of the best in the country. The

museum's great Maori-style hall boasts splendid displays of greenstone and whalebone weapons, jewellery, feather cloaks, tattooing methods and a war canoe that held a crew of 70 and still has bullets embedded in its hull. Upstairs in the natural history section are the reassembled skeletons of several species of moa ranging in size from tiny to enormous. Open Monday to Saturday 10 am–4.30 pm and Sunday 1 pm–4.30 pm. Phone (06)345-7443. Two blocks east is **Wanganui Riverboat Centre and Museum**, home to the *Waimarie*, a paddlesteamer raised in 1992 after spending 40 years on the riverbed then restored, and now used for trips and dinner cruises. Phone (06)347-1863.

At **Durie Hill**, directly across City Bridge, a tunnel connects to an elevator that rises 66 metres (216 feet) to the summit through a vertical shaft drilled into bedrock. A carved Maori gateway marks the entry to the tunnel. (A road also leads to the top.) At the summit, the War Memorial Tower, built of rock containing fossilized seashells, gives an unparalleled panorama of the city, the river, the coast as far as Kapiti Island to the south and the distant volcanoes to the north.

Virginia Lake, on the Great North Road 1.5 kilometres (one mile) north of the city, is a lovely, quiet, parklike area of gardens, walks, and bird-filled woods. Highlights include an aviary, fountains and the tranquil lake itself. The place is imbued with Maori legends.

Whanganui National Park stretches along parts of the Whanganui River between Wanganui and Taumarunui. A road, unsealed along some of its length, branches west off Highway 4 north of Wanganui and follows the river for 80 kilometres (50 miles). It passes through the small settlement of Jerusalem—where James K. Baxter, New Zealand's best known poet, was buried in 1972—and continues on past Maori hamlets and an abandoned flour mill that dates from 1854. It ends up in **Pipiriki**, a one-time resort destination that is now a quiet hamlet, with a museum to browse through and a restored riverboat high and dry on the edge of town. From Pipiriki, a gravel road crosses over mountains to rejoin Highway 4 at Raetihi, 90 kilometres (56 miles) north of Wanganui.

The most easily navigable stretch of the Whanganui River is upstream of Pipiriki, where the river is also at its most beautiful. Bridge To Nowhere Jet Boat Tours runs a four-hour trip from Pipiriki to their namesake, the Bridge to Nowhere, which was built with grand intentions in 1936. The trip includes lunch and a short hike through forest to the bridge. Phone (06)385-4128. It is best to confirm arrangements before leaving Wanganui. Similar tours also run from Taumarunui, the King Country township near the source of the Whanganui. Taumarunui lies at the junction of Highway 4 and Highway 41.

FOCUS

Egmont National Park is somewhat disappointing for bird-watchers, but common forest species such as tui, bellbird, pied tit, pigeon and fantail are found in the dense lower-level bush. Grey warblers breed in the higher subalpine scrub. The self-introduced silvereye is probably the most common bird in the park and the rare blue duck has been released for breeding in the rivers.

Some 15 kilometres (nine miles) west of Wanganui on Highway 3 is Kai-Iwi, from where you travel north eight kilometres (five miles) to arrive at **Bushy Park Homestead**, a magnificent native forest where many types of bush birds can be seen from the forest paths. An interpretative centre in a converted horse stable and an Edwardian-era mansion also grace the park. Phone (06)342-9879.

New Plymouth has a heritage walkway that leads past 30 of the town's historic buildings and points of interest, drawing attention to both the Maori and European past. Highlights include the Egmont Steam Flour Mill, dating from 1865 and recently restored; a boulder that once marked the fishing boundary of two adjacent Maori tribes; and the grave of Charles Armitage Brown, who was, as his headstone proudly declares and as subsequent scholarly research has proven, a friend of the poet Keats. Allow three hours.

Trails can be found in **Egmont National Park** along all three access roads. You can hike to the summit of Mount Taranaki/Egmont from North Egmont Visitor Centre in six to eight hours for the return trip. Ask for track and weather conditions before setting off. For the less-ambitious, Veronica Walk and Veronica Track are both good, well-marked circular walks starting at the western edge of North Egmont's upper car park. Get a map at the visitors' centre before starting out. Allow one and a half to two hours for Veronica Walk, which leads through forest up the mountainside to a high ridge with grand views. Veronica Track is easier but longer, branching from the Veronica Walk after 20 minutes and following a ridge for two kilometres (1.2 miles) before ending along the main access road. Allow about three and a half hours. The delightful Patea Walk (marked yellow) starts at Stratford Mountain Lodge and goes through a moss-filled 'goblin forest,' crossing and recrossing the Patea River. Allow about two hours. South Egmont, accessible from Highway 3 by turning off at Eltham, has the short and popular Kapuni Walk (marked pink), which starts from Manaia Road just below Dawson Falls Lodge and follows the bank of Kapuni Stream through the forest to the 18 metre (60 foot)-high Dawson Falls. A steep path leads down the side to the base of the falls. Another short path leading off before the falls crosses the stream to a fine lookout. The main track emerges lower down Manaia Road. Across the road, clearly marked Cossey's Track is a ten-minute hike through rainforest back to the lodge.

From the Brink of Extinction

In 1980 the rarest bird in the world was undeniably the Chatham Island black robin. Only five of the bright-eyed little bush birds remained on earth. That New Zealanders were aware of the impending loss—and cared—was due to a tragic irony. New Zealand had once been the exclusive realm of bird life, a paradise without predators, where many birds forgot how to fly. For millions of years species unknown elsewhere in the world lived in peace in the country's forests and grasslands. But a thousand years ago, human beings arrived, bringing rats, cats and fire. Since then, fully half of New Zealand's native birds have become extinct, and many more perch precariously on the brink today. Awareness came almost too late.

Officers of New Zealand's Wildlife Service took their first census of the Chatham Island black robins in 1972. They climbed the forbidding cliffs of a tiny islet off the remote Chatham Islands, 800 kilometres (500 miles) east of Christchurch, to a small patch of deteriorating forest known to be the bird's last refuge. The men counted only 18 individuals and marked each one with a coloured leg band. Four years later there were only seven. With infinite care the wildlife team caught the robins, wrestled their cages down the cliffs and ferried them by rubber boat to a bigger, better-forested island nearby. There, the two remaining breeding females, named Old Blue and Old Green for their coloured leg bands, each raised chicks, but the older birds died one by one. Time was running out. The wildlife team took up residence on the forsaken, windswept island and, in desperation, decided to try a technique called cross-fostering. As soon as Old Blue or Old Green laid eggs, they were whisked away to the nests of warblers, who were known to make good foster parents. Saddened to find their nests empty, the robins laid again, and once more the eggs were given to warblers. Ten eggs were hatched by the warblers, but only four chicks survived. The warblers were not able to feed the babies sufficiently, and the robin population fell to five.

Southeast Island, 15 kilometres (nine miles) away, was a nature reserve. Its forest included tits, who are close relatives of the black robin. This was the last chance. Old Blue was now the only remaining female. She had lived almost 13 years, twice a normal lifespan, but she kept laying. The wildlife team mustered the help of fishermen, who ferried each newly laid robin's egg across open sea in a tiny incubator. Within two hours it was on Southeast Island, placed in a nest under a warm mother tit. When Old Blue died in 1984, there were 19 black robins—six of which were her

> children and 11 of which were her grandchildren. Today the descendants are numerous, but all descended from valiant Old Blue.
>
> Cross-fostering, using specially trained bantam hens as adoptive mothers, saved the takahe from certain extinction in the 1950s, and a number of them now live under official protection. Little Barrier Island and Kapiti Island, guarded by the vigilant Department of Conservation, serve as a last refuge for nearly vanished species such as the stichback, saddleback, kakapo, black petrel and Cook's petrel. Other rare birds are carefully monitored and protected in the national parks.

Wanganui has a particularly fine city-and-river walk along the Whanganui River. Start at the Whanganui Regional Museum, follow Victoria Avenue across the Wanganui City Bridge and turn left. Across the road is the carved Maori gateway to Durie Hill. Go into the tunnel, take the elevator to the summit and climb Durie Hill Memorial Tower for a breathtaking view. Return to the river by the road, turn right and follow the river to the next bridge. You will go through James McGregor and Kowhai Parks and a scenic natural reserve, and see the imaginative Kowhai Children's Playpark. Cross Dublin Bridge and turn left along Somme Parade. Turn away from the river on Bates Street, then at Moutoa Gardens cross Ridgeway Street and climb to the top of Queen's Park, where you might want to stop at the Sarjeant Art Gallery and Alexander Library. From here you look down on to your starting point at the museum. Allow two to two and a half hours.

North of Highway 3 between Hawera and Wanganui is **Lake Rotorangi**, a reservoir created in 1987 behind a hydroelectric dam on the Patea River. When Lake Rotorangi was first stocked with rainbow and brown trout, fingerlings got out through the floodgates and have since established themselves below the dam in the river's deep holes. The resulting excellent fishing is one of the region's best-kept secrets. Turn inland from Highway 3 at Manutahi or Kakaramea (both of which are between Hawera and Patea) toward Alton. A good unpaved road goes from Alton to Hurleyville, where signs lead to Lake Rotorangi, 11 kilometres (seven miles) further. A car park and camping facilities are near the dam.

New Plymouth Golf Club (Ngamotu Links), on Devon Road in New Plymouth, offers an excellent links-style course that has hosted the New Zealand Open. The fairways are lined with the distinctive red bloom of pohutukawas, and views of snowcapped Mount Taranaki/Egmont and the Tasman Sea are pervasive. As at all seaside courses, the wind adds an interesting and challenging dimension. Par 72. Phone (06)755-0424. **Westown Golf Club**, on Mangorei Road, is an inland course surrounded by native forest and offering good views of the volcano. Par 72. Phone (06)758-6933. The rolling course at Normanby's **Te Ngutu Golf Club**, five kilometres (three miles) north of Hawera off Highway 3, also has fine views and claims to be the best 18-hole course in south Taranaki. Phone (06)272-8039.

In Wanganui, the Belmont Links course at **Wanganui Golf Club** is a mature championship course—very challenging and enjoyable. Par 70. Phone (06)349-0559.

 East of New Plymouth on Cross Road in Lepperton is **Sentry Hill**, the West's only operating winery. It's best known for a sweet kiwi-fruit wine. Phone (06)752-0778.

The South

The southern point of the North Island is dominated by Wellington (population 167,000), located on a fine harbour at the island's southwestern tip. As the national capital, Wellington is first and foremost a centre of government. But the city is also a destination in itself, boasting one of the world's great museums, a thriving cultural scene, stately buildings sandwiched between the water and the hills, and wilderness on the back doorstep.

Northeast of Wellington and neighboring Hutt Valley, the rugged Tararua Range runs north-south, splitting the region in two. East of the mountains lies the Wairarapa, a peaceful, prosperous plain with its centre at Masterton. To the west, the mountains descend steeply to the Tasman Sea, leaving only a narrow strip bordering a sandy coastline; small towns are strung along Highway 1 as it wends its way north to a broad, built-up triangle with corners at Levin, Bulls and Palmerston North. The people on the west side of the mountains are mainly suburbanites—a different breed from the farmers of the Wairarapa.

WELLINGTON

According to Maori legend, Kupe, the great Polynesian explorer, was the first to see the excellent, hill-encircled harbour around which the capital sprawls. By 1773, when Captain Cook sailed by, Maori settlements lined the shore. The local Maori tolerated the English colonists who arrived in 1840 because they appeared less dangerous than some of their neighbouring tribes. As a result, the city took root as a trading centre. A massive earthquake in 1855 raised the coast and harbour floor by as much as one and a half metres (five feet), making it relatively easy to reclaim much-needed flat land for building, a process that is still going on. Wellington was chosen as the nation's capital in 1865 (to the chagrin of Auckland residents) in recognition of its central location, convenient to both islands. It is now New Zealand's fifth largest city.

Wellington is often compared to Chicago as one of the world's windiest cities. It stands in the path of the Roaring Forties, which funnel through Cook Strait at an average of 90 kilometres (56 miles) per hour for at least 40 days a year. These strong winds, blowing mostly in spring and autumn, are credited with keeping the air fresh and smog-free. The city is also compared to San Francisco for its beautiful setting on hills around a harbour, its cable car, and its frequency of earthquakes. But Wellington is unique. Old buildings jostle with contemporary concrete and glass structures up the hillsides, and the downtown business centre is forever changing its appearance as new flat land is drained and built up, leaving the original quays further and further inland from the present docks.

A large part of the population works in the government or in businesses with head offices in the capital, which makes the downtown scene more homogeneous, formal and citified than in many other New Zealand cities. Foreign embassies provide a cosmopolitan flair. Yet this attractive city is small enough to walk around and get acquainted with quickly.

GETTING THERE

Wellington Airport is eight kilometres (five miles) south of the city centre. The only international flights into Wellington are from Australia. Domestic flights between Wellington and all major cities are currently provided by Air New Zealand. Other carriers, including Soundsair, make the short hop over Cook Strait, saving a sometimes rough ferry ride. Super Shuttle runs a regular service between the city and the airport.

Tranz Scenic offers train service to Wellington from Auckland, Napier and points in between. Wellington Railway Station is on Bunny Street at Waterloo Quay.

Ferries carry passengers, vehicles and railway rolling stock between Wellington's Aotea Quay and the South Island terminal at Picton. The Cook Strait crossing takes about three hours and 20 minutes. (See page 36 for more information).

Bus services linking all points north with Wellington are run by Intercity, Newmans and a number of smaller bus lines. Most services depart from beside Platform 9 of the railway station and also stop at the ferry terminal.

Cruise liners tie up at the Overseas Passenger Terminal in the harbour.

INFORMATION AND ORIENTATION

The Wellington Visitor Centre is in Civic Square, right downtown at the intersection of Wakefield and Victoria Streets. The helpful staff here will ensure you make the most of your stay in the capital, providing information, all kinds of maps, and many types of bookings (including onward travel). Open weekdays 8.30 am–5.30 pm and weekends 9.30 am–5 pm. Phone (04)802-4863. The De-

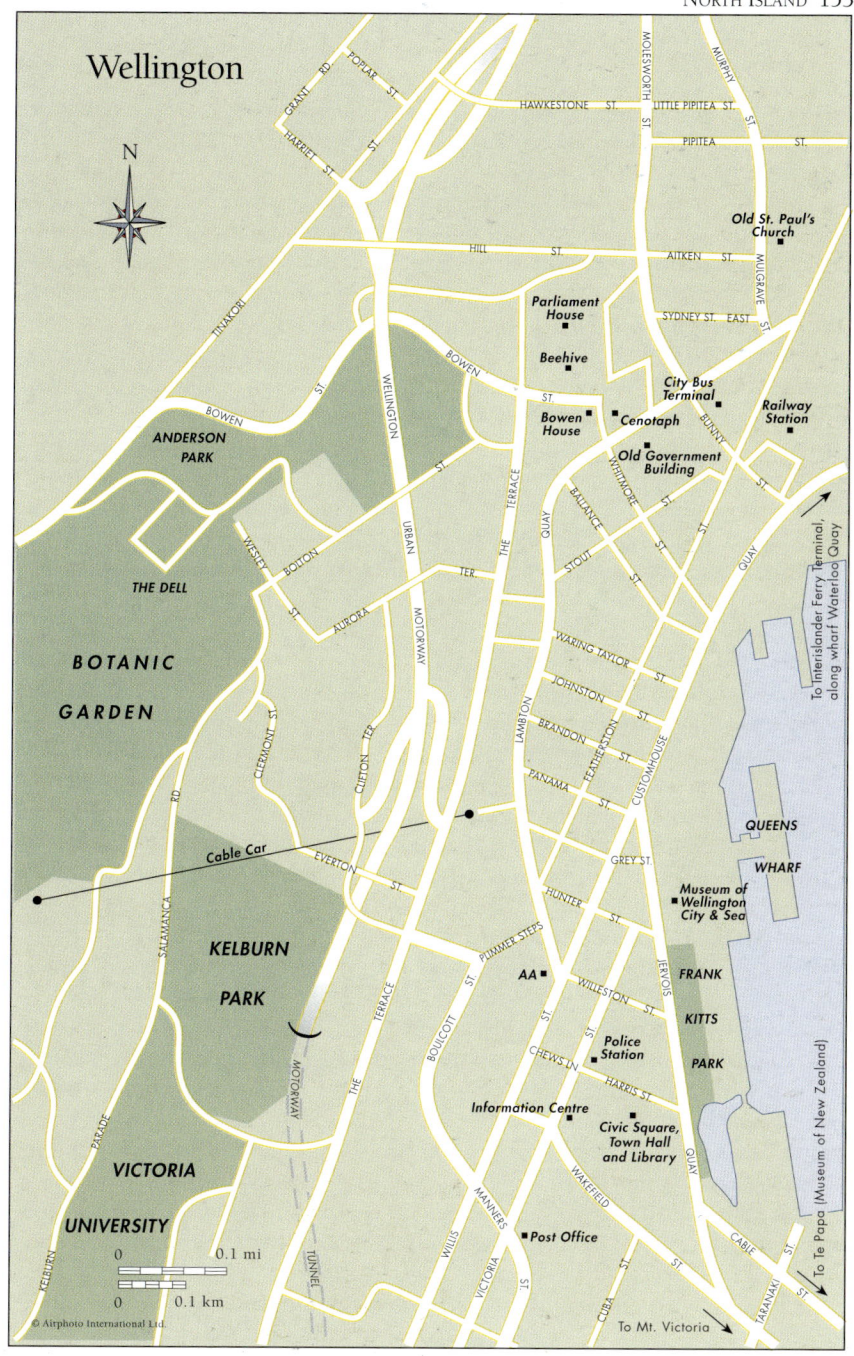

The Old Government Buildings are the epicentre of New Zealand politics and one of Wellington's most popular sightseeing attractions.

partment of Conservation information centre is in the Old Government Building at 15 Lambton Quay. Phone (04)472-7356. The AA is at 342 Lambton Quay. Phone (04)470-9999.

Car rental companies have offices in downtown Wellington, at the airport and at the ferry terminal. Taxis can be found at the railway station, or phone (04)388-8888. The excellent city bus service, run by various operators, provides 50 routes to all corners of the city. Phone (04)801-7000. Newsstands sell a bus map with timetables, and you can pick up individual timetables for each route from the information centre.

Wellington's shopping area of department stores, restaurants and boutiques runs for almost two kilometres (1.2 miles) from downtown Lambton Quay—the original waterfront in pre-earthquake days—along Willis and Manners Streets, with a detour on Cuba Street, to Courtenay Place. Be sure to get a city map from the information centre or a newsstand, as it is easy to get lost. The hills cause streets to run at unexpected angles, and the different levels are often connected by flights of steps. Sometimes you enter what you think is a low building on one side, ride down an elevator, and come out at the bottom on the other side to find it is a skyscraper!

SIGHTS

Te Papa (The **Museum of New Zealand**), one of the world's most modern and spectacular national museums, opened its doors on 14 February 1998 was expanded in 2001. Te Papa, meaning 'Our Place,' rises five storeys from the harbourfront and is surrounded by artificial wetlands, a rushing stream and over 12,000 plants, all connected by a raised boardwalk. The interior is no less impressive, with galleries totalling 38,500 square metres (4.1 million square feet) and encompassing the entire natural and human history of New Zealand. The excellent Maori collection is a highlight, along with relics from Polynesian exploration and Captain Cook's voyage. The story of European settlers is told through historic photographs, moving tributes and an eclectic collection of memorabilia. Some exhibits detail the country's intriguing flora and fauna, while others tell the story of the volcanoes and earthquakes that have shaped the land. Cutting-edge technology is used in the Time Machine, an audio-visual simulator that takes visitors on a journey through time from the pre-European settlement days to a modern-day, heart-stopping bungy jump. Art galleries catalogue the work of New Zealand's many artists; one contains a collection of Maori art. One of the museum's unique features is a marae, where Maori ceremonies take place through the day. The museum is on Cable Street. Phone (04)381-7000. Open daily 10 am–6 pm, until 9 pm Thursdays; free admission.

Mount Victoria, which rises 194 metres (636 feet) above a beautiful old residential district near Courtenay Place, offers the best view of the whole city and harbour. Drive up the winding road, or take bus number 20 to the summit. On a clear day, the panoramic view stretches all the way to the northern tip of the South Island. Several paths lead back down to Courtenay Place for a nice half-hour walk.

Katherine Mansfield

It's a small town, you know, planted at the edge of a fine deep harbour like a lake. Behind it on either side there are hills. The houses are built of light painted wood. They have iron roofs coloured red. And there are big dark plumy trees massed together breaking up those light shapes and making a composition of it well worth looking at.

Katherine Mansfield (1888–1923) is New Zealand's best known writer. She spent her childhood years in Wellington, and her thoughts and feelings for the city are reflected in later writings, such as this excerpt from *Daphne*.

For five of her formative years she lived in a stately home built of locally milled timber at 25 Tinakori Road in Thorndon. Visitors to the restored property can view a video biography of Mansfield's life, as well as excerpts of her work relevant to Wellington, historic photographs and the house and gardens planted as Mansfield wrote of them in *Prelude*. The house is open to the public daily 10 am–4 pm. Tel:(04)473-7268.

Another way to appreciate the city's spectacular setting from above is to take the **Wellington Cable Car** up to Kelburn Lookout. It leaves from Cable Car Lane, off Lambton Quay opposite Grey Street. The cable car was built in 1902 to provide a link up the steep rise between downtown and the suburb of Kelburn. It makes three stops and passes through three short tunnels in the course of the five-minute ride. At the top is the entrance to the **Botanic Garden**, a beautifully laid out,

26-hectare (64-acre) preserve with formal gardens, wild native forest, shrubs and flowers. At the top of the cable car is **Carter Observatory**, which holds interactive computer displays, videos and an observatory. Open 10 am–5 pm daily with telescope viewing Tuesday, Thursday and Saturday at 6.30 pm. Phone (04)472-8167. Near the garden's northern entrance, **Lady Norwood Rose Garden** contains not only thousands of sweet-scented roses that bloom from November to April, but also a camellia garden, a begonia house, a sunken garden, a waterfall, a teahouse and many lookouts over the city. The ivy-covered buildings and manicured campus of **Victoria University** overlook the city from the hilltop south of the Botanic Garden, an easy walk from the cable car's Salamanca Road stop.

Wellington Harbour, a source of city pride, is a deep, circular basin protected by hills and opening onto Cook Strait through a narrow channel. A walk on the waterfront along Jervois Quay (see *Focus*, page 163) gives a taste of the busy harbour life. The fine old Wellington Harbour Board building on Queens Wharf is now the **Museum of Wellington, City & Sea**. Its main floor is full of boat models, charts, relics from wrecks, photographs and paintings, all of which chronicle the port's history. Open daily 10 am–5 pm. Phone (04)472-8904.

Government Centre, the political heart of New Zealand, sits atop a parklike knoll near the north end of Lambton Quay. The most striking building is the **Beehive**, a circular 11-storey structure that serves as the Parliament's executive wing. It was completed in 1981. The adjoining **Parliament House**, built of marble and granite in 1922, holds a debating chamber and offices for the House of Representatives. The old building reopened in 1996 after extensive renovations that returned the building to its original look. Fifteen-minute tours of both the Beehive and the Parliament are conducted Monday to Friday 9 am–4 pm, Saturday 9 am–3 pm, at hourly intervals. Phone (04)471-9999. The tours are not given when Parliament is in session (look for the flag flying above the building), but you're welcome to watch from the visitors' gallery. Alongside the old Parliament House is the stone, Gothic-style **Parliamentary Library**. Built in 1897, it has also been renovated and serves today as the parliamentary research library and repository for all New Zealand books and publications.

THE HUTT VALLEY

Tucked between the Tararua Mountains and the Rimutaka Range, the Hutt Valley lies just northeast of Wellington at the head of Wellington Harbour. The cities of Lower and Upper Hutt sprawl up its length beside the Hutt River until a steep gorge blocks the way. Wellington's first European settlers landed at Lower Hutt and

---

(preceding pages) Wellington, one of the world's great harbour cities

would have established their city there if the Hutt River had not flooded and persuaded them to move further around the bay. For a while the valley served as Wellington's hinterland, with market gardens planted on its rich alluvial soil to feed the city. As the population grew, the city had nowhere but the Hutt Valley to expand into. New housing projects created suburban dormitory communities. Manufacturing enterprises and research institutes soon followed, the market gardens vanished and the communities swiftly grew into important industrial and commercial cities in their own right. They are attractively laid out with trees, parks, and golf courses. Especially in Upper Hutt, residences are so luxuriantly landscaped that they create the illusion of being far from any city.

THE WAIRARAPA

This wide, sheep-filled plain at the eastern foot of the Tararua Range is a world apart from the sophisticated city of Wellington, a couple of hours' drive to the south. The Wairarapa boasts some three million sheep, which makes the ratio of sheep to people here almost as great as that in the South Island. It also has the distinction of being the North Island's only region of peace during the Land Wars of the last century.

Masterton, on Highway 2, is a tree-lined agricultural centre with a beautiful park, but its claim to fame is the annual Golden Shears Championship, held amidst carnival exuberance for four days in the first week of March. New Zealand teams vie with Australians for the coveted first prize, as 8,000 professional sheep shearers show their speed and accuracy. Thousands of sheep lose their fleece in the process, some in the course of barely a minute, and oceans of beer are drunk as hordes of spectators gather to watch the excitement.

Mount Bruce National Wildlife Centre, 30 km north of Masterton towards Palmerston North on Highway 2, is a fascinating stop for any nature lover (see *Focus*, page 162).

The intriguing little town of **Martinborough** lies off the main road on Highway 53, midway between Masterton and Upper Hutt. (Take a good road map with you.) Its main square was designed in 1870 in the shape of the Union Jack, with eight streets converging to form the crosses of Great Britain's patron saints. The old post office on the square has been turned into a delightful little restaurant, and in the last decade the town has gained fame as the centre of an excellent wine-producing region (see *Focus*, page 165).

Nearby **Greytown**, on Highway 2, is worth a stop for **Cobblestones Museum**, on Main Street. This early-settlers' museum on the site of the town's first stables is full of memorabilia from the days of stagecoaches—a reflection of Greytown's one-time importance as a way station. Open daily 9 am–4.30 pm.

Wellington's neo-Gothic Parliamentary Library dates to the 1920s.

THE KAPITI COAST

The western coastline north of Wellington, known as the Kapiti Coast, is famed for its golden, sandy beaches backed by the forested Tararua Range. Not surprisingly, given the area's beauty, the shore is lined with city-dwellers' beach cottages. **Paekakariki**, about 30 kilometres (19 miles) north of Wellington, has a swimming beach strewn with shells, as well as an interesting museum. The **Wellington Tramway Museum** displays antique trams that operated along Wellington streets until 1964. Many are still operational, and one runs through adjacent Queen Elizabeth Park on summer weekends.

Paraparaumu, about ten kilometres (six miles) further north, is the main gateway to Kapiti Island, described below for bird-watchers (see *Focus*, page 162). The town itself features a fine swimming beach and a world-famous golf course (see *Focus*, page 164). The Kapiti Visitor Centre, in the Coastlands Shopping Centre Carpark, has maps and brochures on the region and is helpful for hiring boats to Kapiti Island. For antique car buffs, the **Southward Car Museum** on Otaihanga Road merits a visit. It holds Australasia's largest collection of antique cars. Open daily 9 am–4.30 pm. Phone (04)297-1221.

A mural brightens an old brick building that now holds Wellington's Il Casino Restaurant.

PALMERSTON NORTH

The North Island's eighth largest city can be reached quickly from Wellington via the west coast on Highway 1, or more pleasantly through the Wairarapa—take Highway 2 as far as Woodville, then head west on Highway 3 through the magnificent **Manawatu Gorge**. Palmerston North, a major population centre on the level Manawatu Plain, is an attractive city with a large green park in the middle of its commercial district. Other gardens and parks abound. Massey University is renowned for veterinary and agricultural sciences. The town holds no outstanding tourist sights, but it is a nice place to stop, relax and look around. This is the home of the New Zealand Rugby Institute where the country's best players hone their skills. Sports fans shouldn't miss the **New Zealand Rugby Museum**, at 87 Cuba Street. Open Monday to Saturday 10 am–4 pm. Sunday 1.30–4 pm. Phone (06)358-6947.

FOCUS

Around **Wellington Harbour** you may see reef herons and flocks of shearwaters. Take the ferry across Cook Strait to Picton and along the way look for giant petrel, diving petrel, cape pigeon, varieties of shearwater, prion, albatross, mollymawk and gull. It is surprising that with such a wealth

of seabirds New Zealand has only three species of gull. The large Dominican gull is widespread in the southern oceans; the red-billed gull is also found in Australia and South Africa; and the black-billed gull, usually found inland, is strictly endemic. **Otari Native Botanical Garden**, on Wilton Road, is a delightful sanctuary of bird-filled bush on the edge of the city. Viewing the population of tui is a highlight, although casual bird-watchers are more likely to spot fantails, wood pigeons, and kingfishers.

Pukaha Mount Bruce lies about 130 kilometres (80 miles) northeast of Wellington, between Masterton and Eketahuna on Highway 2. Founded in 1962, it continued the efforts of an individual bird-lover who devised a method for fostering rare takahe chicks with bantam hens. Today Mount Bruce enjoys an international reputation for the management, study and captive breeding of endangered species. The large aviaries and enclosures set in native bush allow bird-lovers to see rare species that they are unlikely to find in the wild, including saddleback, kaka and kokako. Mount Bruce is open daily 9 am–4.30 pm. Phone (04)375-8004.

At **Castlepoint**, east of Masterton, a large coastal lagoon provides a resting ground for a variety of seabirds, including whitefronted terns, red-billed gulls and black shags. This wild and remote stretch of coast is also home to a seal colony.

Enchanting **Kapiti Island**, five kilometres (3.1 miles) from the mainland, ranks second only to Little Barrier Island (see *Focus*, page 63) as a sanctuary for rare native birds. The pride of Kapiti is its great variety of bush birds, some of which are extinct on the mainland. The island is home to whiteheads, North Island robins, pied tits, grey warblers, tuis, bellbirds and best of all, a good population of the strictly nocturnal little spotted kiwi, the rarest of the species. Kaka can be viewed feeding near the ranger station. Water birds frequent the shores and the lagoon at the northern tip. A few rare brown teal hide in the swamp near the ranger's house, and blue penguins nest all over the island. A permit to visit Kapiti Island can be obtained from the Department of Conservations, Wellington Conservancy office . Phone (04)472-7356. Visitors cannot stay overnight, and only 50 people are permitted on the island each day, so apply early for your permit; it will be issued for the date you want, if available. A fee is charged for the permit and you will also have to pay for your boat trip to the island. Two companies in Paraparaumu charter boats to Kapiti; for a current listing call Kapiti Coast Information Centre at (04)364-7620.

Wellington, in spite of its hills, is a good city to see on foot. Many stairways and footpaths link the various street levels. The streets run at odd angles, so be sure to get a free street map from your hotel or the visitor centre. The visitor centre also offers several different one-and-a-half to two-hour guided walks by prior arrangement.

For a city walk at your own pace through the heart of the capital, start at the Citizens War Memorial (Cenotaph) at Lambton Quay and Bowen Street. Cross Parliament grounds, with the Beehive, a statue of Richard John Seddon (who was prime minister 1893–1906), Parliament House and the Parliamentary Library on your left. Walk to the top of Molesworth Street and take the underpass to Murphy Street, where a small garden serves as a memorial to Katherine Mansfield, the New Zealand-born writer. Head back toward the harbour down Murphy Street, visiting Old Saint Paul's Church on Mulgrave Street. Then continue past the National Archives to Lambton Quay. End up opposite the War Memorial again, at the huge Government Building, the second largest wooden building in the world (after Todaiji Temple in Japan). This walk can take up to one and a half hours.

For a harbour walk, start at the visitor centre and go across Civic Square to the waterfront and Frank Kitts Park. Follow Jervois Quay to the Maritime Museum at Queens Wharf and on to Customhouse Quay. A left-hand turn into any side street will take you to Lambton Quay and the heart of Wellington. Allow 45 minutes.

The **Northern Walkway** runs 16 kilometres north from the Botanic Garden. After traversing the garden, the trail climbs steadily to Tinakori Hill, for views extending across the harbour. Continuing north, it passes through Khandallah Park—where a lookout provides more great city and harbour views—and ends in the suburb of Johnsonville. Catching a train back to the city centre completes a pleasant half-day adventure.

Colonial Knob is at Porirua, 20 kilometres (12 miles) north of Wellington on Highway 1. The 7.5-kilometre (4.7-mile) circular trail starts at the car park at Broken Hill Road, passes a reservoir in a scenic reserve and then climbs through pastoral farmland to Colonial Knob Radio Station (for civil aviation). The track is steep in places, but the reward at the top is a spectacular view—all the way to Mount Taranaki/Egmont in the north and the Marlborough Sounds, across Cook Strait, to the west. Allow three to four hours return.

Cannon Point Walkway is on the outskirts of Upper Hutt, 32 kilometres (20 miles) northeast of Wellington. The ten-kilometre (six-mile) circular trail starts behind Totara Park subdivision, north of the Hutt River. It provides a pleasant walk through regenerating vegetation and native bush to the top of a prominent ridge with a splendid view over the Hutt Valley. Allow two to three hours. A shorter walk of five kilometres (three miles) can be followed directly to the stone trigonometric survey marker known as Cannon Point Trig. Allow one and a half to two hours.

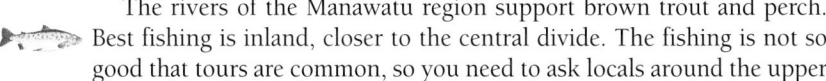

The rivers of the Manawatu region support brown trout and perch. Best fishing is inland, closer to the central divide. The fishing is not so good that tours are common, so you need to ask locals around the upper reaches of such rivers as the **Hautapu**, **Rangitikei** and **Manawatu** to find good locations.

In the Wairarapa, the main fishing river is the **Ruamahanga**, which empties into a coastal lagoon called Lake Onoke. The river north of Martinborough has a rocky bed, as do most of its tributaries, including the **Kopuaranga River**, which is open only to fly-fishing. Brown trout are fairly abundant. If you feel like a change from trout, angle for perch. Near the river's mouth are whitebait and the occasional flounder. The **Waiohine River**, something of a local secret, is beautiful and wild as it comes off the Tararua Range. Inquire at the sports shop at Greytown.

Wellington is not particularly well endowed with angling rivers, but the **Wainuiomata River**, accessed from the eastern side of the harbour near Wainuiomata township, yields brown trout.

Wellington has over 20 golf courses within an hour's drive, and two of them rank amongst the top ten in New Zealand. The New Zealand Open is usually a low-key affair, but in 2002 all eyes were on **Paraparaumu Beach Golf Club**, 70 kilometres (43 miles) north of Wellington off Highway 1, when Tiger Woods made an appearance. It is a classic, sand-based links course that is generally regarded as New Zealand's best. The course is exposed to the winds of the Roaring Forties, making it one of the greatest challenges anywhere. Par 71. Phone (06) 902-8200, website <www.paraparaumubeachgolfclub.co.nz>.

Opposite in style but almost equal in quality is the **Wellington Golf Club** at Heretaunga, 32 kilometres (20 miles) from the city, between Lower and Upper Hutt. This picturesque, parklike course winds past beautiful trees and clear streams. Interesting contours put a premium on accuracy. A casual visitor must be invited by a member to play, but a letter of introduction from your home golf club will assure you a welcome on weekdays. Par 72. Phone (04)528-2640.

Two other courses near Wellington are worth noting. The **Hutt Golf Club**, on Military Road in the middle of Lower Hutt, is a good inland course, mainly flat but attractive. Par 70. Phone (04)567-3714. **Manor Park Golf Club**, between Lower and Upper Hutt, shares some of the characteristics of nearby Wellington Golf Club, with straight hitting required as Out of Bounds comes into play on 13 holes. It is a very fine course. Par 72. Phone (04)563-8558.

At Palmerston North, the national-championship **Hokowhitu Golf Club**, on Centennial Drive, is an excellent inland course beside the Manawatu River. Difficult and windy, it is characterized as unrelenting—a real challenge. Par 72. Phone (06)357-8793.

The Wairarapa, the sleepy farming region northeast of Wellington, has sprung into prominence with a very promising wine area around Martinborough, 50 kilometres (31 miles) from Wellington on Highway 53. A climate similar to the Burgundy region of France—warm summers and dry autumns—first attracted the attention of viticulturists to the Wairarapa. After extensive research and viability studies, the first plantings were made in 1980. The first significant vintage was produced in 1986 and confirmed suspicions that the region could be unique. The area's vintners formed an association—Winemakers of Martinborough—which delineated the limits of the area, established its own appellation and laid down regulations against contract grape-growing, which is widely practised elsewhere.

The Martinborough region is only small in terms of production but has contributed greatly to the country's reputation for quality wine. Pinot Noir is the most planted and most highly acclaimed of local plantings. Chardonnay, Sauvignon Blanc and Cabernet Sauvignon also have a local reputation for quality. Production is still small and quickly absorbed by Wellington, so it is hard to find these wines elsewhere in New Zealand. As the vineyards develop and business settles down, more wine will be cellared. Now most of the wine is sold either at the winery or by mail order as it is bottled.

Martinborough, on Princess Street, is emerging as the foremost winery of the region. Best-known for Pinot Noir, the winery also produces Riesling and Sauvignon Blanc. Phone (06)306-9955. Palliser Estate is the premium label of the **Palliser** winery, on Kitchener Street; its Chardonnay and Sauvignon Blanc are in high demand and are priced to match. Palliser's winemaker, Allan Johnson, has been making wine in the Martinborough region as long as anyone. Phone (06)306-9019. Also on Kitchener Street is **Lintz**, owned and operated by Chris Lintz, a descendent of long-time German winemakers. Since the first vintage in 1991 his wines have won many awards, including one for a well-priced Sauvignon Blanc. Phone (06)306-9174, website <www.martinborough-vineyard.co.nz>.

Benfield and Delamare, on Cambridge Road, is a typical Martinborough operation—small, and with production of fine wine more important than commercial success. The winery specializes in red wine only, with grapes coming from two small organic vineyards. Phone (06)306-9926. Most wine from **Margrain**, on Ponatahi Road, is sold at the cellar door, but it is the lodging at this small winery that is most appealing to visitors. Eight luxurious villas and a café are set amongst the vines. Phone (06)306-9202, website <www.margrainvineyard.co.nz>.

Gladstone, on Gladstone Road, south of Masterton in the town of Gladstone, is a particularly picturesque winery, with vines planted along an alluvial terrace above the Ruamahanga River. An award-winning Sauvignon Blanc is the pride of this winery. Phone (06)379-8563, website <www.gladstone.co.nz>.

South Island

From the deep, still fiords of the southwest, to the glaciers flowing off the snow-capped Southern Alps, to the rocky coastlines softened with sandy coves—the South Island is a place of awesome natural beauty. While the North Island has always exerted a magnetic pull on southern youth—who see it as the place to go for action, advancement and a taste of a wider world—those who choose to remain on the South Island prefer its open spaces, slower pace, and isolation from the outside world's intractable problems. Efficient air transportation and good roads make even the most remote parts of the island easily accessible, but South Islanders, in love with the land, tend to stay close to home. Their sincere caring for strangers and warm smiles speak of a kinder, more generous era than the one we now know.

Though the South Island, at 150,460 square kilometres (58,093 square miles), is nearly a third larger than the North Island, it holds less than a quarter of New Zealand's total population (980,000). Christchurch (population 320,000) and Dunedin (population 119,000) are the only sizeable cities. Christchurch serves the rich farmland of the Canterbury Plains, while Dunedin is the focus of the Otago Province sheeplands. Along the west coast and on Stewart Island, people are more scarce.

Cook Strait, though only 23 kilometres (14 miles) wide at its narrowest point, is a formidable barrier between the two islands. A ferry carries cars, passengers, and railway rolling stock across the choppy, windy strait. Whether by ferry or by air, hordes of travellers make their way to the South Island every year. They come to enjoy the sunshine and beaches of Nelson, the grandeur of the island's nine national parks, the rugged coastline alive with birds and marine mammals, and the island's great wilderness, where ranger stations, well-maintained tracks and overnight huts make backcountry travel safe and convenient.

The North

The beautiful northern part of the South Island, facing Cook Strait, is often bypassed by foreign visitors, who rush straight down the east coast to Christchurch. But this region of superb scenery, intricate waterways and golden beaches is treasured by New Zealanders as a favourite holiday destination. Abel Tasman National Park protects a magnificent coastline, while Nelson Lakes National Park preserves a forested mountain wilderness around two deep glacial lakes. Orchards and vineyards grace the green valleys and hillsides sloping down to the sea. The people are creative, friendly and easy-going, as befits the benevolent climate. The region comprises two provinces: Marlborough, on the east, centred around the substantial township of Blenheim; and Nelson, on the west, spreading expansively north from the pocket-sized but near-perfect city of Nelson.

GETTING THERE
Tranz Scenic offers passenger and vehicular ferries across Cook Strait between Wellington and Picton. The 83-kilometre (51-mile) journey usually takes a little over three hours. The *Arahura* and newer *Aratere* are each modern vessels capable of carrying upwards of 800 passengers and 100 vehicles each. They both have a choice of eateries, a Club Class lounge, and an information centre. A third Tranz Scenic vessel plying this route is the *Lynx*, which makes the crossing in a little over two hours. Between two and four departures are scheduled daily in each direction. Foot passengers usually secure tickets easily, but the car decks on the ferries are heavily booked during holiday seasons, particularly the summer holidays (late December to January). It pays to book ahead. Phone (04)498-3302 or (0800)802-802, website <www.interislander.co.nz>. You can also make your arrangements through most visitor information centres. Keep warm clothes handy because Cook Strait can be cold and blustery.

Air Nelson, part of the Air New Zealand network, flies from Wellington to Nelson. Soundsair offers regular floatplane service between Wellington and Picton.

You can book a train right through from a North Island main trunk city to Blenheim or points south but not to Nelson. The daily rail service running from the Picton ferry terminal through Blenheim to Christchurch is called the Trans Coastal. Its 2 pm Picton departure meshes with the interislander ferry's 10 am sailing from Wellington. From Christchurch, the return service connects with the 2.20 pm ferry to Wellington.

Intercity coaches connect Picton with Blenheim and points south twice daily. The company runs at least five buses daily between Picton and Nelson and two daily between Nelson and Christchurch. At least half a dozen other companies operate regular services between Picton, Blenheim and Nelson. Abel Tasman National Park is also easily reached by public transportation.

Two highways serve the region. Highway 1 runs from Picton through Blenheim, to Christchurch and points south. Highway 6 branches off Highway 1 at Blenheim to access Nelson. Winding but scenic Queen Charlotte Drive leads from Picton around the convoluted shoreline of the sounds to join Highway 6 at Havelock.

South Island

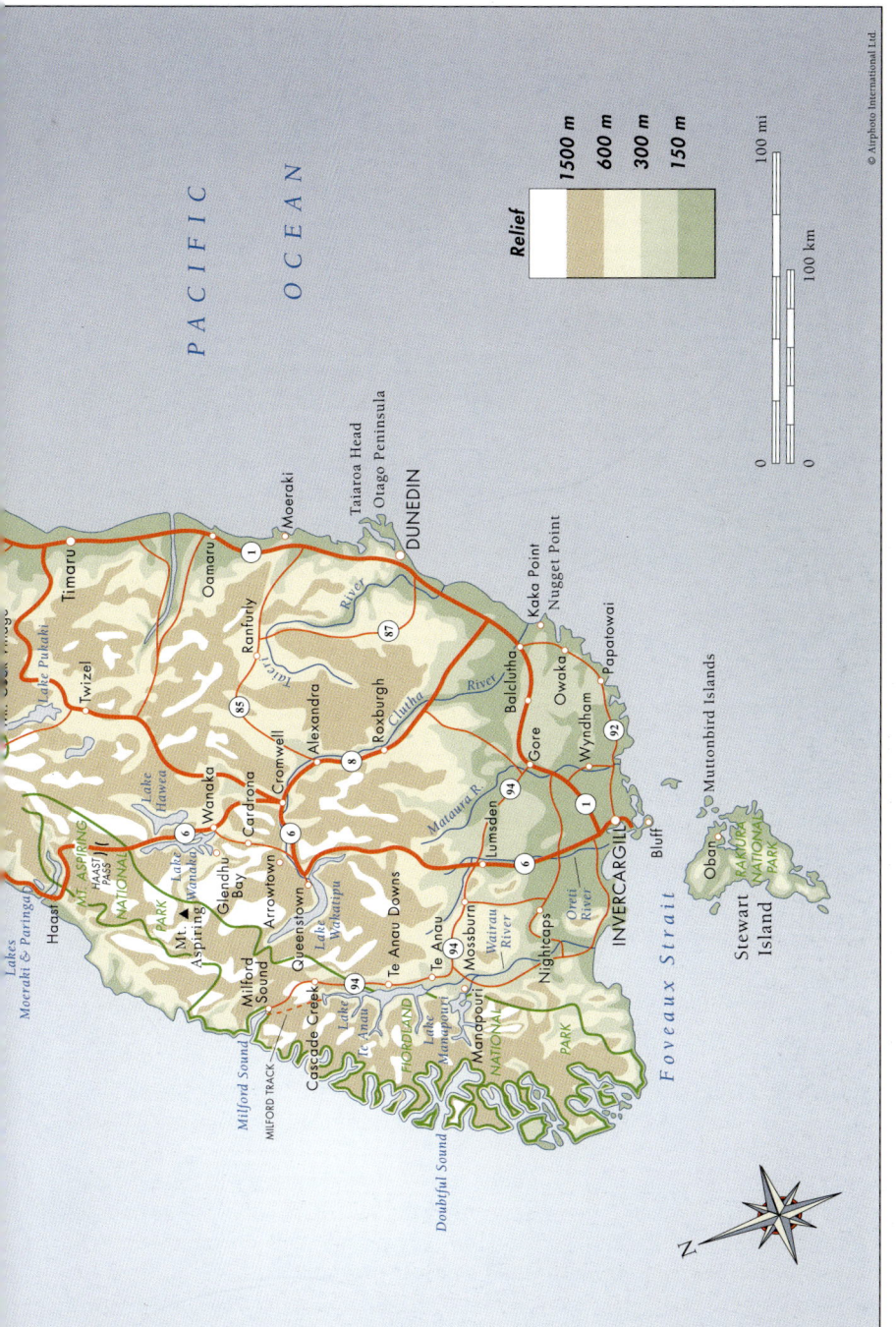

Marlborough Sounds

The South Island's northeast corner is dominated by the beautiful Marlborough Sounds, a half-submerged mountain range revealed as a labyrinth of waterways, inlets, coves, bays and islands. The result is a marvellous recreation area for boating, swimming and fishing. The loveliest areas are protected in **Marlborough Sounds Maritime Park**, comprising many small reserves interspersed with private land. Ship Cove, in Queen Charlotte Sound, was Captain Cook's favourite anchorage, to which he returned for rest and safety again and again.

Picton, the terminus for the Cook Strait ferry, is the main town of the Sounds. This pretty little port at the head of Queen Charlotte Sound is backed by forested mountains rising dramatically from the sea. Picton's ferry dock and freight-handling facilities are at the harbour's western end, reserving a lively marina in the east for small craft. Between the two ends is a palm-studded park facing London Quay, which shares much of the town's tourist activity with High Street, at right angles to it. Picton Visitor Centre, along the foreshore between the ferry terminal and downtown, supplies maps and information on tours, walks and local events, and helps with accommodation and bookings. Phone (03)520-3113. In the same building, the Department of Conservation is a source of information for travel through the Sounds. Phone (03)573-7582.

Get a taste for life in the Sounds by wandering down to the harbourfront, the departure point for cruises, fishing trips and water taxis. Dominant on the foreshore is the sailing ship *Edwin Fox*. Built in 1853 to transport tea to England from India, it's the ninth oldest ship in the world. An ambitious restoration project will eventually see the three-masted teak barque returned to her former glory. Open daily 8.45 am–5 pm. Phone(03)573-6868. A narrow footbidge at the east end of London Quay spans the marina and ends near the *Echo*, an old cargo scow built entirely of kauri. The boat is now an art gallery with a maritime theme. The **Picton Museum**, on London Quay, holds fascinating displays recalling Picton's early whaling days, along with interesting Maori antiquities and curiosities. Phone (03)573-8283.

Picton is the main departure point for cruises around **Queen Charlotte Sound**. Beachcomber Cruises offers the widest variety of options for taking in the tranquil beauty of the region. Phone (03)573-6175. The Cougar Line operates a Twilight Cruise, as well as making drop-offs to points throughout the Sound. Phone (03)573-7925, website <www.cougarlinecruises.co.nz>. A more challenging way to

> *It was an exquisite day. It was one of those days so clear, so still, so silent, you almost feel the earth itself has stopped in astonishment at its own beauty.*
>
> —from the journal of Katherine Mansfield, on Marlborough Sounds

travel is by sea kayak, either on your own carefully planned itinerary or on a guided expedition. Marlborough Sounds Adventure Company, based at the marina, offers both options. Phone (03)573-6078, website <www.marlboroughsounds.co.nz>. For a stunning aerial view of Marlborough Sounds, try flightseeing with Soundsair. Phone (03)573-6078, website <www.soundsair.co.nz>.

Havelock, 70 kilometres (44 miles) west of Picton, is a peaceful old fishing village at the head of Pelorus Sound. The Pelorus Mail Boat, operated by Beachcomber Cruises, takes mail and supplies to isolated homes and settlements scattered throughout the Sounds, departing Picton every Tuesday, Thursday and Friday. The full-day Wednesday run to the Outer Sounds is recommended for bird-watchers (see *Focus*, page 175). Phone (03)573-6175. If you are a confident driver and have plenty of time, consider taking winding Queen Charlotte Drive between Picton and Havelock; the route will reward you with lovely views of coves and bays. It is faster, though further, to reach Havelock from Picton via Blenheim on Highways 1 and 6.

The largest town of Marlborough province, **Blenheim** is a tidy commercial and agricultural centre that stands on an open plain near the Wairau River. Until about 15 years ago, the local economy centred around sheep ranching and light industry. Then a major wine industry blossomed here, further south than conventional wisdom had thought grapes could ripen (see *Focus*, page 179).

NELSON

Overlooking V-shaped Tasman Bay at the top of the South Island, Nelson (population 73,000) is a neat, pocket-sized city with a distinctly English grace. Its green hills rise from the bay's sandy beaches and lead up to the oak-shaded Anglican cathedral, which seems to preside over the brightly painted and sun-soaked city. Drawn by the sun and the pleasant, relaxed lifestyle, many craftspeople have come to live around Nelson; shops sell their high-quality wares. The fertile farmland surrounding the city produces potatoes, hops, tobacco, and fruit, especially grapes.

GETTING THERE

Air New Zealand connects Nelson to Christchurch, Wellington and Auckland. Intercity uses Nelson as a hub, offering scheduled bus service to Picton, Christchurch and Greymouth. Newmans operates daily buses to and from Christchurch through Picton. Small bus lines run to Abel Tasman National Park. The road from Havelock to Nelson, following the valley of the Rai River through the Richmond Range, takes about two and a half hours—longer than one might expect from looking at a map. The scenic drive twists through beautiful forests and parallels an enticing stream. Anglers may be sorely tempted to stop and try their luck.

INFORMATION AND ORIENTATION

Trafalgar Street is the main thoroughfare through Nelson's compact city centre. At the top of Trafalgar, the modern Anglican cathedral was built largely of local Takaka marble. Nelson's busy, natural harbour is formed by a slim boulder bank 13 kilometres (eight miles) long. The old lighthouse on the bank, dating from 1862, was put out of business by a new, shore-based light in 1982. Suburbs stretch out on all sides of the city. Large city maps are available at the Nelson Visitor Information Centre at the corner of Trafalgar and Halifax Streets. Phone (03)548-2304.

SIGHTS

The **Suter**, at 208 Bridge Street, houses a very good permanent art collection, including a painting of Ship Cove by one of Captain Cook's official shipboard artists. The gallery offers rotating exhibitions, a pleasant restaurant, and a crafts shop selling quality weavings, pottery and prints by local artists. Open daily 10.30 am–4.30 pm. Phone (03)548-4699, website <www.thesuter.org.nz>. Adjacent to the Gallery **Queen's Gardens**, an extensive stretch of parkland bursting with colour through summer, is filled with many plants endemic to New Zealand. A stroll around Trafalgar Square, Nile Street and Collingwood Street will take you past colonial houses and many more craft exhibits. The most-noted historic houses from colonial days are south of town toward Richmond. At **Isel Park**, off Marsden

Road in Stoke, rhododendrons, azaleas and century-old trees surround a landowner's mansion full of antiques. On Nayland Road in Stoke, **Broadgreen**, dating from 1855, is a two-storey colonial cob (clay-and-chopped-straw) house completely furnished with artifacts from the period. Open daily. Phone (03)546-0283. For sun and sea, **Tahunanui Beach**, at the end of Rocks Road, is the city's safe, sheltered seaside playground.

Nelson's potters are renowned as the best on the South Island, if not in the whole country. New Zealanders in general do not relegate fine pottery to the display shelves. Average families use it on a daily basis, much as people in other countries use plastic ware. Various superior clays and minerals for glazes occur naturally near Nelson, and a profusion of small potteries with showrooms dot the back roads and small valleys of its hinterland. A free brochure called *Tourist Guide to Nelson Potters*, available at the information centre, tells you how to find them. One place to see a variety of crafts in the process of creation is **Craft Habitat**, at the Stoke end of the Richmond Bypass. Established by well-known British potter Jack Laird, the cooperative community features pottery, leadlighting, weaving, wood- and metal-working, glass-blowing, jewellery, basketry and Maori crafts. A coffee house rounds out the imaginative melange. Phone (03)544-7481.

Abel Tasman National Park

On the headland between Tasman and Golden Bays, Abel Tasman National Park is one of the smallest and loveliest of all New Zealand's national parks. It's best known for its coastal tramping track (see *Focus*, page 178), but the park's magnificent beaches and dense forests can also be enjoyed by day-trippers aboard one of the many launch trips that take in the park's roadless coastline.

The drive to Abel Tasman National Park from Nelson is as enjoyable as the park itself. Highway 60 leaves the main Highway 6 at Richmond and branches northwest to run parallel to the coast of Tasman Bay. Out in the country, smaller roads lead to the shoreline around Mapua and Ruby Bay, the heart of the apple district. Orchards are in full blossom in October and laden with ripe fruit in March. Ruby Bay also boasts an attractive little vineyard (see *Focus*, page 181). At **Motueka**, the road is lined by fields of hops and tobacco. Beyond Riwaka, a side road leads to the beach at Kaiteriteri and then on to the southern entrance of the national park, where it ends. Highway 60 continues north, looping around the back of the park to **Takaka**. You'll need to cross the steep Takaka Hill—known locally as Marble Mountain—to get there. Near the summit, watch for a sealed road turnoff to Harwood's Hole, an awesome 370-metre(1,214-foot)-deep sinkhole in the limestone. It's a 40-minute walk in from road's end to the gaping hole, whose mouth is wide enough to swallow a ship. From Takaka you can drive 33 kilometres (20 miles) to Totaranui along the only

A tangle of coastal forest bent at impossible angles by a prevailing wind.

road that actually enters the park. It passes along a sweeping coastline of cliffs and forests, with safe, beautiful beaches at Pohara, Ligar Bay and Tata, beyond which the road has a gravel surface. A park office at Totaranui provides maps and information. Splendid short walks are possible in the area, and the Coastal Track is unbeatable.

Abel Tasman Wilson's Experiences is the main transportation operator within the park. Phone (03)528-7801 or (0800)223-582. The company's launch service departs daily from Kaiteriteri, at the south end of the park, stopping at many of the beaches en route to **Totaranui**, a cruise of five and a half hours. Passengers can alight at any point, relaxing with a picnic lunch on a remote beach or walking a section of the Coastal Track while awaiting the return service. For those with less time, consider the three-hour sightseeing cruise. Highly recommended. You need no experience for kayaking the sheltered waters of Tasman Bay. Abel Tasman Kayaks at Marahau Beach leads a variety of guided trips, including an easy paddle to view the seals that frequent the waters off Tonga Island. Phone (0800)527-8022.

THE FAR NORTHWEST

Beyond Takaka, Highway 60 continues to its end at Collingwood. Beyond is crescent-shaped **Farewell Spit**, a 35-kilometre (22-mile) stretch of sand that forms a natural barrier between the Tasman Sea and Golden Bay. The spit is accessible only by four-wheel-drive. Farewell Spit Tours pioneered tours along the beach to the lighthouse at the end of the spit. The company's five-hour tours leave from Collingwood and are tide-dependent. Phone (03)524-8257 or (0800)808-257. The spit is also a bird-watcher's paradise (see *Focus*, page 175).

Encompassing 450,000 hectares (1,125,000 acres) of the wild and remote region west of Highway 60 is **Kahurangi National Park**. Meaning 'Treasured Possesion,' Kahurangi is New Zealand's second largest national park. The **Heaphy Track**, a justly famous four- to five-day walk, crosses this utter wilderness of forest, red tussock, rivers, and valleys, ending up at the densely bushed coastline.

NELSON LAKES NATIONAL PARK

Covering a remote, untamed area at the northern end of the Southern Alps, this inland park holds within its boundaries the gem-like, glacial-fed **Lakes Rotoiti** and **Rotoroa**. St. Arnaud, the park's sole village, lies beside Lake Rotoiti and holds the park headquarters and a visitor centre. Phone (03)521-1806. The village is along Highway 63, 103 kilometres (64 miles) from Blenheim (take Highway 6 west to Renwick, then Highway 63 west) or 119 kilometres (74 miles) from Nelson (take

Highway 6 west to Kawatiri, then Highway 63 east). Lake Rotoiti is somewhat developed and offers sailing, water sports, no-frills skiing in winter and good walks around the lake through pristine scenery. By contrast, Lake Rotoroa, an angler's joy (see *Focus*, page 179), is hardly touched by civilization.

FOCUS

The **Marlborough Sounds** are a haven for birds. Spotted shags are common, while Australasian gannets and terns often follow the ferries through Queen Charlotte Sound. Long Island, a reserve near the mouth of Queen Charlotte Sound, is inhabited by the rare little spotted kiwi. And the rare king shag breeds in several places in the Outer Sounds, including Duffers Reef in Forsyth Bay, the islands of French Pass, and Sentinel Rock beyond the Chetwolde Islands. Birders can see many varieties of shore and sea birds by taking the Pelorus Mail Boat on its Wednesday trip to the Outer Sounds. It leaves Havelock Wharf at 9.30 am and returns at 6.30 pm. Buy tickets from Beachcomber Cruises in Havelock. Phone (03)573-6175.

East of Blenheim, the **Wairau River** estuary forms lagoons where royal spoonbills nest and can be seen through the summer. White-faced heron, pukeko, South Island pied oyster-catcher, duck, teal and other waders and waterfowl also gather in the lagoons. Beyond the lagoons is the historic Wairau Boulder Bank, where the Maori would hunt the now-extinct moa, the world's largest flightless bird. The Maori would drive the birds into this cul-de-sac before killing them for food. The site is on private land and inaccessible to visitors.

In **Nelson**, shore birds and waders such as pied oystercatcher, banded dotterel, godwit and pied stilt are found around the city's river estuaries. Fifeshire Rock, lying just off the port, is home to a large number of spotted shags.

The forests of **Abel Tasman National Park** are home to plenty of bush birds, including kaka, weka, pigeon, bellbird, tui, yellow-breasted tit, robin, brown creeper and rifleman. West of Upper Takaka, a road leads into remote **Kahurangi National Park**, where you might spy kaka, kea, parakeet, western weka and tui.

The tidal mud flats of **Farewell Spit**, a 35-kilometre (22-mile)-long sandbar at the north end of Golden Bay, support huge numbers of waders, especially godwits, knots, turnstones and banded dotterels. Rare migrants such as whimbrel frequently visit, and black swan and several kinds of duck share the area. A sparsely inhabited shore road leads from Collingwood past Pakawau to its end beyond Puponga. The local information centre at Puponga offers binoculars for viewing the many waders of the expansive tidal flats, but keen birders will want to continue on foot 2.5 kilometres (1.5 miles) along the inner beach. Many land species such as pipit,

(following pages) Lake Rotoiti, in Nelson Lakes National Park, is popular for fishing, boating and, with the younger set, feeding the ducks.

goldfinch and California quail frequent the plants amongst the sand dunes. The South Island's only mainland Australasian gannet colony lies near the end of the spit. Farewell Spit Tours runs four-wheel-drive ecotours designed especially for bird-watchers; one across the edge of the tidal flats, the other out to the gannet colony. Numbers are strictly limited, so book ahead. Phone (03)524-8257.

The **Queen Charlotte Track** traverses the isthmus between Queen Charlotte and Kenepuru Sounds. Lush forests, protected coves and high ridges make this trail nothing short of spectacular. The trail begins at Ship Cove, used by Captain Cook as a resting point on many occasions, and ends 67 kilometres (42 miles) southwest at Anakiwa. It takes three to four days to walk the entire length, but water taxis provide transportation to many points, making it possible to hike just a short section. Another unique feature of this track is the string of ten lodges spread out along the way. Almost every lodge has a restaurant, and you can even arrange to have your luggage moved from one lodge to the next. For trail information contact the Picton Field Centre of the Department of Conservation. Phone (03)573-7582. For transportation and accommodation information call Picton Visitor Centre. Phone (03)520-3113.

Abel Tasman National Park, between Tasman and Golden Bays, protects a spectacular coastline made up of sandy coves, headlands, reefs, lagoons and sparkling beaches backed by rugged hills. Like Marlborough Sounds, this park has a **Coastal Track**, which, at just over 40 kilometres (25 miles), can easily be hiked in three days. The trailheads are at Marahau (north of Kaiteriteri) in the south and Totaranui in the north. Water taxis provide access to many points, so you can follow the track for a while through lovely forest glades, explore a few coves, swim and then come back. Torrent Bay is an easy four- to five-hour walk from Marahau. One lodge lies along the track, but most overnight hikers rough it, either camping or staying in one of four rustic cabins. Water-taxi services are provided by a number of companies, including Abel Tasman Aquataxis at Marahau, phone (03)527-8083, and Abel Tasman Wilson's Experiences at Motueka, phone (03)528-7801.

The **Wairau River**, which flows into Cloudy Bay near Blenheim, affords good fishing along its whole length, as well as on its tributaries. Sea-run trout frequent its mouth, but fly-fishers head to the upper Wairau, near Nelson Lakes National Park. Roads provide access to both sides of the river. Highway 63, on the south bank, connects Blenheim to the Nelson Lakes, passing several interesting tributaries. But at holiday times this is a noisy, bustling route, so many fly-fishers recommend instead the quiet little north-bank road that peters out after about 40 kilometres (25 miles).

In the **Nelson** area, the mouths of rivers and creeks along the north coast between Havelock, Nelson and Motueka all provide good fishing. Highway 61, inland from Motueka, follows the Motueka River Valley and offers access to many good fishing spots. The western side of the old suspension bridge that leads up the Graham Valley to Flora Hut, on Mt. Arthur, is one.

Fishing is suberb in the lakes and rivers of remote **Nelson Lakes National Park**. Quiet, unpopulated and crystal-clear Lake Rotoroa is favoured by anglers for its abundant brown trout, lack of powerboats and water-skiers, and relative lack of sandflies. (Take plenty of insect repellent nonetheless.) The best fishing is at the lake's south end, near the mouths of the Sabine and D'Urville Rivers. Smaller streams entering the lake on both sides are all full of fish. The tiny settlement of Rotoroa holds little more than a fishing lodge; St Arnaud, on Highway 63 at Lake Rotoiti, is the park's main centre of activity and amenities. The season for fishing the rivers in and around the park is usually 1 October to 30 April. Fishing is permitted year-round in the lakes.

Rarangi Golf Club, 15 kilometres (nine miles) north of Blenheim on Highway 1, is an attractive, well-groomed links-style course, flat and well-treed with a lovely shoreline view. Par 72. Phone (03)570-5709. **Marlborough Golf Club**, six kilometres (four miles) southwest of Blenheim at Fairhall, is a partly undulating, parklike course. Par 72. Phone (03)578-7646.

Nelson Golf Club offers a long, challenging links course with tree-lined fairways and fast greens. It overlooks Tasman Bay from the seaside close to Nelson Airport. Par 72. Phone (03)548-5029.

Along with Gisborne and Hawkes Bay, Marlborough is one of New Zealand's top three wine-producing regions. It is also without doubt the most fashionable one. The white wines and Pinot Noir here are now internationally famous; the local Sauvignon Blanc was the first varietal to gain acclaim, followed by Chardonnay. Marlborough's sparkling wines are the latest entries to win a strong international and local following, with both Cellier Le Brun and Montana, in alliance with French company Champagne Deutz, now producing a world-class méthode traditionelle. Riesling is the next up-and-coming varietal here. This success is surprising considering that wine making in the Marlborough began only in the 1970s. Today, the Malborough is New Zealand's largest wine growing region, with 4,000 hectares (10,000 acres) planted and 60 wineries. The assumption until then was that the region was too far south to allow grapes to ripen. Actually, Blenheim, at the centre of the region, often records the highest number of sunshine hours in New Zealand. It is not intense sunshine, however, so it gives the grapes a long, slow ripening period. The summer of 2001 was drought-like in its conditions, but fruit quality was excellent. Marlborough is well aware of its attraction as a wine centre and welcomes visitors. Wine tours can be made by coach or minibus from Blenheim. Tour schedules and a brochure with a map of winery locations are available from the Blenheim Visitor Centre, in the railway station. Phone (03)577-8080.

Marlborough's one huge operation is **Montana**, New Zealand's biggest wine company and, many say, its best. Montana began as a small winery in the Henderson Valley in 1943, founded, like so many others, by a Yugoslav family from Dalmatia. Thirty years later, two sons were producing millions of gallons of wine, much of it from Gisborne contract grapes. In 1973, on the advice of two grape experts from California, they planted a new vineyard in Marlborough—an action for which they were roundly ridiculed by the New Zealand wine industry. The next year, Montana established a full winery on Highway 1 at Riverlands, just east of Blenheim. The vineyard has grown to a massive 530 hectares (1,310 acres). Head of Montana's Marlborough operation is Andy Frost, voted White Winemaker of the Year at the 1997 International Wine Challenge in London. Tours of the winery operate from Monday to Saturday 10 am–3 pm. You'll see wine made on a scale that far surpasses any other winery in the South Island, and you'll have the opportunity to taste and buy. Phone (03)578-2099.

Montana's success immediately attracted others. **Hunter's**, on Rapaura Road, three kilometres (two miles) north of Blenheim, produces méthode traditionelle using, unusually for New Zealand, Meunier grapes, that is as good as any produced in the country. The excellent vineyard restaurant makes this an attractive port of call on the Marlborough wine trail. Phone (03)572-8489, website <www.hunters.co.nz>.

Small **Cellier Le Brun**, on Terrace Road, 3.5 kilometres (2.2 miles) north of Renwick (off Highway 6 towards Havelock), was the creation of Frenchman Daniel Le Brun, whose family in Champagne has been making wine since 1640. On behalf of the owners, vintner Mark Inglis still uses the classic grapes of Champagne, including, like Hunter's, Meunier grapes. The result is a méthode traditionelle that is closer to the Champagne standard than any other New Zealand sparkling wine. Phone (03)572-8859, website <www.lebrun.co.nz>.

Cloudy Bay, on Jacksons Road in Rapaura (just northwest of Blenheim), is owned by the Western Australian company, Cape Mentelle, whose majority shareholder is Veuve Cliquot. Its 'Pelorus' méthode traditionelle was produced first in 1992 and is highly rated. But the winery's reputation still rests on its Sauvignon Blanc, and a sweet, late harvest Reisling. The winery is open daily for tastings and sales, and tours are available by appointment. Phone (03)520-9140, website <www.cloudybay.co.nz>.

Across the road from Cloudy Bay is **Allan Scott**. Scott's wines—Chardonnay, Sauvignon Blanc, Riesling, and, more recently, Pinot Noir—are vinted at a modern onsite winery that includes a restaurant open daily. Phone (03) 572-9054, website <allanscott.com>.

Wairau River, on Giffords Road in Blenheim, previously supplied the contract market with grapes but in 1991 first produced its own wine, and in 2002 opened a new winery. The winery runs a restaurant, open daily for lunch. Phone (03)572-9800, website <www.wairauriverwines.com>.

Forrest Estate, on Blicks Road in Renwick, is a small vineyard known for high-quality red wines. It began production only in 1991, crisp Chardonnays and Merlot have already reaped awards. It offers cellar-door sales. Phone (03)572-9084, website <www.forrest.co.nz>.

Te Whare Ra, on Anglesea Street, off Highway 63 beyond Renwick, produces botrytized dessert wines from specially selected grapes. Husband and wife team Allen and Joyce Hogan don't often sell to retail outlets, and it is worth a trip to try their wide range of wines, which include an oak-aged Sauvignon Blanc and a mellow Chardonnay. The winery's Maori name means 'House in the Sun,' and a Maori motto inscribed in the winery's leaded windows, 'Na Te Ra Nga Mamahi,' means By Sun and Hard Work. Phone (03)572-8518, website <www.te-whare-ra.co.nz>.

Vavasour is a 20-minute drive south of Blenheim down Highway 1; turn off at Redwood Pass Road near the township of Seddon. Set in the sunny Awatere Valley, the winery's first vintage was bottled in 1989. High-quality red wine was the aim—achieved in an excellent Cabernet Sauvignon. Now the winery's Sauvignon Blanc and Pinot Noir are attracting critical acclaim. Phone (03)575-7481, website <www.vavasour.com>.

Nelson is even more blessed in its weather than Marlborough, having less rain at harvest time. Vineyards are usually irrigated. This small wine area is the most beautiful of any in the country, surrounded by orchards and green hills. The industry here is unlikely to expand, however, because of difficult transport over the mountains to Blenheim. A brochure called *The Nelson Winemakers*, available in Nelson, has more information and a good map.

Seifried, on Redwood Road in Appleby, is the biggest of Nelson's wineries. Austrian Hermann Seifried established his first winery in the Nelson region in 1974. Today Scott's best-known wines are Riesling, Chardonnay, and Cabernet, but the Gewurtraminer—with a spicy, intensely concentrated flavour—is worth searching out. The winery is worth a visit for the restaurant alone, which enjoys a beautiful setting amongst the vines. Phone (03)544-5599, website <www.seifried.co.nz>.

Small and friendly **Neudorf**, on Neudorf Road in Upper Moutere, was started in 1978. The winery produces an extremely fruity late-harvest Riesling. Its Chardonnay, Pinot Noir, and Sauvignon Blanc are also outstanding. Much of the wine is sold on the spot. A pleasant wine and lunch bar is open from September to the middle of May. Visits are available by appointment the rest of the year. Phone (03)543-2643.

Ruby Bay is a small vineyard on the coast at Ruby Bay, 34 kilometres (21 miles) west of Nelson near Mapua, off Highway 60. Production is small but of high quality, the Pinot Noir and Pinot Rosé being especially notable. The winery's popular outdoor wine bar and restaurant is open November to May. Visits are available by appointment the rest of the year. Phone (03)540-2825.

The West

The region's proper name is Westland, but South Islanders call it 'The West Coast.' The narrow strip of lush wild land between the Southern Alps and the rocky shoreline of the Tasman Sea follows the great geological rupture of the Alpine Fault, which runs along the western base of the whole range. Heavy rainfall on the west side of the Alps produces a landscape very different from the tussock grass on the rain-shadowed eastern side of the divide. Magnificent rainforests laced with waterfalls cascade down the lower slopes of the mountains and spill out onto part of the narrow western plain. This natural beauty is protected in four national parks along the coast, ranging from Paparoa National Park's distinctive limestone formations in the north to the splendid glaciers of Westland National Park in the south.

Highway 6 runs down the coast past rivers, marginal farmland, lakes, forests and glaciers. Three sizeable towns lie at the northern end. Farther south the population becomes increasingly sparse and the settlements increasingly small. Perched precariously on an ancient, uncaring landscape, the smaller towns have an ephemeral look. Life here is hard, and though the people are few, they are wonderfully warm and friendly.

Before the Europeans came, Maori tribes lived in small fishing communities along this coast. The riverbeds on this side of the Southern Alps hold greenstone, a fine jade, which the Maori learned to shape and sharpen to a keen, long-lasting edge. Beautifully shaped fighting clubs and ornaments of all sorts were fashioned from greenstone. Tribes from the east side of the island crossed mountain passes to get the precious stone, which, more valuable than gold, was traded with the North Island tribes across the strait.

The first Europeans on the west coast were whalers and sealers, alerted to opportunity by Cook's published journals. They set up temporary shore stations and slaughtered seals for fur and oil, but they did not stay to put down roots. When ill-prepared English colonists came to hilly Nelson in 1843, hoping for flat farmland, they quickly investigated Maori rumours of plains to the southwest.

Expeditions with Maori guides followed the Buller River and explored the west coast, but their findings were utterly discouraging. Almost casually, the government bought the west coast from Maori tribes in 1860 for £300. But then gold was discovered along the coast, and the Europeans came pouring in.

By 1864, the gold stampede was in full swing. The town of **Greymouth** sprang up around a Maori settlement at the mouth of the Grey River. New gold strikes further south brought Hokitika into being almost overnight, and it rapidly grew into the west coast's biggest, busiest port. Ships suffered wrecks with appalling frequency, but the brawling, boozing prospectors kept coming. New towns mushroomed, and in three years the population had grown to 40,000—12 per cent of New Zealand's total at the time.

The gold rush ended when the easy gold was gone and new strikes were made on the North Island. The west coast kept producing gold until 1895, but the population declined. Today only 30,000 people—one per cent of New Zealand's total—live here, and coal and timber are the mainstays of the regional economy.

GETTING THERE
Because Westland holds so many tempting places to stop and explore, renting a car is by far the best transportation option here. Rental cars are available in Westport and Hokitika. Nevertheless, scheduled buses run the length of the west coast. Intercity coaches run from Nelson to Fox Glacier, with an overnight stay necessary for travellers continuing south to Queenstown. The same applies for northbound travel. Intercity also connects Christchurch to Greymouth via Arthur's Pass. Tranz Rail's TranzAlpine, a luxury train with panoramic windows, makes the spectacular coast-to-coast journey between Christchurch and Greymouth daily. Air New Zealand flies to Westport from Wellington and to Hokitika from Christchurch.

From the north, the most direct route to the west coast is Highway 6, which runs from Nelson through the Buller Gorge to Westport. Most travellers continue south along the coast to Haast, from where the highway climbs to Haast Pass then descends through Mount Aspiring National Park to Wanaka. By this route it's 590 kilometres (370 miles) between Nelson and Wanaka, but allow at least 11 hours to navigate the narrow, winding road.

Two roads cross the Southern Alps from Christchurch. Highway 73, the more southerly route, crosses Arthur's Pass. This is the most direct and spectacular route, but it's also very demanding. Highway 7, usually called the Lewis Pass Road, is easier to drive. It links Christchurch and the Canterbury Plains to Greymouth, with a second road breaking north to Westport from Reefton. Towns along this route are few and far between. The road runs near delightful Hanmer Springs (see page 218) on the eastern side of the divide before climbing to Lewis Pass, where

The Curious Kiwi

I have very little to say regarding this bird, as I have only seen two of them, and being pushed with hunger, I ate the pair of them, under the circumstances I would have eaten the last of the Dodos. It is all very well for science, lifting up its hands in horror, at what I once heard called gluttony, but let science tramp through the Westland bush or swamps, for two or three days without food, and find out what hunger is. Besides at the time, which was many years ago, I was not aware that it was an almost extinct bird. Had I known so, I would at least have skinned it and kept the head and feet.

—John Pascoe, Mr. Explorer Douglas, *1957*

Everybody knows the flightless kiwi. You see it on tins of shoe polish and crates of kiwi fruit all over the world. Modest, humorous and one of a kind, the bird has become a symbol for New Zealand itself, and New Zealanders proudly call themselves Kiwis.

When the first kiwi skin was brought to Europe in 1813, the scientific community flatly refused to believe that a wingless, tailless bird could exist. When further proof trickled back, some scientists assigned the kiwi to the penguin family while others related it to the extinct dodo. It took 20 more years before a missionary with a scientific bent took note of the hairlike feathers on this 'most remarkable and curious bird' and correctly linked it to the emu. Today, scientists know that the kiwi is New Zealand's last surviving member of the ratite family, a group of flightless birds that also includes the cassowary, emu, rhea and ostrich.

Unlike most birds, kiwis have weak eyes but a strong sense of smell. With nostrils at the tip of their long beak and sensitive catlike whiskers at its base, they poke around purposefully in the dark for grubs, worms and berries. The female, bigger and stronger than the male, lays one enormous egg weighing up to 20 per cent of her body weight. (An X-ray of a female about to lay is an astonishing sight.) In a hidden burrow, the male sits on the egg for ten weeks or more, sleeping away the time. The chick emerges fully feathered and with eyes open. Within a few days it's ready to leave the nest and start hunting with its parents.

The kiwi was deemed sacred by the Maori, who called the birds the hidden children of Tane, god of the forest. Only chiefs were allowed to eat or sacrifice the kiwi, and the bird's tough, leathery skin covered with warm, waterproof feathers was treasured for chiefs' cloaks. Unfortunately, Europeans held no such reverence for the hapless kiwi, and their arrival seriously endangered the bird's survival. The European settlers destroyed kiwi habitat to create farmland, and slaughtered the birds by the tens of thousands to feed miners and bushmen and to provide feather trimmings for ladies' hats.

Today all kiwis are protected. One of the six species, the little spotted kiwi, is firmly established on Kapiti Island but is now extinct on the mainland. Because they are both rare and nocturnal, your chances of seeing a kiwi in the wild are slim. But New Zealand holds a number of 'kiwi houses' where day and night are artificially reversed, allowing you to watch these strange birds by simulated moonlight as they stalk through the underbrush.

you'll find picnic places and walks of varied lengths, but less spectacular scenery than at **Arthur's Pass**. On the western side of the pass, Highway 7 runs high above the Maruia River and soon comes to Maruia Springs, where a lone hotel provides a restaurant, bar and hot mineral pools.

BULLER GORGE

To reach the west coast from the northern region, the most direct, dramatic and beautiful route is Highway 6, which runs alongside the big **Buller River** through two spectacular gorges to the river's mouth at Westport. The Buller flows west out of Lake Rotoiti deep and swift, already a fully formed river teeming with fish (see *Focus*, page 202). Along the way you'll pass through **Murchison**, 130 kilometres (80 miles) southwest of Nelson. This pleasant farming centre, tucked away behind a ring of distinctly seismic-looking hills, was all but destroyed by a violent earthquake in 1929. Now it's a mecca for adventure sports. The Upper Buller Gorge begins just west of town. Here the river's green waters plunge between cliffs overhung with evergreen and fern. The road hugs the river closely, crossing the century-old Iron Bridge, where a punt once ferried horses and coaches over the water. A major tributary, the Inangahua River, joins the Buller near Inangahua Junction (halfway between Murchison and Westport), adding its force to the torrent that soon plunges through Lower Buller Gorge. Even more magnificent than the upper gorge, the lower gorge funnels the thundering river under crags and a canopy of emerald rainforest, past old gold-mining settlements to the coast. Pull-off places dot the road, and short, well-marked paths lead to lookouts, waterfalls and the remains of the once-thriving township of Lyell.

WESTPORT

This town of 4,200 lies at the foot of the steep, coal-bearing Paparoa Mountains. Here the mouth of the Buller River forms a natural port, out of which is shipped timber, coal and products from the huge Millburn Cement Works nearby. When the gold petered out, coal was found to be the true wealth of Westport. **Coal Town**, a museum housed in an 1890s-era brewery at the end of Queen Street South, tells a tale of pioneering spirit and technical ingenuity with relics, audio-visual shows and a realistic, walk-through coal mine. Open daily 8.30 am–5 pm. Phone (03)789-8204. Westport is also becoming something of a centre for adventure activities. Norwest Adventures runs two trips for daredevils: the Underworld Rafting trip, where brave souls plunge headlong down an underground river on an inflatable raft; and an Adventure Caving trip, which involves abseiling 30 metres (98 feet) into a cave containing a fossilised whale skeleton. Phone (03)789-6686. North of Westport, the Karamea River delivers what is probably the best white-water rafting ride on the west coast. Buller Adventure Tours offer a variety of trips. Phone (03)789-7286.

Cape Foulwind, ten kilometres (6.5 miles) west of the town, was named by Captain Cook during a storm. A lighthouse caps the high granite promontory. Tauranga Bay, further around the south side of the headland, is home to New Zealand's northernmost breeding colony of seals. The bay can be reached by an easy four-kilometre (2.5-mile), one-hour walk along the cliff tops from Cape Foulwind, with fine views on the way.

About 100 kilometres (62 miles) north of Westport, the road ends at **Karamea**. This little dairying centre boasts a uniquely mild climate for the region. The town is backed by the rugged, forested mountain ranges that take up the whole northwest corner of the South Island. This wilderness can be crossed only by a five-day tramp on the Heaphy Track, through Kahurangi National Park. North of Karamea, in a valley carved by the Oparara River, are the Honeycomb Caves, where the bones of extinct birds such as the moa have been found.

Punakaiki, 56 kilometres (35 miles) south of Westport on the road to Greymouth, is the headquarters of **Paparoa National Park**, a good stop for bird-watchers and walkers (see *Focus*, pages 198). The sight not to be missed at Punakaiki is Pancake Rocks, 30-million-year-old cliffs of thin limestone laid down in layers like immense stacks of pancakes. When rough weather brings high swells, the surf crashes up through blowholes here. The ten-minute Dolomite Point Walk leads from the highway through an enchanting tree-fern forest to the top of the cliffs.

GREYMOUTH

Westland's largest town, Greymouth (population 10,000) is a bustling commercial centre and port at the mouth of the Grey River. The river, well known to anglers, carves a cleft in the mountains known as the Gap, through which a cutting wind (appropriately called 'the barber') sometimes funnels into the city. From the end of the breakwall at the river mouth, views extend south across a long beach to the snowcapped peaks of the Southern Alps. A trail leading from Mount Street up into tree-filled King Domain also affords panoramic views. Up the Grey Valley northeast of Greymouth is the eccentric almost-a-ghost town of **Blackball**; for a true New Zealand experience, stop in and have a drink at the local pub.

A major attraction near Greymouth is **Shantytown**, a meticulously reconstructed gold-mining town of the 1860s, complete with assay office, bank, church, hospital and gaol. A few of the buildings are original. A steam locomotive puffs into the bush,

(following pages: top) Rafting is an enjoyable way to travel down the Buller River. (bottom) Dense rainforest extends right to the ocean within Paparoa National Park. (opposite page) Take the Dolomite Point Trail, in Paparoa National Park, to reach the unique limestone formations known as Pancake Rocks.

Gold Rush

If you think New Zealanders are an unexcitable, well-regulated people by nature, take a look at their history. The glint of gold brought as much turmoil, craziness and change to the South Island of the 1860s as ever it did to California or Australia.

When the Californian and Australian gold rushes were in full swing, New Zealand was a dull backwater; many settlers pulled up stakes to seek wealth in the foreign goldfields. Amongst them was Charlie Ring, who left his sawmill near Coromandel to try his luck in California. When he got home again in 1852, a committee in Auckland was offering £500 to anyone who could find a 'payable' goldfield in New Zealand. Within two days Charlie raced to Auckland with gold-bearing quartz from Coromandel to claim the prize. Unfortunately his find was not 'payable'—expensive machinery would have been required to extract the gold—but it was New Zealand's first recorded strike and it set off an epidemic of gold fever.

Provincial governments on the South Island offered rewards for local finds, and prospectors fanned out. In 1861, Gabriel Read, a miner from Tasmania, found gold in a gully in Otago, the wild hinterland of Dunedin. Read had experienced the brawling goldfields of California and Victoria and loathed the violence he had seen there. Hoping to set things on a better course in Otago, he generously made his discovery public, collected his prize money and set out to uphold decency and maintain law and order amongst the 11,000 prospectors who swarmed to 'Gabriel's Gully.' Read personally settled disputes, defended miners' rights and even paid to bring out a preacher.

Nobody else was so public-spirited. After Gabriel's Gully was mined out in 1862, two close-mouthed prospectors appeared in Dunedin with bags containing 1,392 ounces of gold. Bribery and sharp guesswork traced the new strike to Lake Wakatipu. A secretive loner named Fox was ferreted out on the Arrow River. Soon the mighty Clutha River and many of its tributaries were giving up hidden hoards, and 80 new goldfields mushroomed. Queenstown, Arrowtown, Cromwell and a host of smaller towns sprang into being. In two years the population of Otago increased fivefold.

The canny Scots of Dunedin harvested a fortune from the newfound business coming to their port, breweries and banks. They built a splendid stone city, the biggest and richest in 19th-century New Zealand. But by 1865 Otago was fading. When news came of gold in remote Westland, half the miners in Otago swarmed over the Southern Alps at Arthur's Pass. Thousands more came by sea from Australia, helping to swell Westland's population from 800 to 30,000. Greymouth and Hokitika sprouted banks, shops and hotels; Hokitika even had an opera house. But the gold diminished and the rush turned north to the Coromandel Peninsula. Gold fever began anew there in 1867, with discovery of gold-bearing quartz lodes near Thames.

In a mere decade the big gold rushes were over. The European population of New Zealand had doubled, but the flow of gold, which had accounted for 70 per cent of all exports in 1863, fell to a trickle. Wool remained the only source of wealth until an 1882 experiment in refrigeration saved New Zealand from depression and emigration; suddenly meat and butter could be shipped unspoiled around the world, and New Zealand came into its own. Agriculture, the new source of prosperity, would last to the present day. But new open-cast methods have made gold recovery once again a viable quest. In 1988 the Martha mine at Waihi on the base of the Coromandel Peninsula reopened to produce NZ$40 million of gold and silver annually. Further sites on the Coromandel Peninsula and in Otago have begun small-scale production, and prospecting licences have been taken out in many of the old gold regions, including Westland.

taking visitors to the Chinese gold works, and an original Cobb & Co. stagecoach harnesses up for rides in summer. Shantytown is well signposted from Paroa, ten kilometres (six miles) south of Greymouth on Highway 6. Open daily 9.30 am–5 pm. Phone (03)762-6634. www.shantytown.co.nz.

ARTHUR'S PASS NATIONAL PARK

This park of dramatic peaks, high alpine meadows and glacially carved U-shaped valleys straddles the Southern Alps 100 kilometres (63 miles) southeast of Greymouth. The road into the park from the west coast is nothing short of heart-stopping, as the road climbs steeply by hairpin turns through the Otira River Gorge to the 924-metre (3,050-foot) pass. The pass is named after Arthur Dudley Dobson, a surveyor and explorer who found the pass in 1864 and chose it as the best route for road and rail from the east coast to the west. He was knighted for his pioneering work—but not until 1931, when he was 90. Beyond the pass is the small village of **Arthur's Pass**, where a very good Department of Conservation visitor centre displays one of the original stagecoaches that regularly made the journey. The centre also shows an entertaining audio-visual programme on the

This little country pub in Blackball traded for many years as the Blackball Hilton, but a lawsuit from the international hotel chain meant a name change—to Formerly the Blackball Hilton.

building of the road and railway. Phone (03)318-9211. The village offers lodgings to suit all budgets and a couple of restaurants. Tramping (see *Focus*, page 199) and mountaineering draw most visitors in summer, while the steep terrain of Temple Basin ski field keeps the park busy in winter.

HOKITIKA

Hokitika sprang to life with the gold rush and was once known as the 'Capital of the Goldfields.' In its heyday it boasted grand hotels and an opera house. Prospectors poured in from Australia, and scavengers grew rich from the many shipwrecks dotting the beaches around this treacherous port. Hokitika has kept some of its old character, although prosperity now comes from timber, not gold. The **West Coast Historical Museum**, on Hamilton Street, exhibits all manner of gold-mining equipment and shows an excellent 20-minute audio-visual show on Hokitika's early days. Phone (03) 755-6898. The mountains backing Hokitika are renowned for greenstone, the tough jade that the Maori carved into clubs, sharp implements and jewellery. Greenstone is still commercially important today and is the speciality of a dozen or so craft shops around Tancred, Weld and Revell Streets.

Lake Moeraki, alongside Highway 6, is renowned for brown trout fishing.

Westland Greenstone, on Tancred Street, demonstrates how raw rocks of the hard nephrite jade are converted into finely crafted, polished jewellery of Maori design. The shop is open daily, but the jade workers are there only on weekdays. Across the road is the Hokitika Craft Gallery, an interesting cooperative that always has an exhibition and is well worth a look. At **Plane Table Lookout**, one kilometre (half a mile) north of town on the airport road, a panoramic view of the Southern Alps is augmented by a pointer and map identifying over 50 peaks. Five kilometres (three miles) south of Hokitika on the main highway, you can take a paddleboat cruise down the river to Lake Mahinapua.

The little town of **Ross**, 28 kilometres (17 miles) from Hokitika, sits amidst what were once Westland's richest alluvial goldfields. Ross was still busy long after other boom towns had become ghost towns. The biggest nugget ever discovered in New Zealand was found near Ross in 1907 and bought by a tavern keeper for £400—£100 more than the purchase price of the whole west coast a few years earlier. The nugget was christened the 'Honourable Roddy,' after the minister of mines, and eventually was presented to King George V, who had it fashioned into tableware for Buckingham Palace. A restored miner's cottage (near a working gold mine) now serves as the local museum, providing some colourful history. For more history, take the easy walk to an old cemetery, in which the dangerous lives led (and lost) by gold miners are recorded on the gravestones.

Westland National Park

Centred around Franz Josef and Fox Glaciers and surrounded by some of the most majestic scenery in the Southern Alps, this park is the highlight of a trip along the west coast. The glaciers, which are separated by a distance of 25 kilometres (15 miles), are closer to the ocean than any other glaciers in the world at the same latitude. And given their low altitude they are unusually large, together covering over 4,000 hectares (10,000 acres). Heavy snowfalls dumped by prevailing westerly winds onto the west face of the mountains feed the glaciers. The weight of the snow compacts the deeper layers into pure blue ice, which slowly creeps down the valleys dragging rock and rubble with it. At the toe the glacier steadily melts, leaving the accumulated rock behind and sending run-off down the mountain. The streams of run-off are full of rock 'flour'—bits of rock finely ground by the moving ice—which gives the water a unique appearance akin to dirty milk. Through history the glaciers have advanced and receded many times. During the past century the retreat has been very fast, interrupted by three or four short surges forward. At present both glaciers are advancing, with Franz Josef creeping forward around one metre a day.

The villages of Franz Josef Glacier and Fox Glacier (known locally as simply Franz and Fox) have restaurants and lodging but tend to be overcrowded in summer, so book accommodation well in advance. Franz is larger, but both villages have big, well-managed visitor information centres offering displays, information, maps of walks (see *Focus*, page 199) and advice. Both also have small airstrips where flightseeing companies are based; the information centres can help make arrangements for the expensive but spectacular flights up the glaciers. A popular flightseeing variation is 'heli-hiking,' in which a helicopter lands passengers and a guide high on the glacier for a hike amongst dazzling pinnacles, blue-green ice caves and crevasses. (Take good sunglasses.) Flightseeing excursions of varying duration and price are available around the glaciers, Mount Cook and other mountain peaks. Several companies operate tiny planes from both centres, but the changeable weather makes cancellation a constant threat. Early morning and late afternoon tend to be clear (photographers take note), with clouds coming down in the middle of the day. March and April are usually the sunniest months.

Franz Josef Glacier was named by Julius von Haast for the Austrian emperor in 1865. It's 12 kilometres (7.5 miles) long, and both steeper and shorter than Fox Glacier. To reach it from the Franz visitor centre, go about half a kilometre (0.3 miles) south on Highway 6, turn left on Glacier Access Road (immediately after the bridge) and continue another 5.5 kilometres (3.7 miles). Signposts along the lovely, forested valley record the glacier's retreat and advance and point to various short walks. The ten-minute walk to Sentinel Rock, four kilometres (2.5 miles) along Glacier Access Road, gives a magnificent view up the Waiho Valley to the glacier. From the car park at the end of the road, a trail leads across the gravelly riverbed and several streams to the glacier's rubble-strewn toe. Be sure to take a jacket and plenty of insect repellent. Allow at least an hour for the walk. The village of Franz Josef Glacier holds the pretty little St. James Anglican Church. The church's altar window once framed a perfect view of the glacier, which since retreated out of sight.

Fox Glacier is a bit more accessible. From Fox village, take Highway 6 south for about two kilometres (a mile) and turn left on Glacier Access Road, just before the bridge. The road follows the Fox River for about five kilometres (three miles) to a gravelly car park. An easy, 20-minute walk across the riverbed leads to the grey terminal ice. Keep to the track and do not try to climb on the ice. Cheeky grey-green mountain parrots called keas often frequent the car park. They will try all their tricks to persuade you to feed them. Please don't, or they will become dependent on tourists and will lose the ability to feed themselves properly. You'll enjoy their antics though—they are real clowns.

From Westland National Park, Highway 6 follows a winding inland route to the coast at Knights Point, then heads back inland at Haast. The section of the highway between Haast and Haast Pass is particularly scenic, offering views of lakes, waterfalls, forests and snowcapped mountains, as well as numerous places to pull off the road for a picnic or walk. **Haast Pass**, in Mount Aspiring National Park, was first crossed by a gold prospector named Cameron while racing to the

Franz Josef Glacier (pictured) and nearby Fox Glacier are currently in a state of advance, the closest such glaciers to the equator.

goldfields in 1863. But it was the Austrian geologist-explorer Julius von Haast, who paused here long enough to name the pass after himself. The stretch of Highway 6 that crosses the pass opened in 1965.

Focus

Paparoa National Park encompasses much of the coast and mountain area between Westport and Greymouth. Park headquarters is in Punakaiki. The birds in the park are typical of those along the west coast. Near the ocean are yellow-breasted tit, tui, pigeon, bellbird, silvereye, grey warbler and others. Inland are kaka, brown creeper, rifleman and yellow-crowned parakeet. You might see blue duck along mountain streams. Near Barrytown, about 15 kilometres (nine miles) south of Punakaiki, the rare Westland black petrel breeds in winter along the forest-covered cliffs of the **Paparoa Mountains**. The birds can sometimes be seen at dusk in winter, flying along rivers and creeks.

Above the treeline in **Arthur's Pass National Park**, mountain birds such as the kea are easily observed. Rock wren are present but rare. In the beech forests below

Franz Josef Glacier is just a small arm of a 4,000-hectare ice field within Westland National Park.

the treeline, kaka, bellbird, grey warbler and the endangered great spotted kiwi find a home. Descending from the park to the Canterbury Plains, the road follows the Waimakariri River—where Canada geese congregate in late spring—then passes right beside Lake Pearson and Lake Grasmere on the Canterbury side, where crested grebes are common.

At **Okarito Lagoon**, 115 kilometres (71.5 miles) south of Hokitika, or 60 kilometres (37 miles) north of Franz Josef, a wildlife sanctuary protects the site of New Zealand's only breeding colony of Kotuku (white herons). The birds nest between November and February, before heading off to spend the rest of the year elsewhere. The lagoon is also New Zealand's largest unmodified tidal wetland. The bird life of the wetland is incredible, even non-bird-watchers will be enthralled as the tidal flats come alive with activity on the outgoing tide. The best way to view the nesting colony is with White Heron Sanctuary Tours. Phone (03)753-4120. The tours start in Franz Josef and head to the sanctuary via a jet-boat ride down the Waitangi-Taona River. At the sanctuary, a short walk leads to a hide from where the birds can be viewed in all their glory. Okarito Nature Tours, based at the seaside village of Okarito at the southern outlet of the lagoon, offers guided kayak trips on the lagoon and also rents kayaks. Phone (03)753-4014. You can paddle across to the heron sanctuary from Okarito, but you must first obtain a permit from the Department of Conservation.

The **Haast Pass** road over the Southern Alps provides good opportunities to see bush birds of all sorts; stop at Thunder Creek Falls or Fantail Creek Falls or take the 20-minute Makarora Bush Walk.

Starting some 32 kilometres (20 miles) northeast of Westport in Ngakawau, the unforgettable **Charming Creek Walkway** follows the route of an old bush railway built during the early coal-mining days. The walk begins a short distance upstream from the Ngakawau Bins, where a car park is provided. It threads through a dramatic gorge with giant river boulders to Mangatini Waterfall, one hour along. (An S-shaped tunnel in the gorge area shows where construction crews, working from both ends, almost failed to meet.) The path continues over a suspension bridge above the falls, then through another tunnel, finally emerging on the road to Seddonville (three hours). Try to arrange in advance to be picked up here.

Paparoa National Park, 57 kilometres (35 miles) south of Westport, combines limestone, sea and forest in several irresistible walks. The Truman Track, signposted on the main highway 2.8 kilometres (1.7 miles) north of the visitor information centre, is one of the most beautiful 15-minute walks anywhere. An impressive forest with some giant trees leads to a magical section of the coast with blowholes, reefs and pools. At low tide you can continue the walk north past reefs, caves and waterfalls as far as Perpendicular Point. Starting a further nine kilometres (six miles) north along Highway 6 is the Fox River Cave Track, which leads along the north bank of the Fox River to a deep cave that can be explored with a reliable torch. Allow one hour each way. Maps, brochures and information are available at the Punakaiki Visitor Centre. Phone (03)731-1893.

Westland National Park is best known for its glacier walks. The park offices at Franz Josef Glacier, phone (03)752-0796, and Fox Glacier, phone (03)751-0807, have hiking maps of the park. Alpine Guides offer walks on the ice with experienced glacier guides. Phone (03)751-0825. (It is dangerous to walk on the glaciers without a guide.) Walks leave twice daily. Boots, socks, poles and transportation to the glacier are included in the price. Half-day or full-day 'heli-hikes' (see page 195) are also available, at considerable cost. At **Franz Josef Glacier** you'll find many well-marked walks around the valley. At **Fox Glacier**, the Chalet Lookout Walk starts from the car park at the end of Glacier View Road and follows an old access track to the glacier that was used until the 1930s. A shelter (the Fox Chalet) once stood just below the present lookout, which offers a panoramic view of the lower glacier and its terminal moraine. Since the 1930s, the glacier has receded more than a kilometre (half a mile), leaving the valley floor far below. Allow 40 minutes each way for this excursion.

Lake Matheson, a glacial 'kettle' lake famous for its reflection of Mount Cook, is beloved by photographers. Take Cook Flat Road left off Highway 6 just north of Fox, toward Gillespies Beach. Follow it for 5.5 kilometres (3.4 miles) to a well-marked turnoff to the lake. A pleasant trail circles the lake through native bush, but you need good hiking shoes for the return section. The best time for photographers to catch a mirror-like reflection of the mountains is very early in the morning. Allow one and a half hours for the circular walk.

The **Buller River**, the West Coast's biggest, is a fishing delight along its whole length. The river flows from Lake Rotoiti to Westport, closely paralleled by Highway 6. The town of Murchison, on a small plain at the junction of the Upper Buller and Matakitaki Rivers, is surrounded by fine trout streams. The Mangles River, close to Highway 6, and the nearby Tutaki River are especially worth fishing. Ask about the best localities from local people in Murchison. The old gold-mining boom town of Reefton (turn off Highway 6 at Inangahua Junction and continue south down Highway 69) is now the centre of **Victoria Forest Park**, where the swift, boulder-strewn rivers teem with brown trout. Be sure to ask landowners' permission when crossing private property and leave all gates as you find them.

This climbing hut high above Franz Josef Glacier makes an ideal base for those brave souls who venture high onto the ice field.

The rugged west coast offers excellent fishing in its smallish lakes and its swift rivers, where sea-run brown trout predominate. In the Greymouth district, the extensive **Grey River** system boasts the best fishing waters. Nearby **Lake Brunner**, the biggest lake on the west coast, lies in a glaciated hollow among untouched forest about 40 kilometres (25 miles) southeast of Greymouth. The well-known Lake Brunner Lodge, at Mitchells, offers accommodation. Phone (03)738-0163.

The **Hokitika River** system attracts a run of sea-run brown trout and salmon in February and March. Perch, good to eat but scorned locally as a poor sporting fish, are also found here. The upper reaches hold rainbow trout.

Other good fishing spots in the area include: **Harihari**, 74 kilometres (47 miles) south of Hokitika (keep to the clear streams; avoid those with milky glacier-water); **Whataroa**, 35 kilometres (22 miles) south of Harihari; and **Lake Wahapo**, ten kilometres (six miles) south of Whataroa, which holds brown trout and increasing numbers of salmon.

Near Haast, two seaside lakes with views of snowcapped mountains are well supplied with sea-run brown trout averaging 2.25 kilogrammes (five pounds) and recently established salmon. Access to the sea makes these lakes a good source of whitebait, too. **Lake Moeraki** lies beside the main road 32 kilometres (20 miles) north of Haast. Its fishing lodge rents boats, rods and nets for whitebait. **Lake Paringa**, on the sea side of the road 45 kilometres (28 miles) north of Haast, has a lakeside motel that doubles as a fishing lodge with similar services. The dead-end road heading south from Haast crosses several streams that are hardly fished and supposedly very productive.

Regulations here are kept to a minimum to encourage anglers to come to the west coast. Most lakes and rivers are open all year, but Lakes Moeraki and Paringa have a closed season for salmon. The mixed-bag limit is seven fish per day, be they trout or salmon. However, anglers on Lake Brunner may take just one rainbow trout per day.

The **Westport Golf Club** challenges golfers with its excellent links course south of the Buller River. Watch for the deep bunkers. Par 72. Phone (03)789-8132. **Greymouth Golf Club** offers a course on undulating terrain with a backdrop of fern-filled native forest. It's pleasant and fun to play. Par 72. Phone (03)768-5332. The links course at **Hokitika Golf Club** lies ten kilometres (six miles) south of Hokitika. Its narrow fairways behind windswept sanddunes and beach make it a fine test of accuracy. Par 72. Phone (03)755-8549.

The only wine found on the rugged, rainy and windy west coast is in its restaurants and hotels. But fans of fermented beverages can instead tour **Monteith's**, on Turumaha Street in Greymouth, one of New Zealand's oldest and best-known small-town breweries. Tours run Monday to Friday. Phone (03)768-4149.

The East

Comprising the largest area of flat land in New Zealand, the fertile **Canterbury Plains** extend more than 200 kilometres (125 miles) along the east coast of the South Island, from Amberley in the north to Timaru in the south. The plains lie in the rain shadow of the Southern Alps, so unlike the wet, lushly forested west coast, the landscape here is relatively treeless. When the first European settlers arrived, the plains were covered with grey-gold tussock grass, feathery toi-toi, flax and scrub—a landscape well-suited to dairy farming and sheep ranching. Soon the settlers had drained swamps, irrigated dry areas, and turned the plains into New Zealand's granary as well. The city of Christchurch grew up at the centre of this vast patchwork quilt of green and gold.

Today Christchurch, the South Island's largest city, attracts visitors with its appealing English-style architecture and gardens. Visitors with a Gallic bent can head just south of the city to Banks Peninsula, which juts into the Pacific Ocean like a fat thumb. Tucked into one of the peninsula's many safe harbours is the French-influenced village of Akaroa. Highlights north of Christchurch include the soothing hot springs of Hanmer and the whalewatching mecca of Kaikoura.

CHRISTCHURCH

New Zealand's second largest city and one of its most important industrial centres, Christchurch (population 340,000) is often called the most English city outside England. But if so, the city belongs to an England that no longer exists except in nostalgic memory. It manages to hum along, the undisputed hub of the South Island, without the ugliness, congestion and hustle-bustle that characterize other modern cities, in England or anywhere else. It devotes an enviable amount of space to leafy parks and flower gardens, and has ample time for music, alfresco lunch hours and top-quality cultural pursuits. In addition, the active role of citizens' groups in every phase of city life provides an almost small-town sense of community. The perplexing problems faced by other metropolitan areas worldwide seem barely to have raised their head in Christchurch, making it one of the most pleasant cities on earth.

GETTING THERE

Airlines serving Christchurch's large and convenient international airport, 15 minutes from the centre of town, link the city with Australia, North America, Southeast Asia and Europe. The airport's domestic terminal is served by Air New Zealand, which provides frequent flights daily to New Zealand's other main cities as well as to other towns and scenic resorts in the south. The Airport Shuttle Bus departs hourly for all downtown destinations. Since 1955, the airport has also been a base for America's Operation Deep Freeze, which flies about 1,500 scientists and others

(following page) Driving across the Mackenzie Basin, it's impossible to lose your sense of direction, as the snowcapped Southern Alps are ever-present to the west.

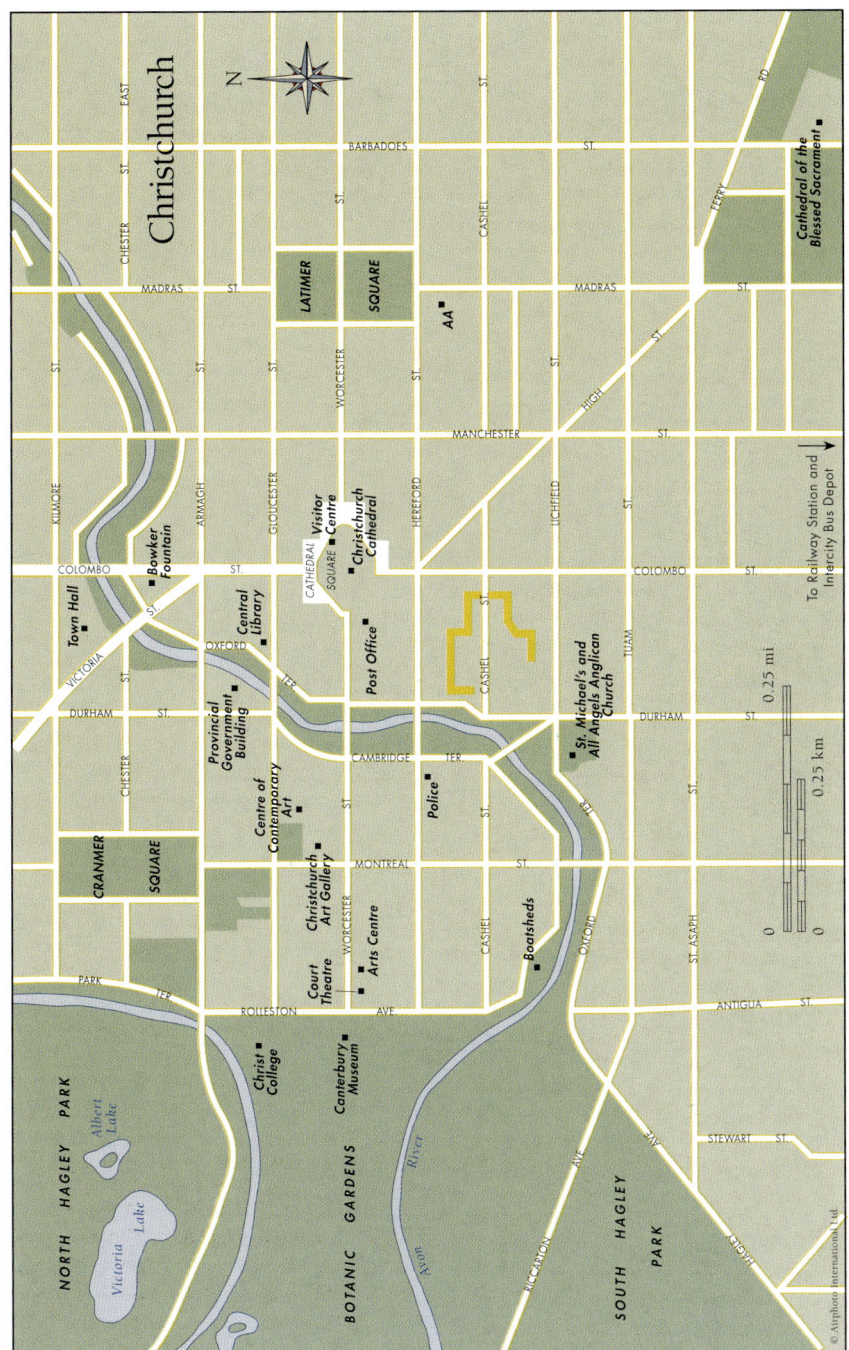

non-stop to McMurdo Base in Antarctica every year. American support staff live at the airport, and a large American Indian totem pole on the road to the airport is America's token of thanks for the city's hospitality.

Tranz Scenic's daily Tranz Coastal service connects Christchurch with the ferry terminal at Picton, by way of Kaikoura. The Tranz Alpine is the most spectacular rail journey in New Zealand. It runs west from Christchurch—across the plains, through gorges, over the snowclad peaks of Arthur's Pass (see page 194) and down through rainforest to Greymouth, on the west coast. On-board bar and buffet services are available.

Intercity offers daily bus service north and south along Highway 1. The other major carrier using Christchurch as a hub is Newman's, which stops at Christchurch on its Picton-to-Dunedin run. To travel by bus over the Southern Alps to the west coast, take Coast To Coast's daily bus service.

INFORMATION AND ORIENTATION
For city maps and information about accommodation, restaurants, excursions and entertainment, consult the Christchurch Visitor Centre, in Cathedral Square. Open daily 8.30 am–6 pm. Phone (03)379-9629. Out at the airport, both the domestic and international terminals have an information centre. The Department of Conservation office is at 133 Victoria Street. Phone (03)379-9758.

Christchurch has an excellent city bus system that takes in the outlying suburbs. Timetables and maps together with bookings for many half- or whole-day bus tours are available at the Christchurch Visitor Centre. Mount Cook Line runs an excellent three-hour Christchurch Highlights tour. Phone (0800)650-373.

The meandering **Avon River** winds through the city's heart and you can hire a punt for a leisurely hour or two; the information centre will make the arrangements. In 1995, after a 50-year hiatus, trams began trundling along the streets of Christchurch again. They can be boarded anywhere along the circular route, which passes Cathedral and Victoria Squares and the Canterbury Museum. Christchurch is flat and seemingly made for bicycles. Many roads have special bike lanes for the city's numerous cyclists. You can rent all kinds of bicycles at Trailblazers 90, Armagh Street. Phone (03)366-6033.

SIGHTS
The large heart of Christchurch, **Cathedral Square**, is for pedestrians only—a place where people meet, sit, snack, show off, sightsee, peoplewatch or deliver orations from a free-speech area. The square is dominated by **Christchurch Cathedral**, which was planned even before the Canterbury Pilgrims arrived in 1850 to found their Anglican colony. The cathedral was finally completed in 1904. A 133-step climb up the bell tower to the balconies on top is rewarded by magnificent views of the

The Founding of Christchurch

Christchurch was the brainchild of an earnest and deeply religious young Tory aptly named John Robert Godley, who feared that the Church of England, like society itself, was collapsing under the new egalitarian ideas current in England towards the middle of the 19th century. Godley hoped to see the old values regenerated in the pristine newness of the Southern Hemisphere. To launch his plan, Godley helped to found the Canterbury Association in London, whose 53 members included archbishops, members of Parliament and peers. He then journeyed to New Zealand to study the terrain with his own eyes and select a site for the settlement, deciding in the end on this place on the Canterbury Plain, on the banks of the Avon River.

Four ships set sail in 1850 with the first carefully selected Canterbury Pilgrims on board. All were under the age of 40, and all bore letters from their vicars certifying them to be 'sober, industrious and honest.' When the pilgrims landed in December 1850, Christchurch was born. Today, ancestry traced to a First-Four-Shipper is as much boasted about in Christchurch as being descended from a Mayflower pilgrim is in Boston, Massachusetts.

By 1855 over 3,500 well-screened immigrants had arrived. The town took shape in accordance with a plan devised long before the first Anglican pilgrim left England. In 1864, construction began on Christchurch Anglican Cathedral, which was sited in the middle of a broad square (Cathedral Square) set precisely in the centre of the city. Building the cathedral proved to be more complicated than anyone anticipated; more clergymen turned up than the community could support, there was a mix-up about bishops, and other urgent, but easier, matters (such as establishing a cricket club) were dealt with first. The impressive stone cathedral was not completed until 1904. Later, earthquakes shook the spire off no fewer than three times.

city, plain and mountains. Choral Evensong takes place in the cathedral on Tuesday and Wednesday at 5.15 pm, and a collegiate choir sings on Friday at 4.30 pm during the school term. Traditional Holy Communion is held on Sunday at 8 am. A visitor centre on the northern arm is open daily. Phone (03) 366-0046.

Worcester Street leads from Cathedral Square to the quiet, neo-Gothic former campus of Canterbury University. (The new, modern campus is in the western suburb of Llam.) In 1982 the campus was turned into the lively **Arts Centre of Christchurch**, which includes three theatres, a cinema, shops, restaurants and the studios of craftspeople, rug weavers and painters. Every Saturday and Sunday an open market spills from the quadrangle into Worcester Street. Vendors sell everything imaginable, including delicious-smelling ethnic food from a dozen countries, while musicians and jugglers stroll by. In one corner of the quadrangle, the den of the great physicist Ernest Rutherford is preserved intact, showing where he performed his first experiments in magnetism with primitive instruments in 1894; he later went on to England to split the atom and win the Nobel Prize in 1908.

The **Canterbury Museum**, a few steps further across Rolleston Avenue, features the Hall of Antarctic Discovery, which records the history of that continent from the explorations of Scott and Shackleton to the present. Another gallery focuses on the extinct moa and the early Polynesians who hunted them, and includes three walk-in dioramas. A large, revolving relief globe is tilted to show the Southern Hemisphere on top, offering visitors from northern countries a

Speakers' Corner

Relatively new to Christchurch's Cathedral Square, Speakers' Corner dates from the early 1970s. It owes its existence to a flamboyant character calling himself the 'Wizard,' who was determined to establish the square as a free-speech area like Hyde Park Corner in London.

Born Ian Brackenbury Channell, the Wizard was a sociologist (some say psychologist) from Leeds University in England who arrived in Christchurch via Australia. He held forth on any and all subjects in the square, only to be arrested for his trouble, such speechifying in the square then being illegal. Undaunted, he had himself carried to the square in a box and, when the police came to arrest him, proclaimed his innocence, pointing out that he was speaking in the box, not the square. This argument failed to impress the arresting officers. Then he delivered an hour-long soundless tirade in mime, which drew an enthusiastic audience. Exasperated but outwitted, the City Council agreed to delineate a free-speech area.

The Wizard is still around, considered by some a loony demagogue. He turns up most weekdays at 1 pm in one outlandish costume or another—a long black robe and cap, sheik's outfit, sackcloth and ashes—and harangues the crowd from a stepladder. Other speakers frequent the area as well. You might hear an ex-drug addict preaching about the evils of drugs and premarital sex, a young man in a frenzy of political fervour or a Maori woman who has found Jesus.

---

jolting new perspective on the world. Open daily 9 am–5 pm, admission free. Phone (03)366-5000. **Christchurch Art Gallery**, on the corner of Montreal and Worcester Streets, is the region's premier art museum., housing an impressive permanent collection that includes classic paintings of the Maori by the noted artists Lindauer and Goldie. Open daily 10 am–5 pm. Phone (03)941-7300. For a look at the work of current New Zealand artists, walk around the corner to the **Centre of Contemporary Art** (COCA), at 66 Gloucester Street. Three floors hold frequently changing exhibitions of modern work, as well as musical concerts. A gift shop sells interesting art works and crafts. Phone (03)366-7261. Just north of Canterbury Museum is **Christ College**, an exclusive Anglican boys' school established in 1850 in imitation of Eton and Harrow. The boys can be seen on the campus or bicycling around town dressed in their school uniform of striped blazers.

Art deco shopfronts, New Regent Street

A statue of Queen Victoria presides over **Victoria Square**, two blocks north of the cathedral. Opposite the Queen, a statue of Captain Cook is backed by the Bowker Electric Fountain, which dates from 1931. The fountain features coloured-light shows at night. Adjacent, at the corner of Armagh and Durham Streets, the Gothic **Canterbury Provincial Government Buildings** recall a time when Canterbury ran its own affairs. These architectural splendours are the only Provincial Government Buildings left in New Zealand. The interior is a replica of Westminster, full of detailed mosaics and stone carvings. The corner building is the ornate Provincial Council Chamber. The buildings themselves are open Monday to Saturday 10.30 am–3 pm and Sunday 2–4 pm. Bordering the river on the other side of Victoria Square, the handsome and modern **Town Hall** is the centre of the city's cultural and civic activities. Opened in 1972, the building holds a concert hall, theatre, auditorium and restaurant. A superb modern fountain facing the square makes water sculptures that reflect the Town Hall's facade.

An architectural gem slightly off the main track, the **Roman Catholic Cathedral of the Blessed Sacrament**, at Barbadoes Street and Ferry Road, was banished to its out-of-the-way site near the gasworks by the Anglican city fathers. The Catholics constructed on the site a five-domed basilica of white Oamaru stone, in neo-Renaissance style, with a mosaic floor and coffered ceilings. It was completed in 1905. In 1934, George Bernard Shaw upset the Anglicans by declaring it the treasure of Christchurch. A fine organ and impeccable acoustics make it a favoured location for concerts. Open daily 8 am–4 pm.

The gardens and greenery of Christchurch have earned it the title of 'Garden City.' Private suburban flower gardens seen from the road often look like competing showpieces. Best of all is the **Botanic Gardens**, set in a loop of the Avon River at the end of Worcester Street, behind the museum. In fine weather, an open, motorized vehicle (dubbed the 'Toast Rack') carries visitors who do not feel like walking through the hectares of gorgeous gardens, flowering trees and lawns. The Cockayne Memorial Garden is devoted entirely to native New Zealand plants. Canoes and pedal boats can be hired by the hour on the river, and a restaurant serves teas and smorgasbord lunches. Surrounding the Botanic Gardens is enormous **Hagley Park**, which is laced with walking, jogging and cycling tracks. It encompasses various sports grounds (including a golf course) and Victoria Lake, a meeting place for racers of remote-controlled model yachts. The City Council stages outdoor concerts and fireworks displays here in summer.

Short of going, you'll never get closer to the world's least-visited continent than by visiting the **International Antarctic Centre** at the airport. This excellent facility is part of the actual staging centre for United States Antarctic operations. The self-guided tour includes a re-creation of Scott's 1912 base hut, a modern-day base camp, audio-visual presentations, and a tank full of Antarctic marinelife. Visitors are also given the opportunity to ride in a Hagglund snowmobile around the actual base. Don't miss this attraction—it's a highlight of any visit to Christchurch. Open daily 9 am–5.30 pm, until 8 pm in summer. Phone (03)353-7798.

The scientifically inclined will enjoy the state-of-the-art interactive displays at **Science Alive!**, housed in the old Railway Station on Moorhouse Road. Open daily 9 am–5 pm. Phone (03)384-0700.

On the southeastern outskirts of the city in the Heathcote Valley, **Ferrymead Historic Park** offers a return to the 1920s, with a reconstructed village and a history of the country's railway engines. Open daily 10 am–8 pm. Phone (03)384-1970.

Past Ferrymead you can take the **Christchurch Gondola** to the summit of 500-metre high Mt Cavendish in the Port Hills. These high hills separate Christchurch from the Port of Lyttelton; from this eyrie, the city and its port, the Canterbury Plains and the Southern Alps spread out before you, maplike. In addition to the great views, the summit station holds a restaurant, café and the Time Tunnel, a historical overview of the area. The gondola operates daily from 10am until well after sundown. Phone (03)384-0700.

The city's most scenic drive, **Summit Road** winds for 26 kilometres (16 miles) along the crest of the Port Hills, starting in the seaside suburb of Sumner. The view is magnificent, looking northward over Christchurch to the Kaikoura Mountains and eastward to Lyttelton and the Southern Alps. An historic roadhouse along the route, named the Sign of the Takahe, was built in the 1930s in old-English style. It makes a convenient, scenic stop for light refreshments or lunch.

Banks Peninsula

This knob of land south of Christchurch is all that remains of two huge volcanoes. Their craters, drowned by the sea, now form two deep ports. Formerly an offshore island, the peninsula was joined gradually to the mainland by alluvial silt and gravel from the Southern Alps. **Lyttelton** is the South Island's leading port. The two-kilometre (1.2-mile)-long tunnel that now connects it to Christchurch is the longest in New Zealand. Wooden houses line the steep streets surrounding the harbour, where the 'First Four Ships' landed with carefully picked Anglican colonists in 1850. The route followed by the Canterbury Pilgrims over the high hills to the flat Canterbury Plain is known as the Bridle Path. Every year in December, hundreds of the original pilgrims' modern descendants make a trek over the Bridle Path to commemorate the landing, while the old stone signal tower in Lyttelton raises nautical flags to simulate the sighting of the first ship.

Quail Island, the cone of an extinct volcano, protrudes from the middle of Lyttelton Harbour, dominating the smaller islands. The scene of several shipwrecks, it has served, at different times, as a quarantine station for migrants, a leper colony and a staging post for the Antarctic expeditions of Shackleton (1907) and Scott (1910). Launches take visitors to Quail Island every half hour in summer. An easy walkway around the island (about two hours) gives a view of the ships' graveyard, the lepers' graves and the kennels that housed Scott's sled dogs.

Akaroa is a picturesque, French-flavoured village near the tip of the peninsula. It was settled in 1840 as part of the first and only attempt by the French to found a colony in New Zealand. If communications had been better and if the French had not dawdled on the way, New Zealanders might be speaking French today. Upon arrival, the French found to their dismay that the Treaty of Waitangi had been signed on the North Island, the Union Jack was flying and hastily assembled British law courts were in session. The British had arrived on Banks Peninsula exactly five days earlier. The French had originally intended to make their settlement into a base for French whalers in the Pacific and perhaps a penal colony, but instead they built a Catholic church and turned their efforts to farming. The sponsors in France sold the colony to the New Zealand Company in 1849.

The town enjoys a fairytale setting on the edge of an ancient sea-flooded volcanic crater. Many of the streets still have French names. The wooden Church of St Patrick and the museum attached to the Langlois-Eteveneaux Cottage are well worth a visit. Across from the museum is the Akaroa Visitor Centre. Phone (03)304-8600. Akaroa Harbour Cruises depart at 1.30 pm from the main wharf, searching out resident seals and dolphins and visiting a sea cave. Phone (03)304-7641. The scenic drive from Christchurch to Akaroa, on Highway 75, passes shallow Lake Ellesmere, a birder's haven (see *Focus*, page 217).

Robert Falcon Scott, a tragic figure in the race for the South Pole, is remembered by this statue beside Christchurch's Avon River.

KAIKOURA

North of Christchurch the Kaikoura Peninsula juts out into the Pacific Ocean, protecting the small seaside town of Kaikoura from the prevailing southerly winds and swells. Here the Kaikoura Ranges come right down to the sea, creating a magnificent landscape. For hundreds of years the peninsula was a Maori stronghold well supplied with seafood—the name Kaikoura means 'crayfish food.' Europeans turned it into a whaling station. Today, the town still depends on fishing, especially of crayfish for export (it's easy to pick up the delicacy locally—watch for the handmade signs advertising crays along Highway 1), but it is best known as New Zealand's premier wildlife-viewing spot. Whales, seals and dolphins inhabit the surrounding waters, and the area's bird life is prolific.

Impressive Christchurch Cathedral was completed in 1904, 40 years after construction began. Even then, earthquakes shook the spire off no fewer than three times.

Getting to Kaikoura is easy. Highway 1, between Christchurch and Picton, runs right past town, and bus and rail services are regular. Start your visit by heading to the Kaikoura Visitor Centre, on the Esplanade. Phone (03)319-5641.

The continental shelf is extremely narrow off Kaikoura. Beyond it, the sea plunges suddenly to over a kilometre in depth. Combined with a confluence of warm- and cold-water currents, this creates an upwelling that brings nutrient-rich waters to relatively shallow depths. Amongst the abundant marine life that shows up for the feast is the sperm whale, a 100-tonne leviathan once hunted with harpoons but now the subject of a far more gentle industry—whalewatching. From the old Railway Station at Kaikoura (nicknamed the Whaleway Station), tours depart regularly in high-speed Niad craft equipped with hydrophones. By monitoring the underwater sounds, the crew can tell where the whales will come up for air. Dolphins, seals and occasionally albatross are also sighted on these three-hour tours. Book at least a week in advance with Whale Watch Kaikoura. Phone (03)319-6767. Wings Over Whales can take you aloft to search out the whales. The company is based at a small airfield eight kilometres (five miles) south of Kaikoura. Phone (03)319-6580.

While whalewatching is Kaikoura's main drawcard, the area offers many other wildlife-oriented activities, of which swimming with dolphins is the most popular. Dolphin Encounter gives you the choice of getting in the water with these magnificent creatures or simply watching from aboard a boat. Phone (03)319-6777. Seal Swim Kaikoura is exactly that—swimming with seals, another unique New Zealand experience. Phone (03)319-6182. Seals can be viewed along the shoreline from various locations around Kaikoura. One colony basks in the sun on the rock shelf at Point Kean, on the northeast tip of Kaikoura Peninsula; other colonies can be found along the coast north of Kaikoura.

Fyffe House, at 62 Avoca Street, is an early whaler's house, constructed partly of whale bones and the timbers of shipwrecks. It dates to 1860. Open daily 10 am–5 pm. Phone (03)319-5837. South of town is **Maori Leap Cave**, a limestone cave carved by waves and wind over the last million years.

NORTH CANTERBURY

Highway 7 curves inland at Waipara, heading toward Lewis Pass and the west coast through hilly country with big sheep runs and open views along the Hurunui and Waiau Rivers. The charming, old-fashioned spa of **Hanmer Springs** lies in a high alpine setting just off Highway 7, some 136 kilometres (85 miles) north of Christchurch. A great forest, hot springs and comfortable accommodation make it a favourite retreat from urban life in Christchurch.

Originally bubbling up from bare tussock-covered land, the thermal pools developed in the 1890s into a fashionable spa for the wealthy. In 1902, a forest plantation was established here, using convict labour, to supply Christchurch with timber from pine and fir trees. The plantation, Now covering 17,000 hectares (42,000 acres), lends a beautiful backdrop to the little town. When fashions changed, Hanmer Springs became a quiet holiday resort, although many people still come to treat arthritis and rheumatism with a regime of thermal baths. Though neither as dramatic nor as extensive as the famous thermal areas of the North Island, it is nevertheless full of charm.

At **Hammer Springs Thermal Pools & Spa**, a large public pool area has changing rooms where bathing suits and towels can be rented for a small fee. Three pools, ranging in temperature from 37° to 40°C (99° to 104°F), have healing waters rich in sodium chloride, sodium borate and lithium. Their built-in underwater benches make them seem like giant hot tubs. A 25-metre(82-foot)-long swimming pool is kept at 28°C (82°F) for exercise and cooling off between soaking sessions, and a safe, shallow paddling pool is provided for children. Open daily 10 am–9 pm. Phone (03)315-7511. Walks in the bird-filled forest, an excellent scenic golf course and good fishing in the nearby rivers add to Hanmer Springs' appeal.

South Canterbury

The richest farmland of the Canterbury Plains lies south of Christchurch. Its rural scenery includes broad, shingly riverbeds, long fields of grain, tidy small towns, thousands of white sheep cropping green grass, cattle grazing and red deer browsing (Germany and Austria provide hungry markets for venison). **Timaru**, midway between Christchurch and Dunedin on Highway 1, at the junction with Highway 8 (which leads to Twizel and Mount Cook), is a busy port that ships out much of the province's meat and grain and serves as the base for a fishing fleet. A fine sandy beach on Caroline Bay, north of the port, draws thousands of holiday-makers in late December for a two-week carnival lasting until the New Year. The Aigantighe Art Museum in a grand 1908 mansion, at 49 Wai-iti Road, is one of the nation's best provincial galleries. Open Tuesday to Friday 10 am–4 pm, Saturday and Sunday noon–4 pm. Phone (03)688-4424. The **South Canterbury Museum** in Perth Street focuses on the region's natural history. Open Tuesday to Friday 10 am to 4.30 pm, weekends 1.30–4.30 pm. Phone (03) 684-2212. The Botanical Gardens here are beautiful.

Focus

In **Christchurch**, bird-watching is good along Avon-Heathcote Estuary, between the suburbs of New Brighton and Sumner. Here you find migrant waders in summer and a good number of coastal residents. An easily viewed colony of spotted shag occupies the cliff top above Sumner. Take Scarborough Road up from the waterfront and turn left at the top. A grass path opposite the pine trees leads to the edge of the cliff. Other spotted shag colonies can be found around the cliffs of Banks Peninsula.

Lake Ellesmere, a huge, shallow lagoon about 20 kilometres (12 miles) south of Christchurch, is an outstanding bird habitat. The main road between Christchurch and Akaroa passes close to the lagoon's northern end, where pukeko, black swans and a good assortment of ducks can often be seen from the roadside. Rare waders sometimes gather along the west shore's wide mud flats. With luck you might see golden plover, pectoral sandpiper, curlew sandpiper, sharp-tailed sandpiper, greenshank, red-necked stint or wrybill. Be sure to take a road map, as it is easy to get lost on the roads around the lake. The outlet of the lake and nearby Lakeside Domain are good places to see welcome swallows.

The middle and upper reaches of the wide riverbeds crossing the Canterbury Plains are home to a variety of birds. The most accessible bird-watching spot is the **Rakaia River**, where you may find banded and black-fronted dotterels and wrybills.

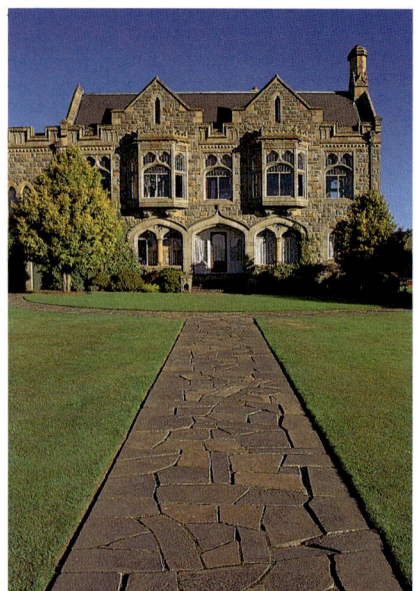

(top left) Relax over a Devonshire tea at the Sign of the Takahe, a grand stone building in the Port Hills high above Christchurch. (top right) Brightly painted buildings and a unique French atmosphere combine to attract visitors to Akaroa, on the Banks Peninsula. (bottom) Christchurch Tramway links many of Christchurch's downtown sights with the outdoor cafés of New Regent Street which provide a pleasant place to break a day's sightseeing.

Fyffe House, now restored, is typical of housing built for whalers and their families in the 1850s, when Kaikoura was a bustling whaling station.

Christchurch offers great urban walking along the winding Avon River. Start at the Information Centre, by the Worcester Street bridge, and take Oxford Terrace downstream along the river bank, through the bustling centre of town. Stop and look at the old provincial government buildings at the corner of Armagh and Durham Streets. Catch a tram back from Victoria Square, with its statues of Queen Victoria and Captain Cook and the old, electric Bowker Fountain. Alternatively walk upstream from the Information Centre back past St. Michael's and All Angels Anglican Church, noting its old campanile dating from 1860. Go beyond the Montreal Street bridge and look for some boatsheds across the river. Cross the footbridge here and bear left. On your left is the entrance to the Botanic Gardens, another beautiful place for a walk. Or follow Rolleston Street to the venerable buildings of the old Canterbury University campus, now housing the Arts Centre of Christchurch and the Canterbury Museum.

The **Akaroa** Visitor Centre offers a large selection of brochures detailing 'village walks' and 'country rambles.' The five-hour 'Round the Mountain Ramble' is one of the most enjoyable. Beginning from the east end of Akaroa, the trail climbs steadily through farmland and a stand of macrocarpa to a lookout offering panoramic views across the open ocean. Returning to town along the Banks Peninsula Track, take time to visit Tree Crop Farm for refreshing drinks in a unique setting.

On **Kaikoura Peninsula**, 191 kilometres (119 miles) north of Christchurch, two invigorating coastal walks take in an important habitat for fur seals, birds and marine life. One of the trails traverses the cliff tops, the other leads along the shoreline. Both are easily accessible from Highway 1, via either Kaikoura township or South Bay. The walks start at the car parks where the roads end. The 3.7-kilometre (2.3-mile) cliff-top walk gives panoramic views of the coastline and a distant look at the seals and sea birds on the rocks below. Allow one hour one-way. A return by the 4.5-kilometre (2.8-mile) shoreline walk around the tip of the peninsula gives a close-up view of breeding colonies of terns and gulls and a large winter colony of fur seals. Allow one and half hours one-way. An old whaler's track at East Head links the highest point of the cliffs with a small bay on the shoreline below. A longer, two- or three-day tramp follows the Kowhai River into the mountains, ascending to Kowhai Saddle at 1,176 metres (3,858 feet) and following the Hapuku River out. Contact the Kaikoura Information Centre about conditions on this track before starting out.

In **North Canterbury**, lovely forest walks and soaks in open-air thermal pools should attract any walker to **Hanmer Springs**, 136 kilometres (85 miles) north of Christchurch, just off Highway 7 about two-thirds of the way to Lewis Pass. A number of excellent walks, some with panoramic views, thread through a huge, 90-year-old forest of pine and fir. The hikes range in duration from 30 minutes to five hours. Hurunui Visitor Centre, on Main Road, has maps and information about all the walks. Phone (03)315-7128.

Rakaia Gorge, off Highway 72, 100 kilometres (62 miles) west of Christchurch and 11 kilometres (seven miles) north of Methven, offers a superb river walk. The Rakaia River funnels through a dramatic, steep-sided ravine whose terraces record seven glacial advances—a geologist's delight. The five kilometre (three mile)-long trail starts at the Rakaia Gorge Bridge and follows the rim, past an 1851 ferryman's cottage and the portals of a long-abandoned coal mine. It ends at a high point with a fine, broad view. The return trail loops towards the river before rejoining the main trail near the coal-mine portals. A side route from the loop goes to a boat landing from which you can take a jet boat back to the bridge. To arrange for a boat, phone (03)318-6515. Allow one and a half to two hours for the walk one-way.

In **South Canterbury**, Peel Forest Park, 51 kilometres (32 miles) west of Ashburton, is an oasis of greenery and waterfalls that offers a forest walk off the main tourist track. At least half a dozen trails, most about one and a half hours long, lead through the fern-filled native forest. The Department of Conservation field centre at tiny Peel Forest township has details on all the walks and also runs a campground at the edge of the park. Phone (03)696-3826.

The snow-fed rivers flowing to the South Island's east coast are famous for salmon fishing. Quinnat salmon (known as chinook in North America) are well established from the **Clutha River** in the south all the way to the **Wairau** in the north. Salmon fishing is best from December to March. Rainbow and brown trout are most numerous from October to December. Hatcheries release fingerlings annually.

The mouth of the broad **Rakaia River** is 60 kilometres (37 miles) south of Christchurch. Rakaia, a town on the south bank, fronts a stretch of water renowned for its salmon. Take Highway 1 south, crossing the river on New Zealand's longest bridge. The century-old South Rakaia Hotel on the river bank has canning and smoking facilities, and guides for trout and salmon fishing are available at the hotel. Phone (03)302-7058. The bigger town of Methven, some 30 kilometres (19 miles) upstream, is another good place to find guides and organized fishing safaris.

Two lakes about an hour's drive from Christchurch offer very good trout fishing. **Lakes Pearson** and **Grasmere** lie three kilometres (two miles) apart beside Highway 73 (the road to Arthur's Pass) in open tussock land with a view of the mountains. Both are known for their brown and rainbow trout.

The season runs from 1 October to 30 April. Consult local fisherfolk about limits because regulations vary widely.

The Canterbury Plains region holds more golf courses per capita than anywhere else in New Zealand, and some of them are magnificent. Christchurch alone has 11 golf courses within easy reach. At Shirley, **Christchurch Golf Club** is one of the top courses in the country, having hosted the National Open over a dozen times. Recently reshaped, this gracious, undulating course is given colour by yellow-blooming gorse and broom bushes under its pine trees. The clubhouse resembles an old English manor. Visitors are welcome on weekdays. Par 73. Phone (03)385-9506. **Russley Golf Club**, at 428 Memorial Avenue near the airport, is a city course bounded on three sides by roads. The challenging course is flat and tree-lined, with fine greens. Visitors are welcome on weekdays. Par 73. Phone (03)358-4612.

Four other Christchurch courses are worth noting. The immaculately groomed **Waitikiri Golf Club** comprises two very different 18-hole courses, the "old course" is an excellent course with flowering shrubs and beautiful trees while the "new course" is more open and undulating. It's in the suburb of Burwood, on the north side of the city. Par 71. Phone (03)383-0729. West of the city in Harewood, **Harewood Golf Club**, at the corner of Harewood and Pound Roads, is another very

A Land of Sheep

Viewed from the air, much of the South Island looks like a sesame bun, with countless sheep sprinkled like white sesame seeds over a golden-brown crust of tussock grass. Sheep are almost synonymous with the southern economy—the island's Merino wool always commands good prices, and South Island breeds like Corriedale and South Suffolk are valued for both their fine wool and their meat. It was from the southern port of Dunedin that the first refrigerated ship sailed to England with a cargo of frozen meat in 1882. Sparks from the cooling mechanism set fire to the sails, and in another incident the captain almost froze to death, but the meat arrived in good shape. The tradition continues: Canterbury lamb is world famous.

Adorable lambs start dotting the hillsides in September, the early spring. Soon their tails are lopped off for cleanliness, the males are castrated, and identification tags are stapled to their ears. A few are spared this treatment and raised unblemished for shipment to North Africa in the care of a shepherd. There, as sacrificial lambs, they meet their end in the Muslim ceremony of Id al-Adha.

Most sheep graze through the summer on 'runs' (ranches) in the South Island's high country. Some of the runs cover tens of thousands of hectares. At the end of April a great 'muster'(round up) takes place and the sheep are brought down below snowline for the winter.

Sheep outnumber people in New Zealand's southernmost reaches.

Muster time is sheep dogs' glory. Descended from border collie stock, the dogs are bred not for bloodlines but for ability. Heading or 'eye' dogs work silently, gathering and directing the scattered sheep. Raucous 'hunt-aways' control the great flocks by barking and chasing them into the valleys. One person can manage half a dozen dogs, guiding them with whistles and the motions of a stick—a great boon in terrain too rugged for riding a motorbike or horse. A big run may use as many as 30 dogs. They eat once a day when they are working (every other day when they are not), and 30 dogs will go through six sheep carcasses in a week. Their work in the high country is over by the age of seven. Most dogs are then sold to lowland sheep farms, where the work is easier and the dogs can carry on until they are 12.

Sheepshearers are the aristocrats of the industry. A good one may shear by hand more than 50,000 sheep in a season. Early in March, a competition called Golden Shears takes place in Masterton, northeast of Wellington, to determine the national champion. Hundreds are eliminated before six finalists struggle to shear 20 sheep to perfection as quickly as they can, which, at this level of the competition, takes little over a minute per animal.

Since the removal of government subsidies to the industry in 1984, sheep numbers have declined. Wool earned 14 per cent of the export dollar in 1986 but just five per cent by 1998. Sheep meat has also declined as an export-earner. Where the land can be adapted, many sheep ranchers are turning instead to horticulture, including growing grapes for the country's burgeoning wine industry.

good course that's reputed to be the friendliest club in the Christchurch area. Par 72. Phone (03)359-8843. The **Coringa Country Club** is also near Harewood, eight kilometres (five miles) from the airport in a relaxed country environment. Its flat, pleasant course is one of the longest in the region. Par 73. Phone (03)359-7172. Right in the centre of Christchurch, spacious **Hagley Park** holds a short and tight 18-hole golf course. Phone (03)379-8279.

In North Canterbury, the one course among many that should not pass unmentioned is the 18-hole **Hanmer Springs Golf Club**, 136 kilometres (85 miles) north of Christchurch, on Argelins Road in Hanmer Springs. The course at this quiet, forested spa is especially scenic, being one of the highest in the country. Par 68. Phone (03)315-7110.

Near Timaru, 164 kilometres (102 miles) south of Christchurch, **Timaru Golf Club** at Levels is celebrated for its beautiful flowers and view of the Southern Alps. Surrounded by farmland, the flat, green course looks easy, but is in fact very challenging. Par 72. Phone (03)688-2405.

In 1972, agricultural scientists at Canterbury's Lincoln College first started research into cool-climate grapes suitable for this region. The first commercial Canterbury wines were produced by Austrian-born Danny Schuster in 1977. Since then, over a dozen wineries have come into production, with a strong bias towards Pinot Noir and Chardonnay. The Waipara Valley (North Canterbury), accessible off Highway 1 some 70 kilometres (44 miles) north of Christchurch, holds the most northerly of the region's vineyards.

Canterbury's first commercial winery, **St. Helena**, is off Highway 1 north of Christchurch, on Dickey's Road in suburban Belfast. Brothers Robin and Norman Mundy were looking for a new type of crop in 1978 after their potato farm suffered setbacks. Daniel Schuster came as their winemaker and stayed for seven years. St Helena's Pinot Noir was awarded Canterbury's first gold medal at the 1983 National Wine Competition. Its finest white wine is Chardonnay. Phone (03)323-8202.

North of Amberley near Waipara (close to the Waipara School), **Glenmark**, on Mackenzies Road, lies on land formerly part of the Glenmark family's sheep station. When irrigation became possible, much of the land was put into wheat and barley. The vineyard was planted in 1980, and the shearing shed became a winery. The first vintage was 1986. Phone (03)314-6828.

Waipara Springs is right off Highway 1 in Waipara. The winery has a restaurant and a reputation for high-quality Chardonnay and Sauvignon Blanc. Phone (03)314-6777.

In the same Waipara area, Austrian winemaker **Daniel Schuster** produces top-quality, self-titled Sauvignon Blanc and Chardonnay and Pinot Noir from two small vineyards in the Omihi Hills, up Reeces Road. Daniel has both written upon, and practises, the art of cool-climate wine making. Tastings are by appointment. Phone (03)314-5901.

Also north of Christchurch, at Fernside, near Rangiora, is **Havill's Mazer Mead Company**, New Zealand's only commercial meadery. Leon Havill took up the ancient art of making wine from honey (mead) in 1964, believing, like everyone else, that grape-growing in Canterbury was impossible. The mead is not sweet but nutty-flavoured, containing the same amount of sugar as a dry table wine. It makes an excellent drink before dinner. Phone (03)313-7733.

Some 35 kilometres (22 miles) south of Christchurch is Burnham, where in 1981 three youthful brothers from Germany planted 25 hectares (62 acres) to start the **Giesen**, on Burnham Road. The winery has emerged as the region's biggest. The brothers Giesen—Theo, Alex and Marcel—work with energy and strict professionalism to obtain top quality wines. Their elegant 2004 Canterbury Riesling is well worth searching out. Open seven days. Phone (03)347-6729.

Larcomb, established in 1980, is on Larcombs Road, off Highway 1 between Christchurch and Rolleston. The charming little winery (formerly a shearing shed) is set in the vineyard, with peacocks, ducks and geese wandering around on the lawn. An unpretentious restaurant serves lunch under pine trees. Four varieties of wine are produced, of which Pinot Noir is the star. Open Wednesday to Sunday in summer, Friday to Sunday the rest of the year. Phone (03)347-8909.

A number of small wineries lie west of Christchurch along Highway 73 near West Melton. On the corner of Weedons Ross Road and Johnson Road is **Sherwood**, whose first vintage was in 1990. Strengths are Chardonnay and Pinot Noir. A pleasant wine bar overlooks the vineyard and serves snack food and lunches in summer. Open daily. Phone (03)347-9060. In the same district is **Sandihurst**, on Main West Coast Road. Much experimentation has taken place since the first 1992 vintage; the Chardonnay shows most promise. Phone (03)347-8289.

The Centre

This high-country region of dry sheeplands, glacially-carved basins, lakes and alpine snow is inevitably dominated by New Zealand's highest mountain, Aoraki Mount Cook. Until 1991 the peak towered 3,764 metres (12,349 feet) above sea level. But in December that year, in what was probably the geological event of this century in New Zealand, the summit cracked and an avalanche of rock and glacial ice estimated at 14 million cubic metres (494 million cubic feet) swept down the mountain. When next they surveyed Aoraki Mount Cook, it was still the country's highest peak but had lost ten metres (33 feet) of height.

East of Aoraki Mount Cook is the **Mackenzie Basin**, its lakes a stunning turquoise, its tussock golden and grazed by sheep, its roadsides alight with flowers in the spring and summer. To the south are the two beautiful lakes, Wakatipu and Wanaka, each with its own resort town.

Queenstown, set on the shores of Lake Wakatipu, the Remarkable Range rising rugged across the water, is New Zealand's best-known resort town. It has something exciting to offer everybody, young or old, day or night, summer or winter. Many find the international razzmatazz of Queenstown a bit too much and prefer to visit other parts of Central Otago, as the lake country is officially called.

The township of Wanaka, nestled on Lake Wanaka, has a quiet charm, with views across the lake to the permanently snowcapped peaks of Mount Aspiring National Park. Small townships in the river valleys surrounding Wanaka cling to vestiges of their glory days—the great gold rushes of the 1860s. Around Cromwell and Alexandra, the numerous orchards put on an extravagant show of blossoms each year before yielding a feast of cherries, apricots, peaches, plums or nectarines, each in its own season.

AORAKI MOUNT COOK NATIONAL PARK

Aoraki Mount Cook National Park, a long, narrow strip of land 65 kilometres (40 miles) long and only 20 kilometres (12 miles) wide, encompasses the highest crests of the Southern Alps. The main divide includes Aoraki Mount Cook (3,754 metres/12,316 feet), Mount Tasman (3,498 metres/11,476 feet) and Mount

(top) A whale of a mural in Kaikoura (bottom) Punting down the willow-lined Avon River is a great Christchurch experience.

(top) The Kaikoura Range provides a stunning backdrop to the seaside resort town of Kaikoura. (bottom) You can see New Zealand fur seals in colonies all along the South Island's east coast.

Dampier (3,440 metres/11,286 feet). One-third of the park's total area is under eternal snow and ice; the rest is covered with alpine scrub, forests and tussock. The weather at Aoraki Mount Cook is unpredictable, with a wide variation between hottest and coldest periods. Fine weather can be marred by biting wind. The park can be fogged in for days—or be sparklingly clear. In winter, snow stays on the valley floors an average of 21 days.

The pristine symmetry of Aoraki Mount Cook tempted the imagination of mountain climbers almost as soon as Europeans learned it was there. The first to try to climb the mountain, in 1882, were a young Irish clergyman and his two Swiss companions. Their first attempts to find a route failed. A third try from the north, by the Haast Ridge, might have succeeded but they were overtaken by storms near the summit and forced to turn back. The excitement generated by this attempt on their prized peak by foreigners may well be what started New Zealanders on their long path to glory in the heady world of mountaineering. Twelve years later, when an English climber headed for Aoraki Mount Cook, accompanied by an Italian guide and much publicity, the New Zealanders were ready; the trio of Fyfe, Graham and Clarke triumphantly reached the summit ahead of the Englishman, on Christmas Day, 1894. The discomfited English climber had to be content with conquering three other peaks instead. Aoraki Mount Cook became a favourite amongst international mountain climbers when it became known as the training ground for Sir Edmund Hillary, who made the first ascent of Mount Everest in 1953.

GETTING THERE
Air New Zealand is the sole operator flying into the park, with direct daily flights from Christchurch and Queenstown. The fights offer stunning aerial views but are sometimes cancelled due to bad weather. Aoraki Mount Cook Landline provides the most regular bus service, though a number of tour companies running between Christchurch and Queenstown schedule a two-hour lunch stop at Aoraki Mount Cook Village. Travelling by car, head first to Twizel—via Highway 8 from Timaru or Highway 6 from Cromwell. The access road from Twizel to Aoraki Mount Cook village runs for 60 kilometres (37 miles) up the Tasman River Valley, much of the way beside man-made **Lake Pukaki**. In fine, windless weather the lake's opaque, glacial water reflects an enchanting panorama of snowy peaks.

INFORMATION AND ORIENTATION
The park access road ends at Aoraki Mount Cook village, which holds a number of lodgings and general service businesses. The excellent Aoraki Mount Cook National Park Visitor Centre, on Bowen Road is part of the Aoraki Mount Cook National Park headquarters. The centre has maps of walks and trails, a great deal of other

information and interesting displays. Phone (03)435-1819. The major hotels—Aoraki Mount Cook Travelodge and The Hermitage hotel—have desks with free maps and brochures where bookings can be made for half-day and full-day excursions in the park. Avoid trying to get anything arranged around noon, as this is when the tour bus crowds thicken. Accommodation at Mount Cook village is tight at most times of the year, so before you set out to visit Mount Cook National Park be sure you have firm reservations.

SIGHTS

Without a doubt, the park's most spectacular sight is **Aoraki Mount Cook** itself. The mountain can be viewed from many points within the village (the lounge bar in the Hermitage Hotel is the classic viewpoint), or take the gravel road to the White Horse Hill Campground and follow the Hooker Valley Trail for a time. (See *Focus*, page 237, for other hiking opportunities.) Flightseeing is possible by ski-plane or helicopter, with or without a landing high on a glacier. These flights are expensive but worth it, offering breathtaking sweeps around snow-clad peaks and along spectacular glaciers. Aoraki Mount Cook Ski planes offers a variety of flights, many of which include a glacier landing. Phone (03)435-1026. Air Safaris also offers flights, which depart from nearby **Lake Tekapo**. Phone (03)680-6880. The Helicopter Line uses Glentanner Park, on the park access road, as a base. Phone (03)435-1801.

The **Tasman Glacier** can be reached by car. (Some rental cars are not insured for this rough route.) Take Tasman Valley Road along the Tasman River for 12 kilometres (7.5 miles), past forests and a waterfall to the glacier. A 15-minute walk up the moraine wall gives a view over the Blue Lakes and the glacier's whole terminal area. Although the ice is over 600 metres (2,000 feet) thick, it's hard to see any of it under the moraine's layers of debris. Alpine Guides, based in the village, runs a minibus tour out to the glacier twice daily. Phone (03)435-1834. Alpine Guides also sells and rents equipment for biking, climbing, skiing and hiking and offers experienced guides for mountaineering.

Queenstown

An attractive resort town of 11,000 perches amidst picturesque mountain scenery on Lake Wakatipu, a 77-kilometre (48-mile)-long lake shaped like an S. The bare face of a serrated mountain range called the Remarkables rises like a wall from the lake, and in the distance the peaks of the Southern Alps raise their eternally snow-capped heads. Like all the towns of Central Otago, Queenstown sprang to life in the gold rush of 1862. As in its gold-rush days, the town is still small and bustling, but the modern source of gold is tourism.

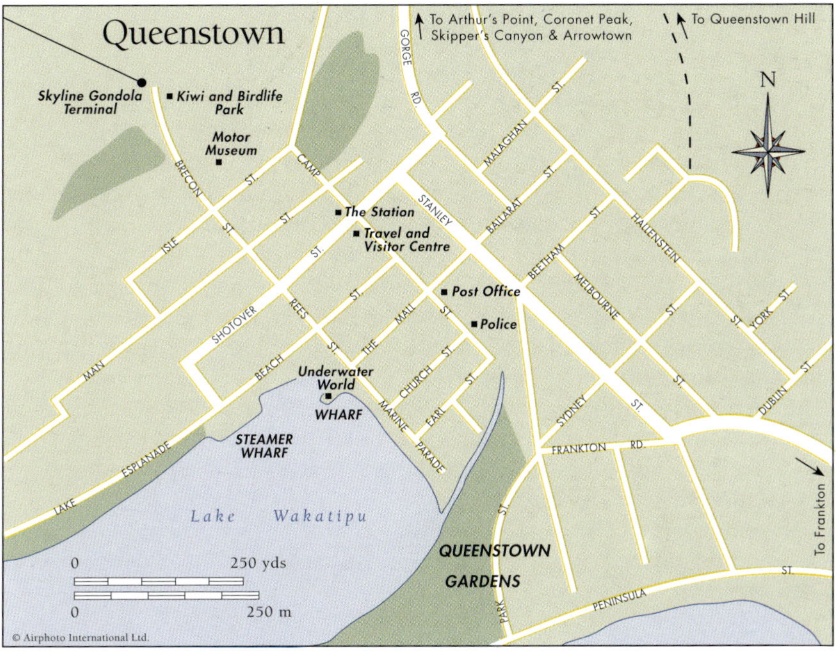

(left) Aoraki Mount Cook rises above the Southern Alps. (above) Breathtaking views extend from the residential streets high above Lake Wakatipu.

GETTING THERE
Air New Zealand flies daily to Queenstown Airport (in nearby Frankton) from Christchurch and Auckland, with connections to other major centres. The airport is tucked tightly between the mountains, and the final descent is either breathtaking or hair-raising, depending on your point of view. Two shuttle companies run between the airport and downtown hotels.

Intercity offers daily bus service to Christchurch, Dunedin, Invercargill and Wanaka. Its booking office is on the corner of Camp and Shotover Streets, and its depot is on the lakefront behind Steamer Wharf. Aoraki Mount Cook Landline operates daily buses to Christchurch via Aoraki Mount Cook from its depot on Church Street. Both companies also run scheduled services and day trips to Milford Sound. Small shuttle buses service all the towns that the large bus companies miss, as well as providing hiker drop-offs and pick-ups. Inquire at the Information Network Office.

Travelling by car, you can take Highway 6 down the west coast of the South Island, or do the long circuit via the east coast, turning inland off Highway 1 at Oamaru.

INFORMATION AND ORIENTATION
The hub of Queenstown is contained within the two-square-block area bordered by Camp Street, Shotover Street, Rees Street (which leads onto Marine Parade and the waterfront), and the Mall (a bustling, pedestrians-only strip geared to tourists). The intersection formed by Camp and Shotover Streets is Queenstown's busiest; on one corner is the Queenstown Visitor Centre, which offers books, free pamphlets and information about the many attractions that vie for the tourist dollar here. Open daily, 7 am–7 pm. Phone (03)442-4100. Across the road is The Station, a massive booking office handling bookings for most adventure activities. Phone (03)441-0073.

SIGHTS
Make your first sightseeing stop a ride up the **Skyline Gondola** to Bob's Peak, 450 metres (1,476 feet) above the town. The Skyline Chalet's observation deck gives a glorious panoramic view of Queenstown, Frankton, Lake Wakatipu, the Remarkables and all the surrounding mountains. In addition to the observation deck, the chalet has a souvenir shop, coffee shop, restaurant and small, wide-screen theatre that shows a 23-minute film titled *Kiwi Magic*. The film takes you riding, flying, sledding, jet-boating and white-water rafting through all of New Zealand's greatest sights. (Besides inducing laughs and thrills, the film's overpoweringly realistic effects help you to decide which of those activities you may want to avoid.) The gondola operates daily 10 am–10 pm. Phone (03)441-0101.

While en route to or from Bob's Peak, catch the excellent **Queenstown Motor Museum** near the bottom of the cableway. Its collection of vintage and classic vehicles is drawn from private collections all over the country. Open 9 am–5.30 pm. Phone (03)442-8059. Also near the base of the cableway is the **Kiwi and Birdlife Park**, where a number of native birds are displayed in nature bushland. Kiwis can be seen feeding by artificial moonlight in a house where day and night are reversed. Open 9 am– 5 pm. Phone (03)442-8059.

The horseshoe-shaped waterfront is a beautiful but busy place with plenty to do and see. On the main jetty at the end of the Mall, **Underwater World** lets you view gigantic trout, salmon and eels from a gallery five metres (16 feet) under the surface of the lake; watch as the hungry fish knife through the clear water to reach the automatic feeders. Open daily 9 am–6 pm. Phone (03)442-8437.

Nearby you'll find the Fiordland Travel Office and the wharf for the venerable **TSS *Earnslaw***, a perfectly preserved, coal-fired, twin-screw steamer built in 1912 to serve the sheep runs around the lake. The ship now takes visitors on lake cruises. Its well-oiled engines are open to view below deck, while incomparable scenery glides past above. The *Earnslaw* also makes a stop at **Walter Peak**, a high-country sheep station across Lake Wakatipu from Queenstown. The farm welcomes visitors to see sheep-shearing and sheep dogs in action, as well as demonstrations of wool-spinning and handicrafts. You'll get a close-up look at highland cattle and have the opportunity for tea. For tour information phone (03)442-7509.

On the peninsula across the waterfront from the *Earnslaw* wharf, the immaculate **Queenstown Gardens** features beautiful flowers by the paletteful, mature trees and greenery, and trails leading down to the waterfront.

For spectacular views of the Shotover River, drive to **Arthur's Point**, about five kilometres (three miles) north of town on the road to Arrowtown. A country pub/restaurant, built in 1863 and rebuilt after a fire in 1880, retains its original colourful character.

Nearby **Arrowtown** is a quiet, well-preserved village dating from the days when the Arrow River served up seemingly endless quantities of alluvial gold. Buckingham Street, with its charmingly restored miners' cottages, century-old sycamore trees, expensive boutiques and restaurants would probably astonish the grubby, rough-and-tumble prospectors of old. The excellent **Lakes District Museum** is well worth seeing. The old jail, a few churches and the Chinese quarter still exist, but Ah Lum's Store is one of the very few Chinese buildings to have survived intact.

Otago Goldfields Park, administered by the Department of Conservation, preserves some 20 sites scattered throughout Central Otago that illuminate the life and work of gold miners. Tours are organized and guides provided during the summer months. Information is available from the Department of Conservation's information office at 37 Shotover Street in Queenstown. Phone (03)442-7933.

Bungy Jumping

Bungy jumping is probably Queenstown's most famous activity. The 'sport' was developed from an ancient ritual on the South Pacific islands of Vanuatu, where young men would throw themselves off a high tower with a vine tied around their feet. The vine stopped them just centimetres before hitting the ground.

In more recent times, this test of manhood was mimicked by various daredevils around the world. One was New Zealander A. J. Hackett, who gained worldwide attention in 1987 when he jumped from the Eiffel Tower. The following year Hackett opened the world's first commercial jump site, at Queenstown's historic Kawarau Suspension Bridge. The site was an immediate success. Adrenaline junkies lined up, handing over their cash to leap off the bridge into the chasm below and then proudly collect a T-shirt proclaiming their bravery. The next jump site to be developed was on the upper reaches of the Shotover River, where a bridge was custom built.

The craze soon spread around the world and took on added dimensions, as people threw themselves off towers and bridges backwards, upside down, naked, on a bicycle, in a wheelchair, just about any way imaginable. A. J. Hackett jump sites can now be found in Australia, Mexico, France, Germany, Las Vegas, and Bali as well as here in New Zealand. In the colder climate of Canada, Edmonton boasts the world's only indoor bungy jump. Though the activity is now very commercialized, each of the Queenstown jump sites follows the strictest of safety guidelines, and accidents are almost unheard of.

A trip to **Skippers Canyon** is a thrilling excursion for gold-rush enthusiasts with nerves of steel. Skippers held the most fabulous gold diggings of the whole Wakatipu region, producing almost one ounce of gold per square foot of riverbed. Thousands of prospectors risked their lives descending the steep cliffs by a precarious bridle track. The narrow modern road follows the same track around the steep gorge, past abandoned claims and other relics. There are no barriers along the road's edge and few passing places. Driving there on your own is not advised; it's quite scary enough to take a half-day coach tour with an experienced driver, who will go only if weather conditions allow. Nomad Safaris offers tours, including those tailored for visitors interested in seeing locations from The Lord of the Rings triology. Phone (03)442-6699, website <www.nomadsafaris.co.nz>. (also *see* special topic page 264).

The world's first commercial bungy jump was at Kawarau Bridge near Queenstown.

ACTIVITIES

Although Queenstown's setting is picture-postcard perfect, the town is best known for the great variety of activities available in the vicinity. Many of these activities rely on an adrenaline rush for their appeal—the town bills itself as the 'Adventure Capital of the World'—but so many choices present themselves that there really is something for everyone. Shotover Street is lined with booking agents, each representing a different group of operators. In addition to daredevil pursuits, Queenstown offers great hiking, world-class golfing, bird-watching and wine-tasting; these activities are covered in the *Focus* section, below.

Bungy jumping—that strange craze of hurling yourself off a high place with a rope bound to your ankles—is available at four sites around Queenstown, three of which are run by A. J. Hackett (see Special Topic page 232). The historic Kawarau Suspension Bridge is a 43-metre (143-foot) jump and is most accessible for spectators. The Skippers Canyon bridge, 71 metres (229 feet) above the Shotover River, is reached by four-wheel-drive, with A. J. Hackett providing transfers from Queenstown. Another Hackett innovation is The Ledge; the bungy cord isn't particularly long, but the height is heart-stopping, as the jump is made from a ledge 400 metres (1,200 feet) above Queenstown. The newest jump is from a gondola 135 metres above the Nevis River. The only non-Hackett bungy is the Pipeline, on the upper reaches of the Shotover River. At 102 metres (330 feet), it is the highest commercial jump in the world.

The ultimate jump is offered by Nzone (www.nzone.biz). Experience the thrill of a 15,000 feet jump, with a full 60 seconds free fall at 200 kph. The Fletcher turbine aircraft takes about 20 minutes to reach altitude; oxygen is available to each customer on board.

Much like bungy jumping, **jet-boating** is a New Zealand innovation. Invented back in the 1950s by C. W. F. Hamilton, the boats are designed for use in extremely shallow water. They don't make use of a propeller; instead water is sucked into the engine and blasted out behind in a jet stream. This allows for almost instantaneous stopping and quick 360-degree turns. Several companies offer hair-raising jet-boat trips through the gorges and shallow rapids of the Shotover and Kawarau Rivers, with the former offering the most thrills. The Dart River is another, tamer option. Some trips leave from the Queenstown waterfront; those operators who use other bases provide transportation. Shotover Jet operates along the most spectacular reaches of the Shotover River. Other well established operators include Helijet, Kawarau Jet and Twin Rivers Jet.

Several companies offer **white-water rafting** along various stretches of the rivers. The trips last anywhere from three and a half to seven hours and are geared to different levels of proficiency and nerve. Rivers are graded from one to six, and sections of the Shotover River are rated five-plus—the most difficult rafted. The Kawarau River is a little tamer but just as enjoyable. The main companies rafting both rivers include Queenstown Rafting, Challenge Rafting and Extreme Green

Rafting. All the companies provide helmets, wet suits, and lifejackets, as well as hot showers and drinks at the end.

Flightseeing is another of Queenstown's much-touted activities. Helicopter flights are often run in conjunction with bungy jumping, jet-boating and rafting, but you can also arrange for just a flight. The Remarkables and Skippers Canyon are popular destinations. Air Fiordland and Air Milford, among others, offer spellbinding flights over the sound, Sutherland Falls, the Milford Track and the coast of Fiordland.

Other options available to the most adventurous include **tandem skydiving**, **parapenting** from the top of the gondola, **tandem hang gliding** from Coronet Peak and **paraflying** behind a boat on Lake Wakatipu.

Queenstown is a year-round resort, and is even busier in winter than summer. The two local ski fields, Coronet Peak and the Remarkables, draw skiers and snowboarders from throughout New Zealand as well as Australia. Queenstown is also the best place in Australasia for heli-skiing. Ski season runs from mid June to early October.

Wanaka

The small resort town of Wanaka, on the southern shore of clear, blue Lake Wanaka, lies in a gentler landscape than that of Lake Wakatipu. It's a more sedate place than Queenstown, but is similarly devoted to outdoor recreation—hiking, biking and water sports in summer, skiing at the Cardrona or Treble Cone ski fields in winter.

GETTING THERE
Aspiring Air flies daily between Wanaka and Queenstown—a spectacular flight on a clear day. Aspiring also offers flightseeing from Wanaka Airport, eight kilometres (five miles) east of town. Intercity is one of nine companies providing bus service between Wanaka and Queenstown. Intercity also runs from Wanaka to the west coast, and east to Christchurch. Two roads lead from Queenstown to Wanaka. Highway 6 goes via Cromwell and the Clutha Valley, a distance of just over 100 kilometres (62 miles); north of Wanaka, the highway continues over Haast Pass to the west coast. The other route, Highway 89, leaves Highway 6 at Arrow Junction, 18 kilometres (11 miles) east of Queenstown, and runs north for 53 kilometres (33 miles) over the Crown Range, passing the ghost town of Cardrona (and the famous ski fields of the same name). This is a marvellously scenic gravel road, but it's steep, rough, and not recommended in bad weather.

SIGHTS
Wanaka is the headquarters of **Mount Aspiring National Park**, named for 3,035-metre (9,957-foot) Mount Aspiring, the park's highest peak. The park visitor centre at the corner of Ballantyne and Main (Ardmore) Streets holds interesting displays and information about walks and drives. This building is also home to the Wanaka Visitor Centre. Phone (03)443-1233.

From Haast Pass, the Makarora River flows through deep gorges and a wide valley, eventually draining into Lake Wanaka.

The Wanaka lakefront is a pleasant place to spend a sunny afternoon. Lakeland Adventures rents boats, canoes and bikes, organizes fishing charters, and books Clutha River jet-boat trips. Phone (03)443-7495. **Glendhu Bay**, on Lake Wanaka's south shore, is one of the lake's most scenic points, offering views across the water to snowcapped mountains. Cruises run out to Pigeon Island, which has the distinction of boasting New Zealand's largest lake on an island on a lake.

Puzzling World, two kilometres (a mile) southeast of town toward Wanaka Junction, is an unabashed tourist trap but contains a fascinating array of mazes and puzzles. Amongst the highlights: a three-dimensional maze of over-and-under wooden passages and bridges; and the Tilting House, built on a slant to challenge the wits of old and young alike. Phone (03)443-7489. Beyond Wanaka Junction, at the airport, is the **Skyshow Centre**. Here you'll find a variety of aviation-related attractions, including flightseeing, biplane joy rides and tandem skydiving, as well as the NZ Fighter Pilots' Museum, which houses a large collection of airworthy fighter planes. The airport hosts Warbirds over Wanaka, one of the world's premier warbird airshows, over the Easter weekend of even-numbered years. Phone (03)443-8619.

Cromwell, at the edge of Lake Dunstan, is New Zealand's newest town. In 1985, the entire town was forced to move when New Zealand's most recent large-scale hydroelectric project, the Clyde Dam, created Lake Dunstan and flooded the old town site. The Goldfields Mining Centre is a DOC historic reserve filled with working mine equipment. Open daily. Phone (03)445-1037. The **Cromwell Borough Museum** has displays detailing the old town that is now lost.

FOCUS

Near **Twizel**, the Department of Conservation runs a breeding programme for the black stilt, one of the world's rarest waders. Less than 100 of the birds exist, and all those in the wild inhabit the watersheds of South Canterbury. Tours of the breeding site can be arranged through the DOC. Phone (03)435-0802.

En route to Mount Cook National Park on the road from Twizel, watch for birds along the shore of **Lake Pukaki**. Besides many waterfowl you may see wrybill, pied stilt, white-faced heron and spur-winged plover. The dry riverbed of the Godley River, which flows down to the lake, is a nesting place for banded dotterel and a known habitat of the black stilt. Keep an eye out for falcons. If you leave your car for any length of time in the various valleys of the park, the curious and strong-beaked keas may peck at anything rubber and do a little damage. At night, listen for the little New Zealand owl. The sound of its cry has led Europeans to nickname it 'Morepork' and the Maori to call it 'Ruru.' If you hear it, you can decide which name best fits.

From Queenstown, the best bird-watching is at the head of **Lake Wakatipu**. Follow Glenorchy Road along the north shore of the lake to the broad shingle riverbeds where black-billed gull, black-fronted tern, banded dotterel, pied stilt and oystercatcher nest. Paradise shelduck, spur-winged plover and Canada geese are also common here. The road forks and continues a few kilometres up the valleys of the Rees and Dart Rivers to beech forests full of bush birds. Here you may see rare yellowheads. In Queenstown, you will almost certainly see a flock of black New Zealand scaup diving for food around the wharf.

Aoraki Mount Cook National Park is not only for mountaineers. Beautiful walks along fairly flat valleys give fine views of glaciers, mountains and alpine flowers, including the famous Aoraki Mount Cook lily. Brochures on all walks are available at the Aoraki Mount Cook National Park Visitor Centre, in the heart of the village. Phone (03)435-1819. **Kea Point** is an impressive walk to a lateral moraine overlooking Mueller Glacier, with the icy face of Mount Sefton looming above. The path starts at the Hermitage and passes through the tussock and scrub of the river flats and the dense subalpine shrubbery higher up. Allow three hours return.

The **Hooker Valley** walk, which branches off the Kea Point track, is a glorious hike. The trail crosses the valley floor and after one hour reaches a suspension bridge over the Hooker River, which it then follows upstream. After half an hour it recrosses the river by another suspension bridge. Mount Cook comes splendidly into sight, and soon thereafter you can rest at the Stocking Stream shelter, amidst alpine meadows. From there, another half-hour's walk takes you to the moraine lake of the mighty Hooker Glacier. If you go as far as the lake, allow four hours return, more if the weather is inclement. The winds can get up to speed in these valleys, and weather changes quickly. Take a warm jacket.

Queenstown Hill provides a panoramic view of that city from its 902-metre (2,959-foot) summit. The leisurely 4.5-kilometre (2.8-mile) climb starts at Kent Street, 500 metres (0.3 miles) from the centre of town. Much of the trail is lined by pine, larch, sycamore and mountain ash. Higher up, in an area of burnt manuka, a plaque bears the hill's Maori name: Te Tapunui. A small alpine lake along the last stretch to the summit is surrounded by a profusion of wildflowers in spring. Rocky outcroppings make splendid seats for admiring the ever-widening view. (Much of the track is on rock, so wear sturdy shoes.) Allow two and a half hours return. Also in Queenstown, many paths lead around the shore of Lake Wakatipu.

The **Frankton Arm Walkway** is a flat, pleasant lakeside track between Queenstown and Frankton, which is across the water from Kelvin Heights. Take the walk from either end, starting at Peninsula Street in Queenstown or Frankton Beach, and return by bus. Allow two hours.

The Southern Lakes District is deservedly famous for superb fishing against a backdrop of stunning mountain scenery. Rainbow trout, brown trout and landlocked quinnat salmon abound in its high lakes and rivers.

Unusual **Lake Wakatipu** has a depth over much of its area of around 377 metres (1,237 feet). It's always cold and is subject to seiches, or rhythmic pulses, that gently raise and lower the water level every four and a half minutes, as though the lake were breathing. The best fishing for both brown and rainbow trout is from a boat at the northern end of the lake, near the mouths of the Rees and Dart Rivers. Boats and guides are readily available in Queenstown, which offers all of the amenities for anglers. The district around Wakatipu encompasses eight lakes and ten rivers or streams, all within easy reach by car or boat from Queenstown. Consult the sports shops for up-to-date information on the best spots. Fishing expeditions, with guides, to remote valleys by helicopter can be arranged through Over The Top based in Queenstown. Phone (03)442-2233.

Lake Wanaka, to the northeast, is an even more popular fishing centre. It has good numbers of brown and rainbow trout, and a decreasing population of landlocked salmon. The best fishing is at Glendhu Bay, on the south shore—a lovely spot shaded by forests and with a fine view of the Southern Alps. You'll need waders if you plan on casting from the bank. Excellent fishing is also to be had on the Upper Clutha River, from just north of Wanaka as far as Luggate. A very good free guide to the river is put out by the Department of Conservation on Ardmore Street in Wanaka. Phone (03)443-7660. The guide includes maps and details of some 20 exceptional fishing spots. Wanaka is much quieter than Queenstown but well set up for fisherfolk. Boats and fishing guides are available for hire.

Lake Hawea, across a neck of land from Lake Wanaka, is an incredible 410 metres (1,346 feet) deep at its deepest. The lake is rich in rainbow trout and salmon. Its abrupt shoreline dates from 1958, when the water level of the lake was raised 20 metres (65 feet) as part of an irrigation scheme. As there are no gentle banks, fishing is from boats, which are available for hire.

Sprawling across a narrow peninsula and surrounded by the clear waters of Lake Wakatipu, the **Queenstown Golf Club** is considered the most scenic course in New Zealand and a must on any golfing holiday. It is a short but demanding course, with the photogenic, water-edged fifth hole most famous. Par 71. The course can be reached by road or by water taxi. Phone (03)442-9169.

Millbrook Resort, on Malaghan Road in Arrowtown, has a championship course designed by New Zealand's most successful international golfer, left-hander Sir Bob Charles. The course opened in 1992, but its 120-year-old elms and oaks were already growing—the site was formerly a long-established wheat farm. The course features four different tee options on each hole, golf clinics, electric carts, a driving range, a practise putting green—in short, total seduction for the golfer who wants class and a backdrop of mountains. The resort has a top quality on-course hotel; if you want a serious golfing holiday, or if you didn't get that first round right, stay on. Par 72. Phone (03)441-7000.

Other towns in the region also have very good, though scenically less spectacular, 18-hole courses. All are beautiful, flattish and pleasant to play. Visitors are warmly welcomed, and no reservations are needed. Wanaka is considered the most interesting course. Alexandra, in a less scenic area, is a well-maintained, green oasis, but you find yourself amongst dry stones and boulders if you stray from the fairways. Roxburgh has a lovely, nearly flat course with huge rocks that make for entertaining play. Arrowtown also has another good but short 18-hole course.

Central Otago, the newest wine district to evolve in New Zealand, holds the southernmost vineyards in the world. After Montana's bold experiment introducing vineyards to Marlborough in 1973, Canterbury followed suit, and in the 1980s, so did Otago. As well as a climate similar to France's Burgundy region, the Otago turned out to have excellent soils and nearly as much annual sunshine as Marlborough. The cool climate here can produce

excellent wines. They're distinctly different—crisp with the higher acidity of a grape grown in harsh conditions, but firm flavoured. Locals snap them up, and you won't find them on retail shelves outside the region. But if you're visiting, you can buy at the cellar door and talk with the informed, friendly pioneers of a still-fledgling industry.

Chard Farm is off Highway 6 between Queenstown and Cromwell. From the road you'll see its picture-postcard setting, on a small flat above the dramatic Kawarau River Gorge. In 1992 the winery made New Zealand's first true ice wine, harvesting frozen grape bunches at midwinter. Chardonnay, Pinot Noir and Riesling are available at the cellar door. The owners are currently developing Central Otago's largest vineyard nearby; look for the Lake Hayes label from 1999 onward. Phone (03)442-6110, website <www.chardfarm.co.nz>.

Gibbston Valley, just beyond Arrowtown on Highway 6, was first planted in 1981. Four years later the winery received strong encouragement from the Te Kauwhata Viticultural Research Station for the quality of its first vintage. Its wine selection includes Pinot Gris, Sauvignon Blanc and Chardonnay. The vineyard is close to the Kawarau River, wonderfully scenic, and has an excellent restaurant. Phone (03)442-6910.

Rippon, a lakefront winery two kilometres (a mile) from Wanaka, on the Mount Aspiring Road, produces a Pinot Noir that is one of the top New Zealand reds. Phone (03)443-8084, website <www.rippon.co.nz>.

Near Alexandra some 60 kilometres (40 miles) southeast of Queenstown are two vineyards set either side of the Clutha River, both producing wines that have been compared to the Rhine Valley wines of Germany. **Black Ridge**, set amidst rocky outcrops that concentrate the heat, is a seven-hectare spread that claims to be the southernmost vineyard in the world. If we cannot verify that by the necessary research in Patagonia, we can certainly agree it is New Zealand's most southerly. The climate is harsh and the wine crisp. Pinot Noir, Gewürztraminer, Riesling and Chardonnay are available at the cellar door. Phone (03)449-2059, website <www.blackridge.co.nz>.

William Hill, on Dunstan Road in Alexandra, is smaller but just as heroic. Its first vintage was in 1994. The hoar frosts build up acid content in the grape to help make a firm Pinot Noir, Riesling, Gewürztraminer and Chardonnay. Wine sales are at the cellar door, but ring to say you are coming. Phone (03)448-8436, website <www.williamhill.co.nz>.

(preceding pages) The braided Tasman River flows from high in Mount Cook National Park, draining into man-made Lake Pukaki near Twizel.

The South

The South Island broadens out at its southern end into comfortably rolling hills that end abruptly at a rugged and remote coastline. This was originally a prime oat-growing area, but today sheep ranches and dairy farms dominate the landscape. The university city of Dunedin, up the east coast, is the region's main urban centre; the solid, rock-ribbed Victorian town is the capital of Otago province. South of Dunedin, sheep outnumber people 20 to one. The South's second largest city is Invercargill, in the centre of the south coast.

South of Invercargill, across Foveaux Strait, Stewart Island often gets overlooked. The fishing village of Oban occupies a tiny stretch of the island's 1,600-kilometre (1,000-mile) coastline, which otherwise remains virtually uninhabited—a delight for naturalists and hikers.

A far bigger uninhabited wilderness is Fiordland, which occupies the whole southwestern corner of the South Island. Fiordland National Park is the largest and most remote of New Zealand's national parks. This magnificent, wild region of craggy mountains, dense rainforest and spectacular waterfalls is penetrated by narrow fiords from the seaward side, and by the long-fingered lakes of its landward side. The landscape was carved by glacial ice estimated to have been over 1.5 kilometres (one mile) thick. Fiordland is a paradise for nature-lovers and hikers. Its only sizeable town is Te Anau, which is the jumping-off point for the Milford Track, the famous four-day hike from the north end of Lake Te Anau to Milford Sound. The so-called 'sound' is actually a fiord, glacially carved, 16 kilometres (10 miles) long, its waters plunging deep and blue between precipitous rock walls hung with waterfalls. It is one of New Zealand's greatest sights.

DUNEDIN

The second biggest metropolis of the South Island, Dunedin (population 120,000) spreads in a horseshoe shape over the hills at the head of Otago Harbour. The site is dramatic, and the ornate stone buildings give the city an air of permanence. Scottish settlers came to found a well-planned Presbyterian colony at Dunedin in 1848. The gold rush of the 1860s brought prosperity and a new population that diluted, but didn't drown, the town's original character. As Dunedin boomed, the canny Scots turned the new wealth into a handsome city built of stone, with as many banks as churches. When the gold was gone, sheep took over. Dunedin set up New Zealand's first freezing works and found new prosperity sending frozen meat to England. The city's Scottish origins are visible today in the street names and the statue of poet Robert Burns sitting right at town centre. (The name Dunedin is Celtic for Edinburgh.) The city boasts the country's first golf course, its last-remaining kilt-maker and its only whisky distillery. In March, lads and lasses clad in tartan dance the highland fling to the skirl of bagpipes in The Octagon, as the city throws itself into its annual Scottish Festival.

Historic buildings can be found throughout the Otago Goldfields.

GETTING THERE
Air New Zealand flies to Dunedin from Christchurch and Wellington, with connections from these cities to all points north. The airport is 29 kilometres (18 miles) south of the city at Momona, but a 30-minute ride from any one of five shuttle companies will get you into town. Intercity and Newmans coaches connect Dunedin with the larger east-coast towns between Christchurch and Invercargill. Many bus services run inland to Alexandra, Queenstown and points between. For those travelling by car, Highway 1, the main east-coast artery, runs right through Dunedin, while Highways 85, 87 and 8 run west to Queenstown, each by a roundabout route.

INFORMATION AND ORIENTATION
The city was planned by church members in Scotland before the first settlers arrived. At the centre is The Octagon, whose eight-sided garden holds the statue of Robert Burns. The Dunedin Visitor Centre is at 48 The Octagon. Phone (03)474-3300. Dunedin is a good city to explore on foot (see *Focus*, page 267).

SOUTH ISLAND 245

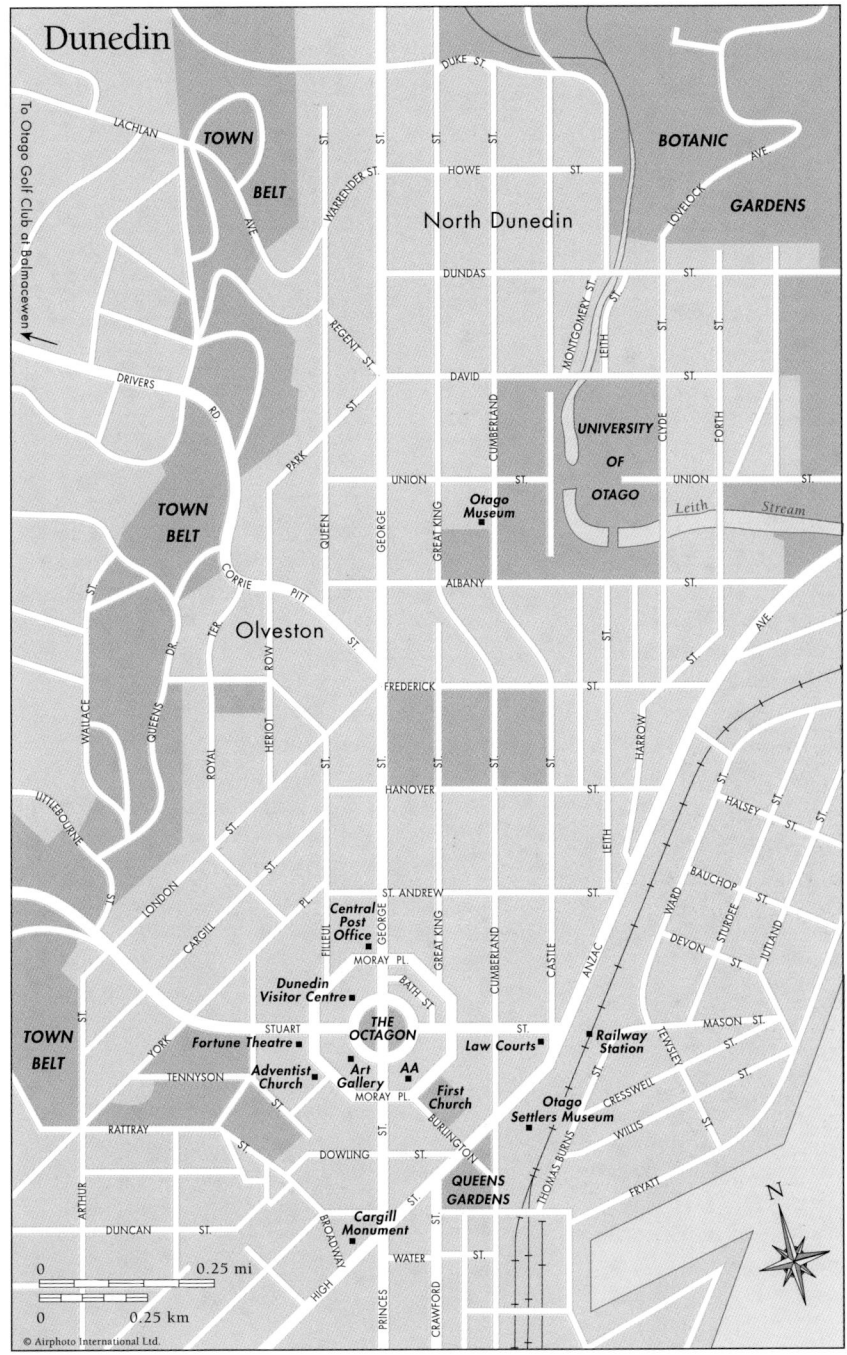

SIGHTS

Otago Museum, at Great King and Union Streets, is one of the South Island's largest and finest museums. It's widely known for its excellent Pacific art collections and cultural displays. The Maori Hall holds outstanding carvings, a reconstructed meeting house, many articles of polished greenstone and more modern displays such as Discovery World, a hands-on exhibit of technological wonders. Open daily 10 am–5 pm. Phone (03)474-7474.

Behind the museum, on Cumberland Street, is the **University of Otago**, New Zealand's oldest campus (1869). Two-toned, ivy-covered stone halls and modern buildings stand amidst lawns and gardens by the Leith Stream. The Hocken Library on campus is well worth a visit for its excellent New Zealand collection. To the north, the beautiful **Botanic Gardens** (New Zealand's first) boast floral displays, superb rhododendrons and a restaurant.

The **Dunedin Public Art Gallery**, at 30 The Octagon, is New Zealand's oldest continuously operated gallery. In its 115-year history it has amassed a collection worthy of inspection, including historical and contemporary New Zealand paintings, Japanese prints, a Monet and other works by foreign artists. Open daily 10 am–5 pm. Phone (03)477-4000.

The **Dunedin Railway Station**, on Anzac Avenue at the east end of Stuart Street, is an astonishing bit of architecture completed in 1906. The outside, faced with bluestone, sports a clock tower and copper dome. Inside you'll find porcelain cherubs, a scroll-enshrined ticket office, intricate mosaics celebrating railway themes, and stained-glass windows featuring steam locomotives. Daily at 2.30 pm an historic locomotive pulling restored 80-year-old carriages departs for the spectacular Taieri Gorge, a four-hour return trip. Phone (03)477-4449.

The **Otago Settlers Museum**, near the railway station at 31 Queen's Gardens, is a treasure house of fascinating objects, from whalebone corsets and antique dental instruments to clocks and velocipedes (early pedal-less bicycles). The museum also has a large research and reading room. Open 10 am–5 pm. Phone (03)477-5052.

First Church, at Moray Place and Burlington Street, was built of Oamaru stone by the first Presbyterian settlers. Bell Hill, which was flattened for the church, is where early services in Dunedin were held.

For a peep at a really splendid old family home, take a guided tour of **Olveston**, a historic 35-room mansion at 42 Royal Terrace. One-hour tours depart five times daily. Phone (03)477-3320.

The **Otago Peninsula** extends south of the city into the Pacific Ocean, enclosing Otago Harbour. It is one of New Zealand's premier wildlife-viewing areas, home to albatross, penguins, seals and sea lions. A 40-kilometre (25-mile) road leads to the end of the peninsula, and many side roads lead to interesting sights. Inquire at the

Dunedin Visitor Centre about the many half- and full-day tours possible, including boat tours departing from downtown wharfs. Yellow-eyed penguins and the royal albatross colony attract the most attention—even non-bird-watchers will be enthralled viewing these two endangered species (see *Focus*, page 262). Seals can be viewed at many spots along the eastern side of the peninsula; one sure spot is at Southlight Wildlife, a privately owned strip of coast near Taiaroa Head. First pay to enter at the owner's residence (well-signposted), then you're on your own to explore. **Larnach Castle**, halfway along the peninsula (12 kilometres/7.5 miles from the city), is a Victorian folly built in 1871 by a rich New Zealand banker for his wife, the daughter of a French duke. (His life reads like a Victorian melodrama.) The building is copied from a Scottish castle, with a lavishly ornate interior, a Georgian hanging staircase and a dungeon. Open daily 9 am–5 pm. Phone (03)476-1616. Portobello, the peninsula's only town, is home to the **New Zealand Marine Studies Centre**, which features audio-visuals and interactive displays. Shallow pools contain live specimens. Phone (03)479-5826.

North Otago

Oamaru, 116 kilometres (72 miles) north of Dunedin, is the chief town of North Otago and is famous for the creamy white limestone quarried nearby. The stone has been used for many impressive buildings, including Auckland's Town Hall, Wellington's Customs house, Christchurch's Catholic cathedral and Dunedin's First Church, Anglican cathedral and Town Hall. Elegant classical limestone buildings dating from the 1870s and 1880s line Oamaru's broad, tree-shaded streets, particularly in the Harbour-Tyne Street and Thames Street precincts. For a good view of the town and coastline, head to Lookout Point, at the eastern end of Tamar Street.

Moeraki, a small fishing port 38 kilometres (24 miles) south of Oamaru, off Highway 1, is famous for another type of rock; huge spherical boulders are scattered over the nearby beaches and protected in the **Moeraki Boulders Scenic Reserve**. These geological curiosities—shaped by chemical action, not wave action—were formed from minerals and salts on the ocean floor 60 million years ago. The boulders appear as the mudstone around them erodes away. Before the site received official protection, many more boulders of all sizes lay upon the beach. All except the biggest were carted off as souvenirs.

The Catlins

The Catlins is an unspoiled scenic region between Dunedin and Invercargill along coastal Highway 92. This wild, windswept and little-visited part of the South Island extends from Balclutha to the Mataura River near Waipapa Point. Rivers and waterfalls, dense podocarp forests, desolate headlands, secluded bays and an

abundance of wildlife make the Catlins one of New Zealand's hidden gems. Award winning Catlins Wildlife Trackers operates two- to four-day tours for groups up to eight people that combine the natural and human history of the area with the friendly hospitality of their small lodge at Papatowai. Phone (03)415-8613.

Nugget Point, reached through the seaside village of Kaka Point, is a wonderful introduction to the Catlins. The point comprises a steep-sided, narrow peninsula rising over 100 metres from rocky islets that extend into the ocean beyond its tip. The rocks below are the only place in the country where fur seals, sea lions and elephant seals coexist; the breeding colony of elephant seals is unique to mainland New Zealand. Bird life is also prolific (see *Focus*, page 262). In the same vicinity is Cannibal Bay, where sea lions occasionally haul themselves onto the beach. Between Owaka and Papatowai, Highway 92 enters Catlins Forest Park, where many points of interest are signposted, including fantailed **Purakaunui Falls**.

Hector's dolphins can often be seen frolicking in the shallow, clear water of **Porpoise Bay**. In adjacent **Curio Bay**, wave action has exposed the fossilized trunks of ancient trees. Related to kauri, the trees are embedded in a rock shelf that shows itself at low tide. It is one of the most extensive such sites in the world. A gravel road leads south from Otara to **Waipapa Point**, site of a lighthouse erected after New Zealand's second worst maritime disaster claimed 130 lives on an offshore reef in 1881. Sea lions can often be seen sunning themselves on the beach below the lighthouse.

INVERCARGILL

New Zealand's southernmost city (population 55,000) sits on a flat plain near the south coast. Invercargill has the same Scottish roots as Dunedin, and the city's wide, tree-lined streets, laid out in a grid, bear the names of Scottish rivers. The city also has its full share of blustery Scottish weather. Its many attractive parks and green areas contrast starkly with the surrounding flat, featureless plains. Two large freezing works, Mataura (south of Gore) and Lorneville (just north of Invercargill), process nearly four million lambs a year, exporting the frozen meat through the port of Bluff.

GETTING THERE

Air New Zealand flies to Invercargill from the major North and South Island cities, with connections through Christchurch. Intercity provides regular bus connections with Queenstown, Te Anau, Lumsden, Gore, Dunedin and Christchurch. For those travelling by car, the flat, well-maintained back roads make this an ideal area to leave the main highways and explore the hinterland. Along the way are a

(preceding pages) Monkey Creek, Fiordland National Park

surprising number of deer farms. Introduced to the wild a century ago, deer eventually became a pest, but now they provide income as venison for export.

If you are driving on a Saturday between October and the end of February, keep an eye out for an Agricultural & Pastoral Society (A & P) show—a kind of county fair held in rural communities throughout the country. The smaller the show the better the fun. You are likely to see prize livestock, sewing and knitting displays, sheep-dog trials, horse-jumping events and wood-chopping and sheep-shearing competitions.

SIGHTS

The **Southland Museum and Art Gallery**, on Gala Avenue, is Invercargill's premier attraction. Housed in a distinctive pyramid-shaped building on the edge of Queens Park, the museum contains many varying displays. One highlight is an interpretive centre for the subantarctic islands, which lie off New Zealand's southern coast (see Special Topic, page 254). Galleries bring the natural and human history of these remote islands to life with photos and displays, while a theatre shows a stunning film about the isles every couple of hours. The museum also has a tuatara house, where you can view live specimens of the rare lizardlike reptile, considered a 'living fossil.' Other local-history exhibits include Maori artifacts and relics from the country's first-recorded shipwreck (in 1795). Open on weekdays 9 am–5 pm and on weekends 10 am–5 pm. Phone (03)218-9753. In the museum foyer is the Invercargill Visitor Centre, open the same hours. Phone (03)214-6243. Adjacent Queen's Park is a lovely area with formal gardens, an aviary, a deer park and many playing fields, including an 18-hole golf course.

Murihiku Marae, close to town, serves as a community house and training centre for arts and crafts. A traditional meeting house has been carved on the grounds, under the supervision of a master carver. It's at Kingswell Heights, off Tramway Road. Phone (03)216-7738.

Seafood from Foveaux Strait is the great speciality in this region. Oysters are dredged from the strait and are a succulent delight during the season (March-August). On Friday evenings the Ascot Park Hotel, at Racecourse Road and Tay Street, puts on an enormous seafood smorgasbord that is a weekly social event. Roasts are also served for non-seafood-lovers. Phone (03)217-6195.

Bluff, 27 kilometres (17 miles) south of Invercargill at the end of Highway 1, is Invercargill's port and the gateway to Stewart Island. From this no-nonsense fishing village, the oyster-boat fleet departs daily to dredge their quotas. A lookout atop **Bluff Hill** provides panoramic views over the harbour, the Southland plains,

Foveaux Strait and Stewart Island. (Turn uphill at the post office and follow the road to the summit.) The view is especially good towards evening, when the fishing boats are heading home. Across the harbour, an artificial island provides docks and loading facilities for the huge New Zealand Aluminium Smelter, the world's eighth largest such smelter. Around the base of Bluff Hill, Highway 1 ends at a sign giving distances to such far-flung places as Antarctica and New York.

STEWART ISLAND

Across shallow Foveaux Strait lies Stewart Island, New Zealand's third largest island. Beyond, the open ocean stretches out all the way to Antarctica. The island is shaped like a large, lopsided triangle 60 kilometres (37 miles) long and half as wide. Rocky coves and sandy beaches line the coast, and virgin forests cover the rugged mountains of the interior. About 420 people call the island home, most of whom live in Oban, which spreads around Halfmoon Bay on the east side. The rest of the island is protected by Rakiura National Park. The weather is mild but is unpredictable from one hour to the next, forever alternating between sun and rain.

GETTING THERE

Stewart Island Flights connects the island with Invercargill year-round and runs as many as four flights a day each way in summer. The flight across the 24-kilometre (15-mile) stretch of water takes about 20 minutes. Phone (03)218-9129. The *Foveaux Express*, a fast, passengers-only catamaran, takes 60 minutes to make the crossing from Bluff to Halfmoon Bay. Phone (03)212-7660. Campbelltown Passenger runs a bus service between Invercargill and the ferry dock. Phone (03)212-7404. Bookings must be made in advance for both sea and air travel. Current timetables are available from the Invercargill Visitor Centre.

The road to Milford Sound skirts Lake Te Anau, a large body of water within Fiordland National Park.

(top) Oamaru's main street features the best-preserved strip of historic commercial buildings in New Zealand. They were constructed of locally mined limestone, which was used throughout the country. (bottom left) First Church, Dunedin, a short walk from The Octagon. (bottom right) Climb the narrow flight of stairs to the top of this 1889 water tower for a 360-degree view of Invercargill. The tower is at the east end of Leet Street.

New Zealand's Outer Islands

New Zealand's territorial boundaries extend well beyond the North and South Islands. As well as Stewart Island (see page 252), government jurisdiction encompasses a number of islands and island groups throughout the southern reaches of the South Pacific.

The **Chatham Islands** lie 700 kilometres east of Christchurch. This wild, remote archipelago is inhabited by 750 people, most of whom live on the largest of the ten islands, Chatham. Volcanic in origin, the islands feature rugged coastlines, windswept forests and large populations of bird life, including the extremely rare Chatham Islands black robin. Polynesians arrived on the Chathams before they landed on mainland New Zealand, while Europeans discovered the islands in the 1790s. Today the islanders are involved in fishing, crayfish processing, and tourism. Tourist services include lodgings, a couple of restaurants, a rental car outlet, a Department of Conservation field centre and scheduled flights from the mainland cities of Wellington and Christchurch.

The **Kermadec Islands** are 1,000 kilometres northeast of New Zealand. They extend from the largest island of the archipelago, Raoul, 130 kilometres south to a group of rocky outcrops. Bird life is prolific; 35 species are present, with five species endemic. Although a whaling station once operated on Raoul, and goats were introduced for shipwreck survivors, the islands have remained unchanged. Apart from a year-round contingent of Department of Conservation officers, the islands are uninhabited.

Also within New Zealand jurisdiction are a number of subantarctic islands, all lying between the southern point of the South Island and the 60th parallel. **Campbell Island**, the site of a meteorological station, is home to 10,000 wandering albatross. Largest of the Auckland Islands, and once the site of a whaling station, **Enderby Island** is now inhabited only by sea lions, albatross, shags, and mollymawks. Named for their location on the opposite side of the world to England are the **Antipodes Islands**, best known for the Antipodes Island parakeet. Closest to mainland New Zealand are the **Snare Islands**, home to around 5,000,000 sooty shearwaters. Northernmost of the subantarctic islands are the **Bounty Islands**, comprising nothing more than rocky outcrops and yet home to permanent populations of crested penguins, fulmar prions, and mollymawks. Aside from actually visiting the islands, the best way to get a feeling for this wild and remote region is by visiting the Southland Museum in Invercargill, where the Beyond the Roaring '40s Subantarctic Experience explores the natural and human history of the islands.

South Island 255

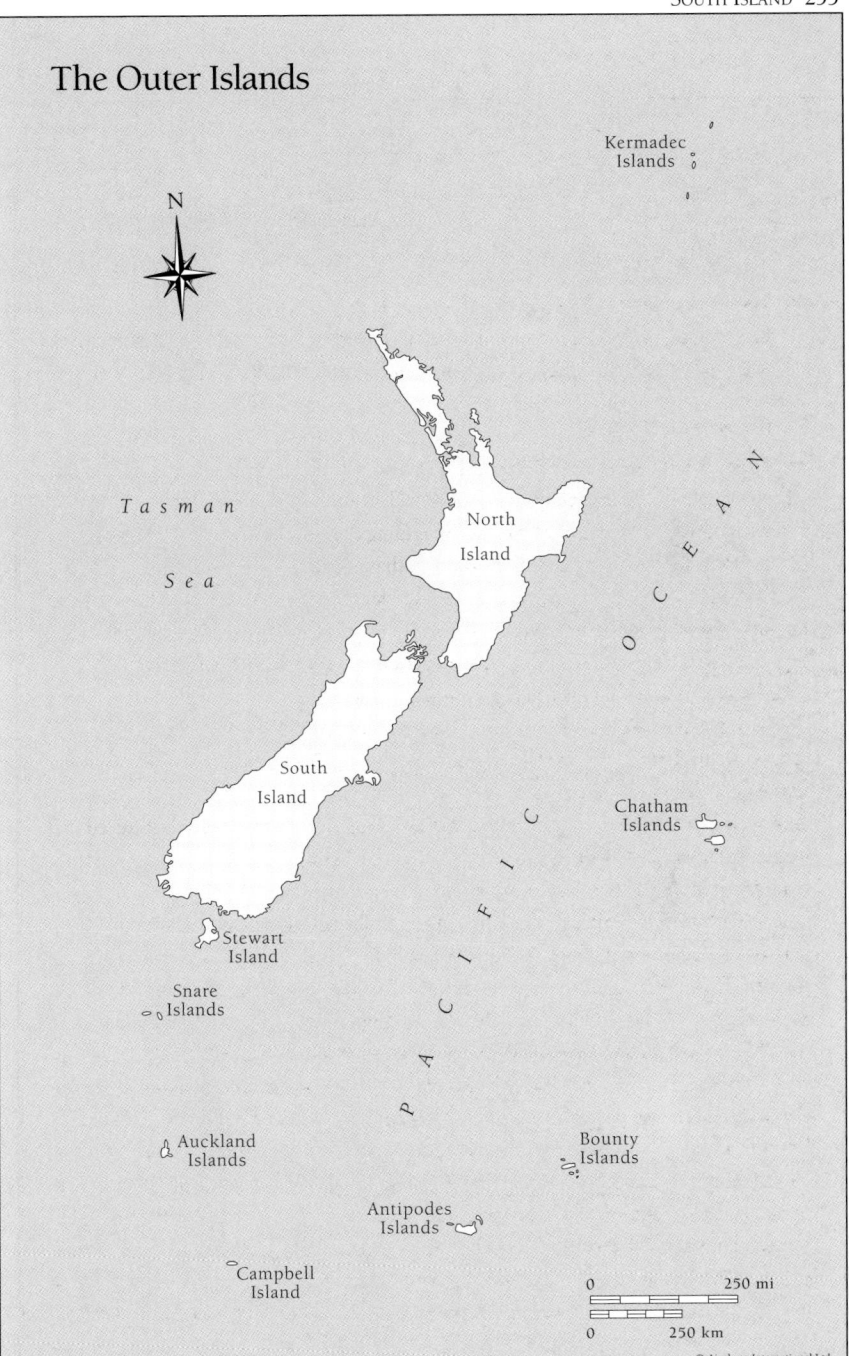

Cruising Milford Sound affords an opportunity to view large bottlenosed dolphins gleefully riding the boat's wake.

SIGHTS

Oban is a tiny, friendly village reminiscent of 1970s-era fishing settlements on the coast of Newfoundland or Maine. Fishing is a far bigger business here than tourism, attested to by the piles of cray pots and fishing nets you'll see. Make your first stop the Department of Conservation's Field Centre on Main Road, which offers an array of good displays, booklets and maps. Phone (03)219-1130. The Field Centre also houses the Stewart Island Visitor Centre; phone (03)219-1218. Various motels and guesthouses dot the village. Book all accommodation from the mainland.

Stewart Island deserves at least a couple of days of exploration. Start with the 90-minute bus tour offered by Stewart Island Travel. Phone (03)219-1269. The tour traverses the island's 32 kilometres (20 miles) of paved roads while offering marvellous commentary. Other possible island activities include charter-boat trips to delightful Ulva Island and the coves most favoured by seals and penguins; magical walks of different lengths through fern-filled forests to sandy beaches; and sunsets and long twilights that are legendary (the Maori name for Stewart Island is Rakiura, meaning 'heavenly glow'). If you're lucky, you might even catch a performance by the amateur Stewart Island Players; so many islanders take part in these productions that they have to bring their audiences from the mainland.

Mount Douglas, Westland National Park

Off the coast from Oban, the **Muttonbird Islands** are the exclusive hunting preserves of the Rakiura Maori and are not open to visitors. The Maori have the right to harvest muttonbirds (migratory sooty shearwaters) from the islands. The fat muttonbird chicks are a prized Maori delicacy, captured by the tens of thousands in April and May and sent to food shops all over the country.

Fiordland

A mere 14,000 years ago, Fiordland was completely covered with ice. Glaciers carved its extraordinary serrated coastline and deep, branching lakes, then retreated to leave behind a magnificent, untamed landscape. Today the region is preserved in Fiordland National Park, one of the biggest national parks in the world. Within the park, huge Te Anau and Manapouri Lakes, along with four smaller ones, create an inland 'coastline' that is almost as daunting as the seaward one.

An immense amount of rain (nearly 6.5 metres/249 inches in Milford Sound, for example) feeds cascading waterfalls and a luxuriant rainforest. Towering beech trees shelter a dense undergrowth of shrubs, ferns and moss, the whole clinging to nearly vertical mountainsides. Lichens and peat moss build up a precarious soil that holds the roots, but when storms dislodge even a few trees, a disastrous 'tree avalanche' can result. Bare scars down every sheer mountain face stand witness. Winter is the driest season, but much of Fiordland's bewitching beauty comes from its wetness.

An incredible insect population lives in this southern region. Most species remain in their forest habitats, but vicious sandflies seek out the few humans around to bite. A Maori legend says that the gods who shaped Fiordland became so entranced by their creation that they stopped working and just sat back to admire it. Hine-Nui-te-Po, the goddess of life and death, created te namu, the sandfly, to goad them back to work. Be sure to apply insect repellent on all exposed skin when you are outdoors.

Te Anau, lying just outside the boundary of Fiordland National Park at the south end of Lake Te Anau, is the region's biggest tourist centre. Manapouri, 19 kilometres (12 miles) south of Te Anau, sits at the mouth of the Waiau River at Lake Manapouri's eastern end. These two towns and the settlement at Milford Sound account for all the urban life in Fiordland.

GETTING THERE
Flying is by far the most spectacular way of getting to Fiordland. Air New Zealand connects Te Anau with Queenstown. Air Fiordland flies to Milford Sound from Queenstown and Te Anau. Intercity run buses to Te Anau and Milford Sound from Queenstown. Other options, such as a fly/cruise/coach combination, can be

arranged through Fiordland Travel in Queenstown. Phone (03)442-7500. Those travelling by car simply get to Lumsden, on Highway 6 (famous for good fishing; see *Focus*, page 271), then take Highway 94 west to Te Anau.

INFORMATION AND ORIENTATION

Te Anau is a small lakeside town completely devoted to tourism. Most of the two dozen hostelries in town are within easy walking distance of Te Anau's main road and waterfront. All will pick up guests from the airport or bus terminal. The Fiordland National Park Visitor Centre, along Lakefront Drive, provides maps, information and permits for all hiking tracks in the adjacent park. The centre also shows a stunning audio-visual presentation on the park, including superb sections on Milford Sound and the Milford Track. Real Journeys, opposite the main road on the waterfront, is the biggest agency for tours on land, lake or sea. Phone (03)249-7416, website <www.realjourneys.co.nz>. Competition is very hot, especially on trips to Milford Sound, and other agencies up and down the main road offer a variety of special deals.

SIGHTS

Real Journeys offers a two-and-a-half-hour trip to **Te Ana-Au Caves**, which entails a cruise across Lake Te Anau and an exciting excursion inside limestone grottoes, part of the way by flat-bottomed punt. These 'young' caves have not yet built up stalactites, but their walls are festooned with thousands of twinkling glow-worms. The trips leave at 2 pm daily, with extra sailings, including one after dinner, in summer. Phone (03)249-7416.

Lake Manapouri is often called New Zealand's most beautiful lake. Its clear, island-studded waters reflect the snowcapped peaks of the Keppler Mountains. A tremendous controversy arose here in the late 1960s when the national government proposed raising the lake's level by 12 metres (40 feet) and installing a gigantic electric power plant to feed the aluminium smelter at Bluff. A nationwide petition sponsored by environmentalists gathered a quarter of a million names and contributed to the government's electoral defeat in 1972. The incoming Labour government agreed to leave the lake intact and put the power plant 213 metres (700 feet) below ground. The **Manapouri Underground Power Station** is an awesome sight. Twice-daily tours take visitors to the site by boat from Manapouri village. A bus spirals down for two kilometres (1.2 miles) through a spooky tunnel to a vast granite cavern in the bowels of the earth, where seven giant generators hum. The trip takes about four hours. Bus transfers between Te Anau and Manapouri can be organized. Phone (03)249-6602.

Organized tours to **Doubtful Sound** take you first by boat over Lake Manapouri, then by bus over picturesque Wilmot Pass to Deep Cove, where the power plant's ten kilometre (six mile)-long tailrace tunnel reaches the sea. A launch then takes

Cruising through Milford Sound on a clear, still day is an unforgettable experience.

you for a cruise on the mirror-like waters of Doubtful Sound, between towering cliffs and waterfalls. Doubtful Sound is much bigger than Milford Sound and is equally beautiful. A combined trip to the power plant and Doubtful Sound makes an excellent day's outing. Also available are flightseeing tours that take in the beauties of Doubtful and Milford Sounds.

Milford Sound is the highlight of Fiordland. You can reach the sound from Te Anau or Queenstown on foot along the Milford Track (you need to have made a reservation many months ahead), by small plane, by road or by any combination of these. An airfield at the head of the sound caters to several companies flying the Te Anau-Milford-Queenstown triangle. Half a dozen competing coach tours in Te Anau and Queenstown offer full-day excursions to Milford Sound, including a cruise up the sound. The road between Te Anau and Milford Sound is spectacular, with lookouts and short walks along the way. The drive, by coach or car, takes about three hours with fairly short stops.

Highway 94 follows the shore of Lake Te Anau north for 28 kilometres (17 miles) to a motor lodge at **Te Anau Downs**, where Milford Track walkers pick up a launch to the trailhead at the north end of the lake. The road turns inland here and climbs over a ridge into the lovely Eglinton Valley and Fiordland National Park. About 12 kilometres (7.5 miles) into the park, a short walkway leads through

The most popular way to see Milford Sound is by boat.

bird-filled forest to the Mirror Lakes, a series of rush-lined pools that reflect the mountains on a clear day. From here, a once-famous stretch of road created the optical illusion of a disappearing mountain; trees have now grown up and obscured the effect. Cascade Creek, with a hotel and campground, is the next stopping place. The 45-minute loop walk from Cascade Creek to Lake Gunn is superb. The road then crests a divide and leads through the most magnificent scenery of all to the Homer Tunnel, which is 1.2 kilometres (0.75 miles) long. The road emerges into the steep Cleddau Valley. A few kilometres further, a ten-minute walk leads to a narrow chasm, where a waterfall plunges under a natural bridge. After a steep descent, the road ends at the head of Milford Sound.

A cruise up Milford Sound is by far the best way to appreciate the sound's grandeur. Real Journeys operates four different vessels on the sound. The fastest are the *Milford Monarch* and *Milford Haven*, which take passengers 22 kilometres (14 miles) to the ocean at the mouth of the fiord (two hours return). The MV *Friendship* is older and slower, but smaller and more personal. Finally, the *Milford Wanderer* takes an overnight cruise, returning the next day to Milford under full sail. Phone (03)249-8090. The Milford Sound Hotel operates Red Boat Cruises that follow the same itineraries as Real Journeys' cruises. Phone (03)441-1137.

The boats glide close to **Bowen Falls** and **Stirling Falls**, which tumble 150 metres (500 feet) down sheer cliffs into the dark, still waters of the sound. Triangular **Mitre Peak** soars 1,692 metres (5,551 feet) straight out of the sea to touch the clouds. Seals play along the rocky shore. Crested Fiordland penguins and their cousins, little blue penguins, can sometimes be seen. Large bottlenosed dolphins are constant companions of the cruise boats. They ride the invisible pressure wave under the bow, skimming along just below the surface with obvious delight. Bring your camera, binoculars, insect repellent, a warm jacket, and something rainproof, just in case.

Focus

The **Otago Peninsula**, near Dunedin, is home to two rare species of birds: royal albatross and yellow-eyed penguin. The peninsula's **Taiaroa Head** is the site of the world's only mainland breeding colony of royal albatross. Access to the headland is restricted; the only way to visit is on organized tours originating from the Royal Albatross Centre, below the colony. Phone (03)478-0499; or (03) 961 5670; www.southpacifictravellers.co.nz. The scene from the observatory depends on the placement of the nests, the weather and the month that you come. An average of 21 pairs nest each year. Incubation takes place through December, chicks hatch around the end of January, parents leave the chicks in March and return only every couple of days for feeding. The full-grown chicks depart in September. The colony is closed during mating and egg-laying season, from 16 September to 25

November. Tickets are sold for a specific date and time at the Dunedin Visitor Centre and at the Royal Albatross Centre. You can also visit the preserve by sea aboard Monarch Wildlife Cruises' *Monarch*, with the option of returning to Dunedin by coach, taking in the land-based sights en route. Phone (03)477-4276.

Also on the Otago Peninsula, an incredible effort by Howard McGrouther and his family has seen the **yellow-eyed penguin**, the world's rarest penguin, rescued from near extinction. The conservation project started when a small colony of the birds began nesting behind sand dunes on McGrouther's coastal sheep farm. In an effort to encourage their presence, and to protect the breeding pairs from predators, he erected small A-frame nesting boxes around the dunes. He began trapping predators and nursing sick or injured birds, even switching eggs from birds that came to be known as bad parents. The results surprised even his most ardent critics; now over 36 pairs of the rare birds call his farm home. The project is funded by visitor fees. You'll walk through camouflaged trenches to reach blinds that provide close-up viewing. The birds are most active around dusk. Open year-round. Phone (03)478-0286. For general information on the project, write Yellow-eyed Penguin Trust, P.O. Box 5409, Dunedin. The adjacent farm also has a few yellow-eyed penguins and a seal colony; known as Southlight Wildlife, you pick up the key to a gate at the farmhouse and then drive until you reach the end of the road (about four kilometres/2.5 miles). An entrance fee is charged. Phone (03)478-0287.

South of Invercargill, shallow **Awarua Bay**, the eastern arm of Bluff Harbour, is an easily accessible bird-rich habitat. As well as recognizable birds such as black swans and Canada geese, the bay is home to rarer species such as the greenshank, whimbrel, and New Zealand dotterel. Access is from a gravel road off the road between Invercargill and the aluminium smelter.

If you approach **Stewart Island** by ferry from Bluff, you may see royal or wandering albatross, mollymawk, sooty shearwater, petrel, prion and any of New Zealand's three species of penguin. On the island itself, Rakiura National Park holds plentiful bird life, including both Stewart Island brown kiwi and little spotted kiwi, which are sometimes diurnal. Remote **Mason Bay**, on the west coast, is a good place to see kiwis in the wild. You can charter a light plane to get there. Pigeons and kaka are found around Oban, and an hour's launch trip from Halfmoon Bay to bush-covered **Ulva Island** can result in a happy day of bird-watching and picnicking. Kakas and Tui are common on Ulva, and the rare Stewart Island robin can still occasionally be found there.

Visitors to **Fiordland National Park** will have a chance to spot a number of unusual birds. The rarest species in New Zealand, the secretive, nocturnal kakapo (an owl-like, flightless parrot), is believed to exist near Milford and Doubtful Sounds. Any signs of kakapo should be reported at once to the Department of Conservation. Twenty-two of the birds were transferred to Little Barrier Island,

Middle-earth Aotearoa

The landscapes of Middle-earth were forged in the imagination of the author JRR Tolkien, from places he had visited and the mythical lands he had encountered during his studies of ancient texts. His detailed descriptions of these lands enabled the reader to imagine them within their mind in great detail.

Since New Zealand Director Peter Jackson released his epic film trilogy '*The Lord of the Rings*', all these thoughts have become three-dimensional, and New Zealand, where all the filming was undertaken, has been transformed into Middle-earth.

The totally diverse and wild landscapes that make up New Zealand, have been called by many, the major star of these films and the opportunity to explore them is a real journey into that mythical world.

It starts less than two hours drive south of Auckland in the rural town of Matamata. With its rolling hills and green hedgerows it was easily transformed into The Shire—the home of the hobbits. The set here still remains and there is the opportunity to visit that most famous hobbit home of all, Bag End.

Ironically the next stop at Tongariro National Park is the total antithesis of this green and ordered landscape and the volcanic mountains of the central North Island became the dreaded home of the dark lord Sauron. In winter, skiers flock by their thousands to this alpine playground, but once the snow has gone this bleak land of volcanic ash and rocks are the personification of Mordor.

The city of Wellington (or 'Wellywood' as it has become affectionately known) is 'production central' for the films. Within this city of harbour and hills are many locations (all accessible by car or tour operator) as well as all the production facilities that created the outstanding sets and props that have helped bring book alive.

A day tour by car or with Wellington Rover Tours (www.wellingtonrover.co.nz) of the locations in and around Wellington is easily achieved and will allow you to see a diverse range of geography as well as some of the most easily recognisable scenes. Grab a map, make an early start and drive initially to Kent Terrace for a look at the Embassy Theatre—location of the Australasian Premiere of *The Fellowship of the Ring* and *The Two Towers* and the World Premiere of *The Return of the King*. Continue on to Alexandra Road, park your car, and venture into the wooded Mt Victoria town belt for a wander (allow an hour—use the book

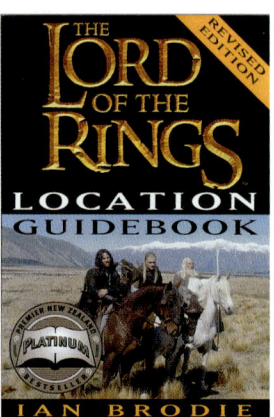

"With the help of this guidebook Tolkien fans, for whom the films were made, can experience their own unique insights into the magic and complexity of Middle-earth, and the adventure we had in order to bring it to life. My only gripe is that this book didn't exist when we started—it would have saved a huge amount of location hunting!"
—Peter Jackson, Film Producer

The mountainous area surrounding Lake Wanaka was used for three locations in The Lord of the Rings. The Matukituki Valley extends to Mt Aspiring.

for reference GPS) around the outskirts of the Shire and the Race to the Ferry.

To maintain your sustenance and savour the tastiest brunch in town, head to the Chocolate Fish Café situated at 497 Karaka Bay Rd (Scorching Bay). Once you're suitably replenished return to Wellington City and drive out on the motorway (SH2) to Kaitoke Regional Park and the location of Rivendell situated 45 minutes north of Wellington.

Down the road (10 kilometres) is Harcourt Park in Upper Hutt, which became the Gardens of Isengard in 2000. Trees, gardens and picnic spots abound.

The nearby Hutt River from Moonshine Bridge to Poet's Park was used for close-up filming of the Fellowship on the River Anduin and is ideal for a short 30 minutes stroll in the area, before returning to Wellington. If you have five minutes spare, pause at Dry Creek Quarry at the bottom of Haywards Hill to see the set for Helm's Deep and Minas Tirith.

The **South Island** boasts some of the most spectacular scenery that can be seen anywhere in the world. It is little wonder then that the majority of the filming was undertaken on this island of precipitous peaks, verdant native bush, azure lakes and brown tussock plains. From Nelson in the north to Te Anau in the south—the island is one huge film set.

The four-hour round trip drive from Christchurch through the spectacular Rangitata Gorge to the location of Edoras is a must. Here in this remote alpine valley the home of King Theoden was created over a ten month period on top of a hill with 360° views and not a house or power pole in sight!

The Southern Lakes Region centred on the adventure capital of Queenstown is the perfect base for a spot of location hunting. Queenstown, eight-hours drive south of Christchurch, is one of New Zealand's most well-known and popular tourist destinations. Nestled in an alpine valley alongside Lake Wakatipu, it's good enough for all the tourist clich's to ring true.

Maori legend tells of a tipua (demon) who seized a beautiful girl. Rescued by her lover while the demon slept, the hero set fire to the area and as the flames licked the demon's body he drew his knees upwards in pain. The enormous amount of fat in his body fanned the fire and a large chasm was dug as he writhed. Rain and snow extinguished the fire, but the demon was destroyed—all except for his heart. Today, the shape of the lake reveals his outline, while his beating heart causes the lake to rise and fall.

The first Europeans to settle in the area were William Gilbert Rees and Paul von Tunzelmann. Cutting their way through the thorny undergrowth for weeks on end they arrived at Lake Wakatipu and decided to go no further. They settled their sheep in the remoteness, not realising their peaceful existence was about to change with William Fox's discovery of gold in the Arrow River. The population exploded and Queenstown became the major service centre supplying the miners.

Tourism is now the 'goldmine' and visitors from around the world descend on Queenstown, also known as The Adventure Capital of New Zealand.

Journey out to Deer Park Heights and you will be amazed at the number of scenes (from all three films including Aragorns Cliff) that unfold, and all within view of the international airport.

The little village of Glenorchy nestles at the northern end of Lake Wakatipu with the jagged peaks of the snow-capped Misty Mountains acting as a spectacular backdrop. Here you can jet-boat up braided rivers to the Wizards Vale of Saruman or amble through the ancient forest of Lothlorien with River Safaris who offer a three-hour trip from Glenorchy (www.riversafaris.co.nz).

Peter Jackson did not let the lack of roads stop a location from being used and some of the most spectacular scenes were filmed, in areas where the cast and crew were flown in by helicopter. You too can visit all of these places using the same means of transport. There are a number of flights available with Heliworks (www.heliworks.co.nz) that can take you across spectacular alpine peaks that became the Misty Mountains, to remote lakes and rivers that doubled as the Great River Anduin or the shores of Nen Hithoel.

Four years after the release of the films, the number of tourists visiting New Zealand to visit Middle-earth locations has only diminished slightly. New Zealanders are proud of their country's accomplishment and recognize the trilogy's influence on decisions to visit. *The Lord of the Rings* and other successful recent films have helped position New Zealand on the world stage as a unique destination inspired by our diverse landscape, unique culture and the creativity of our people.

Figures from Tourism New Zealand for the two years ending in March 2005 suggest that over 21,000 visitors were directly motivated (only or main reason) by *The Lord of the Rings*, and they spent over $100 million dollars on their visits, or more than $26 for each of New ZealandÕs 3.8 million residents.

Although the buildings have gone, Middle-earth remains, as it always has, in the Southern Hemisphere. We call it Middle-earth Aotearoa and all you need is your imagination.

—Ian Brodie 2005

north of Auckland in 1982; the transferred population represents the species' best hope of survival.

The **Te Anau Wildlife Park** has succeeded in breeding the rare takahe, which can be seen here with other native birds. Despite careful protection, takahe numbers have declined from 200 pairs worldwide in 1948 to about 80 pairs today. The culprits seem to be predator stoats and habitat-sharing red deer.

A tourist trip to **Doubtful Sound** offers good bird-watching opportunities: on the cruise across Lake Te Anau you'll probably see falcons; at Wilmot Pass you might spy keas; and during the boat trip on the sound, watch for the Fiordland crested penguin.

The beech forests of **Eglinton Valley**, between Te Anau and Milford Sound, provide some of the best bird-watching in New Zealand. On the walk to Lake Gunn from Cascade Creek, you may well see yellowheads, kaka, robins, yellow-breasted tits and riflemen—and possibly brown creepers, yellow-crowned parakeets and long-tailed cuckoos. At the Homer Tunnel, keas may steal your food or any bright objects. Rock wrens are found around rock falls and scree slopes. On a boat trip to the mouth of **Milford Sound**, you might catch glimpses of the Fiordland crested penguin, if you're lucky.

For an urban stroll in **Dunedin**, first make your way to The Octagon at the heart of the city, where the statue of Robert Burns is surrounded by St. Paul's Anglican Cathedral, the Civic Centre, library and art gallery. From here you can make a nice loop walk taking in a number of city highlights. Follow Stuart Street downhill from the fountain to the severe-looking Law Courts on the third corner and the splendid railway station straight ahead. Continue to the right along Lower High Street to the Otago Settlers Museum, which is worth a stop. Cross the street to Queen's Gardens, with its war memorial and statue of Queen Victoria. Turn left on High Street, noting the elaborate, gothic Cargill Monument, modelled on Walter Scott's monument in Edinburgh. Two century-old hotels stand at the corner of High and Princes Streets. Turn right down Princes Street and walk back towards The Octagon as far as Moray Place. Turn right again and cross Burlington Street to the grounds of First Church, built by Dunedin's founding fathers. Retrace your steps along Moray Place and cross Princes and View Streets. On your left is the city's oldest church. It was originally the Congregational church, now it's Seventh Day Adventist. At the corner of Upper Stuart Street is the Fortune Theatre, once a Methodist church. Turn right past the Anglican cathedral and you are back where you started at The Octagon. Allow one to one and a half hours for the walk. Another nice track west of city centre is the **Flagstaff Walk**, accessible off Whare Flat Road (take Stuart Street from downtown; you'll need a map). Walking to the summit of Flagstaff Hill and back will give you a taste of tussock and subalpine vegetation. The walk takes one hour and provides great views of the city and harbour.

The **Tunnel Beach Walkway** is off Blackhead Road, seven kilometres (four miles) south of the city. Here you will see spectacular sandstone arches, caves and a smugglers' tunnel leading down to the beach. One hour return.

Although **Stewart Island** is famous for its long, difficult tramping trails through uninhabited terrain, several relatively easy walks of various lengths can be taken from Oban. The island's moss-carpeted, fern-filled rainforest, rocky coves and beaches, and scarcity of people make it a delightful place for walkers. The friendly and helpful Department of Conservation office in Oban offers an excellent brochure entitled *Stewart Island Day Walks*, which is all you need for a guide.

In **Fiordland National Park**, a variety of magnificent tracks lie amidst the lakes and mountains. One of them, the 54-kilometre (34-mile) **Milford Track**, is often touted as 'the finest walk in the world'. The four-day tramp crosses the 1,154-metre (3,786-foot) Mackinnon Pass and passes Sutherland Falls, the fourth highest waterfall in the world. You may meet mud or snow before emerging at Milford Sound. Proper preparations are essential. Entry is restricted and permits are required; you'll need

School crossing guard, Murchison Township

to make bookings and obtain instructions far in advance. Hikers must stick to a fixed itinerary, walk in one direction (south to north) and stay in designated huts along the route. Boat transfers are needed to reach both the trailhead and trail end. The permit price includes hut fees and a launch ride on Milford Sound, but you have to carry your own supply of food and a sleeping bag as well as personal gear. A small camping cooker is also recommended—a hot cup of tea does wonders for the morale on a long wet Fiordland day. Get all the details from the Department of Conservation in Te Anau. Phone (03)249-8514. Ultimate Hikes offers guided walks on the Milford Track. Food and bedding are provided—you carry only your personal gear. The trips leave every day from November to late March. Phone (03)441-1138.

The Milford Track is only one of many overnight tracks within Fiordland National Park. The **Kepler Track** is a four-day circuit through the Kepler Mountains, starting and finishing from the southern end of Lake Te Anau. The three-day **Routeburn Track** traverses high alpine areas, linking Highway 94 to the north end of Lake Wakatipu, upon which Queenstown lies. The **Hollyford Track** is a five-day tramp through the spectacular Hollyford Valley between Highway 94 and Martins Bay. For information on these and other tracks in the park, contact the Department of Conservation in Te Anau. Phone (03)249-8514.

Many well-marked, local walks can be found around **Te Anau**. Follow Te Anau Terrace south along the lakefront to its end, turn right on the road to Manapouri and follow the lake to the control gates. Lovely lakeshore walks lead to Dock Bay (one and a half hours return) and Brod Bay (three and a half hours return). At Brod Bay you'll find a well-laid-out nature walk. A fine walk links Lake Te Anau and Lake Manapouri. The gentle track crosses the control gates at the car park, turns left and follows the winding Waiau River downstream through beech forest to Rainbow Reach, where a suspension bridge connects the trail with a side road to the Manapouri-Te Anau Road. This walk takes three to three and a half hours. The trail then goes on for another one and a half hours to a cove on Lake Manapouri's Shallow Bay.

Southland boasts dozens of outstanding rivers full of trout, especially brown trout. Fishing is very good in **Lake Manapouri** but even better in the rivers north and south of Lake Te Anau. To the north, the **Eglinton River** is reached from the Te Anau-Milford Sound road (Highway 94). The best fishing spot on the river is grassy Knobs Flat, 62 kilometres (39 miles) from Te Anau. To the south, the **Waiau River** links Lake Te Anau to Lake Manapouri, winding through ferns and native bush for 19 kilometres (12 miles). Four signposted vehicle tracks lead to the river from the Te Anau-Manapouri Road. Other attractive stretches of river can be reached from the Milford Track (see above).

Lumsden is right in the middle of excellent fishing country. The road from Lumsden to Te Anau (Highway 94) skirts the upper **Oreti River** just west of Mossburn, about 23 kilometres (14 miles) from Lumsden. Its upper reaches are well-stocked with brown trout. A side road runs south from Mossburn to Wrey's Bush, near Nightcaps, which is on Highway 96. The fishing is exceptional along a 30-kilometre (19-mile) stretch of the **Aparima River**, which runs parallel to the road.

The **Mataura River** is a Southland classic; some say it's the finest brown trout stream in New Zealand. The Lumsden-Queenstown road (Highway 6) gives access to the Mataura's fabled upper reaches. (Do not be tempted by Five Rivers, about ten kilometres/six miles from Lumsden. Fish are scarce here.) At Parawa, a right turn on Nokomai Gorge Road leads to easy access on foot to the river. At Athol, the next village, a small road on the right ends near the river. You can also access the river on foot from the main road north of Athol and from the Black Bridge. At Garston, a side road on the left leads to two excellent places. Fairlight Siding offers the last access to the river from the main road.

Gore is within easy reach of a number of fine rivers, and its sports shop has the best, most up-to-date information on the whole region.

Wyndham, 32 kilometres (20 miles) south of Gore (turn off Highway 1 at Edendale), lies close to the rich lower reaches of the **Mataura River**. Nearby, the small **Wyndham** and **Mimihau Rivers** are also highly recommended.

Northeast of Gore is the **Pomahaka River**, whose scenic upper reaches are inhabited by some real lunkers. And in the river's middle reaches, near Tapanui (38 kilometres/24 miles northeast of Gore on Highway 90), resident and sea-run brown trout are plentiful. Near Clinton, 44 kilometres (27 miles) east of Gore on Highway 1, the **Waipahi** and **Waiwera Rivers** are very good. Consult local anglers for the best spots.

In the Dunedin area, at Ranfurly, a power and irrigation scheme on the **Taieri River** (80 kilometres/50 miles northwest of Palmerston on Highway 85) has cleared a willowy swamp and opened up 41 kilometres (25 miles) of river now favoured by anglers. Rumour says the fishing is fabulous, but you should be prepared for wind. Quinnat salmon run in **Otago Harbour** every year between Christmas and Easter. You can catch them anywhere in the channel with a rod and line using bait or lures. Try from one of the wharfs, or you can charter a boat.

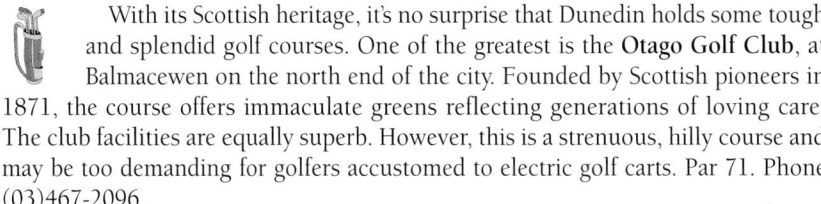   With its Scottish heritage, it's no surprise that Dunedin holds some tough and splendid golf courses. One of the greatest is the **Otago Golf Club**, at Balmacewen on the north end of the city. Founded by Scottish pioneers in 1871, the course offers immaculate greens reflecting generations of loving care. The club facilities are equally superb. However, this is a strenuous, hilly course and may be too demanding for golfers accustomed to electric golf carts. Par 71. Phone (03)467-2096.

St Clair Golf Club, set amongst pine groves above St Clair Beach, is favoured for international tournaments. The 15th hole is rated one of the 18 best in New Zealand, and the greens are excellent. Par 72. Phone (03)487-7076.

Chisholm Park Golf Club, a lovely seaside course in the same vicinity as St Clair, tests all facets of a player's game. Par 71. Phone (03)455-4515.

Invercargill has flat golf courses. Still, the **Invercargill Golf Club**, on Dunns Road in Otatara, is a long, tight and challenging layout. Par 73. Phone (03)213-1133.

Queen's Park, in the centre of Invercargill, has a pleasant, 18-hole public course that is most enjoyable to play. Par 72. Phone (03)218-8371.

Stewart Island boasts the southernmost golf course in the world—the six-hole **Ringa Ringa Golf Course** at Oban. You can rent clubs and a carrier. Phone (03)471-9050.

    The southern end of the South Island holds no vineyards, but Dunedin has a wonderful old brewery to visit. **Speight's Brewery** rolled out its first barrel in 1876, during the gold rush, and has been in business ever since. The small, regional company makes beer in great brewing vessels of burnished copper and open vats of kauri wood. It still makes its own barrels in a cooper's shop on site. The brewery is on Rattray Street at the corner of Dowling Street, three blocks from The Octagon. Guided tours are offered three to four times daily; it is essential to book ahead. Phone (03)477-7697, website <speights.co.nz>.

Practical Information

Tourism New Zealand

Tourism New Zealand operates over 100 information centres throughout the country, as well as seven overseas' offices. Contact the representatives below to receive some good general information on New Zealand. The official Tourism New Zealand site is www.newzealand.com.

Handy Websites

Tourism, Government, and Other Resources

Department of Conservation: www.doc.govt.nz
Destination Lake Taupo: www.laketaupo.com
Explore New Zealand: www.newzealandfocus.com
Meteorological Service of New Zealand: www.met.co.nz
Metservice (weather reports): www.metservice.co.nz
New Zealand Customs Service: www.customs.govt.nz
New Zealand Historic Places Trust: www.historic.org.nz
New Zealand Immigration Service: www.immigration.govt.nz
New Zealand Ministry of Tourism: www.tourism.govt.nz
New Zealand Post: www.nzpost.co.nz
New Zealand Tourism Online: www.tourism.net.nz
Queenstown Visitor & Travel Centre: www.qvc.co.nz
Tourism Auckland: www.auckland.com
Tourism Christchurch: www.christchurchnz.net
Tourism New Zealand: www.newzealand.com
Tourism Rotorua: www.rotorua.com
Tourism South Island: www.visitsouthisland.com
International Association for Medical Assistance to Travelers: www.iamat.org
International Gay and Lesbian Travel Association: www.iglta.org
Society for Accessible Travel and Hospitality: www.sath.org
Wellington Tourism: www.wellingtonnz.com

Airlines

Air New Zealand: www.airnewzealand.com
Air Pacific: www.airpacific.com
Air Paradise: www.airparadise.com.au
Freedom Air: www.freedomair.co.nz
Garuda Indonesia: www.garuda-indonesia.com

Polynesian Airlines: www.polynesianairlines.com
Qantas: www.qantas.com
Soundsair: www.soundsair.co.nz

OTHER TRANSPORTATION AND TOURS

Flying Kiwi Wilderness Expeditions: www.flyingkiwi.com
Foveaux Express: www.foveauxexpress.co.nz
Intercity: www.intercitycoach.co.nz
Interislander: www.interislander.co.nz
Kiwi Experience: www.kiwiexperience.com
Magic Travellers Network: www.magicbus.co.nz
Maui Rentals: www.maui-rentals.com
New Zealand Automobile Association: www.aa.co.nz
Newmans: www.newmanscoach.co.nz
Real Journeys: www.realjourneys.co.nz
Scotties Rentals: www.scotties.co.nz
Tranz Scenic: www.tranzscenic.co.nz

ACCOMMODATION

AA Accommodation Guides: www.nz-accommodation.co.nz
Accommodata: www.accommodate.co.nz
Accorhotels.com.au
Best Western New Zealand: www.bestwestern.co.nz
Budget Backpacker Hostels New Zealand: www.bbh.co.nz
Budget Motel Chain: www.budget-motel.com.au
Choice Hotels: www.choicehotels.com.au
Elderhostel: www.elderhostel.org
Golden Chain: www.goldenchain.co.nz
Heritage and Character Inns of New Zealand: www.heritageinns.co.nz
Holiday Accommodation Parks Association of New Zealand: www.holiday-parks.co.nz
Holiday Inn: www.holiday-inn.com
Jason's New Zealand: www.jasons.co.nz
Mainstay: www.mainstay.co.nz
New Zealand Bed and Breakfast Book: www.bnb.co.nz
Rydges: www.rydges.co.nz
Scenic Circle: www.scenic-circle.co.nz
Top 10 Holiday Parks: www.topparks.co.nz
VIP Backpackers Resorts International New Zealand: www.vip.co.nz
YHA New Zealand: www.yha.co.nz

Other Useful Addresses

Bird-watching
Ornithological Society
 of New Zealand
PO Box 12397, Wellington
www.osnz.org.nz

Royal Forest and Bird Protection
 Society of New Zealand
PO Box 631, Wellington
Phone (04)385-7374
www.forestandbird.org.nz

Walking
Department of Conservation
59 Boulcott Street, Wellington
Phone (04)471-0726
www.doc.govt.nz

Fly-fishing
Fish and Game New Zealand
PO Box 13-141, Wellington
Phone (04)499-4767

Golfing
New Zealand Golf
PO Box 11842, Wellington
Phone (04)385-4330
www.nzga.co.nz

Wine-tasting
Wine Institute of New Zealand
PO Box 90276, Auckland
Phone (09)303-3527
www.nzwine.com

Accommodation

New Zealand is famed for its pristine countryside, fresh air and amiable people. For some people, it may seem to be something of a curious artefact of a bygone tourist world, however this other land down-under harbours some of the cleanest and healthiest locations in our world, which offer respite from the pressure and contamination that beleaguers other continents. In time, New Zealand may rise even higher in status as a safe tourist destination—the quintessential safe haven. The following is a cross-section of lodgings and resorts in major tourist areas and is gathered from personal travel experiences and recommended websites. General information on accommodation is listed on pages 39–43 and 273.

Price Range in New Zealand Dollars
(For a standard double room in high season)
*****   OVER $200
**** $150–200
*** $100–150
** $50–100

Macetown, near Arrowtown, Otago

North Island

AUCKLAND

Stamford Plaza, ***** 22 Lower Albert Street, Auckland. Phone (09)309-8888. Toll free NZ: 0508-658-888. Located in the heart of the central business district and only minutes walk to the sparkling Waitemata harbour, Viaduct Village and Auckland's best shopping, theatre and nightlife.First-class service, timeless décor and excellent inner city location.www.stamford.com.au.

Quay West Suites ***** 8 Albert Street, Auckland. Phone (09)309-6000.
Toll Free (within New Zealand) 0800-782-993.
A boutique hotel, providing guests with 5-star service, facilities and elegantly appointed one and two bedroom suites. This award winning hotel is within easy walking distance of the city's finest bars, restaurants, cafes, Casino, university, art galleries and shopping precincts. www.mirvachotels.com.au.

The Sebel Suites ***** 85-89 Customs Street West, Auckland.
Phone (09)978-4000. Toll Free (within New Zealand) 0800 937 373.
132 spacious studios, marina suites and executive one bedroom suites. Conveniently situated at Viaduct Harbour, Auckland's central business district, the city's finest shopping, restaurants, cafes and recreation activities are all within easy walking distance. www.mirvachotels.com.au

Sky City Hotel ***** Victoria and Federal Streets, Auckland.
Phone (09)912-6000. This full-service hostelry is part of the Sky City complex, which comprises the Sky Tower, a casino and a variety of restaurants. www.skycity.co.nz.

Carlton Hotel ***** Mayoral Drive and Vincent Street, Auckland.
Phone (09)366-3000. Within easy walking distance to shops, galleries, museums and theatres. An underpass links the hotel to the Edge Convention / Entertainment Centre and Aotea Square. www.carlton-hotel.co.nz.

Copthorne Hotel Auckland Harbour City ***** 196–200 Quay Street, Auckland. Phone (09)377-0349. Overlooking the Auckland waterfront, this 12-storey hotel is centrally located and offers fantastic views from every room. www.copthorneharbourcity.co.nz.

Peace & Plenty Inn ***** 6 Flagstaff Terrace, Devonport. Phone (09)445-2925. An elegant bed and breakfast facility, this inn in a magnificently restored Victorian villa (circa 1880), situated in an unbeatable waterfront location in the heart of the historic maritime village of Devonport. www.peaceandplenty.co.nz.

Novotel Auckland **** 8 Customs Street, Auckland. Phone (09)377-8920. Right on Queen Street, just two blocks from the waterfront. Older decor is reflected in the price. www.accorhotels.com.au.

Devonport Villa Inn **** 46 Tainui Road, Devonport. Phone (09)445-8397. This luxurious bed and breakfast occupies an historic Edwardian mansion dating from 1903. Each room is unique, and all have private bathrooms. www.devonportvillainn.co.nz.

Park Towers Hotel *** 3 Scotia Place, Auckland. Phone (09)309-2800. Park Towers is a modern, well-priced accommodation half a block from the top end of busy Queen Street. www.parktowers-hotel.co.nz.

Parnell Inn *** 320 Parnell Road, Parnell. Phone (09)358-0642. This modern, distinctively coloured motel is at the top end of Parnell Road, one of Auckland's restaurant districts. Each of the 16 rooms has a kitchen. www.parnellinn.co.nz.

Oakwood Manor Inn *** 610 Massey Road, Mangere. Phone (09)275-0539. This motel is a five-minute drive from the international airport and offers courtesy airport transfers. Room rates may be a little high, but you can't beat the convenience.

Bavaria Bed and Breakfast Hotel *** 83 Valley Road, Mount Eden. Phone (09)638-9641. German owners have transformed a historic kauri-log house into this comfortable bed and breakfast. Each of the 11 rooms has a private bathroom and rates include a buffet breakfast. www.bavariabandbhotel.co.nz.

Kiwi International Queen Street Hotel ** 411 Queen Street, Auckland. Phone (09)379-6487. Newly renovated, this is the least expensive hotel in downtown Auckland. Rooms are clean, but very basic. www.kiwihotel.co.nz.

THE BAY OF ISLANDS
Paihia Beach Resort ***** Marsden Road, Paihia. Phone (09)402-6140. This luxury resort is rated highest of any New Zealand accommodation by the NZTB's Qualmark Rating System. Each of the casually elegant rooms is furnished with the best money will buy, and each has a large private balcony overlooking the water. www.paihiabeach.co.nz.

Anchorage Motel *** 2 Marsden Road, Paihia. Phone (09)402-7447.
This motel features 14 self-contained units overlooking a small swimming pool. Paihia Beach is directly across the road, and town is just a short and pleasant walk away along the waterfront. www.anchoragemotel.co.nz.
Duke of Marlborough Hotel *** The Strand, Russell. Phone (09)403-7829.
The 'Duke' lies right on the Russell waterfront. Dating from the days when Russell was the national capital, the hotel has held a liquor licence longer than any other hotel in the country. Some of the 27 rooms are small, but many have water views. www.theduke.co.nz.

CARRINGTON
Carrington Resort/Karikari Estate Vineyard and Winery, ***** Maitai Bay Road, Karikari Penisula, RD3 Kaitaia. Phone (09)408-7222.
Carrington provides both lodge and villa accommodations. Lodge accommodations include ten spacious, air conditioned bedrooms with private bathrooms, each containing a California King sized bed and satellite TV. Each lodge room opens onto a wide verandah with views to the ocean or golf course or native bush and vineyard. The lodge connects by verandah walkways to the clubhouse, library, dining room and members lounge. Carrington has a championship, 18-hole golf course, its own vineyard and winery and superb fishing off the Karikari coast. There is a heated swimming pool, tennis courts and skeet shooting with conference facilities.
www.carrington.co.nz; www.karikariestate.co.nz

HAWKES BAY–HASTINGS
Greenhill The Lodge ***** RD4, Hastings. Phone (06)879-9944. Situated a short fifteen minute drive from either Havelock North or Hastings. Close to many outstanding wineries. www.greenhill.co.nz

ROTORUA
Royal Lakeside Novotel Rotorua ***** 9–11 Tutanekai Street.
Phone (07)346-3888. The Novotel is Rotorua's newest and most luxurious hotel. It offers all facilities of a full-service hotel, as well as views across Lake Rotorua. Each evening a *hangi* and concert take place within the grounds. www.accorhotels.com.au.

Prince's Gate Hotel *** 1 Arawa Street. Phone (07)348-1179.
This historic hotel dating to 1897 enjoys a central location across the road from Government Gardens. The 50 elegantly restored rooms feature canopy beds. Chandeliers illuminate the lobby and halls, and the hotel restaurant is excellent. www.princesgate.co.nz.

Mount Philips and Mitre Peak across Milford Sound, Fiordland National Park

Birchwood Spa Motel *** Sala Street and Trigg Avenue. Phone (07)347-1800. Each of the 13 units in this modern complex has a kitchen, dining area, bedroom, and small spa. www.birchwoodspamotel.co.nz.

Cleveland Motel ** 113–119 Lake Road. Phone (07)348-2041.
Extensive grounds and a heated outdoor pool make this 30-room complex a relaxing choice. All rooms have a kitchen.

Eaton Hall Guest House ** 39 Hinemaru Street. Phone (07)347-0366.
Eaton Hall is a large, popular bed and breakfast opposite Government Gardens just two blocks from the information centre. A cooked breakfast is included in the tariff. Only three of the ten rooms have a private bathroom.

TAUPO
Huka Lodge ***** Huka Falls Road, Taupo. Phone (07)378-5791.
The suites are tucked among towering redwoods, firs and pines. The suites are spacious and light, and have outdoor terraces, while the bathrooms feature large, sunken baths. The social focus of Huka is the beautifully appointed Lodge Room with panoramic views over the Waikato River. The lodge, situated in seven hectares of park-like grounds, has a helipad. Located 12 kilometres from Taupo airport; 3.5 hours' drive south from Auckland; 4.5 hours' drive north from Wellington. www.selecthotels.com/hukalodge

Outrigger Terraces Resort ***** 80–100 Napier Taupo Highway (SH5), P.O. Box 741, Taupo. Toll-free New Zealand: 0800-555-075. Tel. (07)378-7080
An historic setting. Most rooms offer views of the thermal valley, or Lake Taupo with the snow-capped volcanic peaks of Tongariro National Park in the distance. Adjacent to the hotel is Taupo Hot Springs Spa, well known for its mineral-rich natural hot springs. It is now a complete day spa with revitalizing, therapeutic treatments. www.outrigger.com

WELLINGTON
Hotel Inter-Continental, Wellington ***** Corner Grey & Featherston Streets Wellington. Phone (04)472-2722.
Just 8 kilometres from the airport. Located opposite Wellington harbour, this stylish contempory hotel is located opposite Wellington's Harbour and at the centre of Wellington's political, commercial and corporate worlds. Located just a short walk to leading attractions, such as Te Papa and Westpac Stadium. www.wellington.intercontinental.com

Hotel Raffaele ***** 360 Oriental Parade, Oriental Bay. Phone (04)384-3450. The Hotel Raffaele stands around the harbour from the city centre, but each room has a private balcony with water views. The restaurant here is highly recommended. www.raffaele.co.nz.

Novotel Capital Wellington **** 133 The Terrace. Phone (04)385-9829. Features an indoor heated pool and 108 modern, stylish rooms. The weekend package deals are exceptional value. www.accorhotels.com.au.

Central City Apartment Hotel **** 130 Victoria Street. Phone (04)385-4166. This hotel is right downtown. All rooms have a separated bedroom, and many feature spacious kitchens. www.centralcityhotels.co.nz.

Shepherds Arms Hotel *** 285 Tinakori Road, Thorndon. Phone (04)472-1320. The Shepherds Arms has been lovingly restored by the descendents of the original owners, who took their first guests in 1870. The 12 rooms reflect a style of days gone by, providing boutique accommodation a ten-minute walk from the city centre. www.shepherds.co.nz.

Abel Tasman Hotel *** 169 Willis Street. Phone (04)385-1304. This is one of Wellington's least expensive downtown hotels. The 76 rooms are comfortable and well-furnished. www.atasman.co.nz.

South Island
CHRISTCHURCH
Outrigger at Clearwater Resort ***** Clearwater Avenue, Harewood, Christchurch. Toll-free New Zealand: 0800-555-075. Phone (3360-1000). Just a 15-minute drive from the beautiful city of Christchurch, this elegant and modern lakeside accommodation offers marvelous lake and fairway views. Clearwater Golf Course is host to the New Zealand PGA championship, a testament to the excellent par 72 course. Natural spring-fed streams meander through the 465-acre resort, teeming with Wild Brown and Rainbow Trout. www.outrigger.com

Fino Casementi All-Suite Hotel ***** 87–89 Kilmore Street. Phone (03)366-8444. Italian-influenced luxury. No expense has been spared in the cavernous lobby and 52 spacious, fully self-contained suites. www.scenic-circle.co.nz.

Chateau on the Park **** 189 Deans Avenue. Phone (03) 348-8999.
This large hotel lies across the road from famous Hagley Park, through which downtown can be reached by a pleasant 15-minute stroll. The hotel comprises 196 rooms, two restaurants, and a swimming pool, all surrounded by landscaped gardens. www.chateau-park.co.nz.

Annabelle Court Motel *** 42 Riccarton Road. Phone (03)341-1189.
This modern motel is particularly good value. Each of the 18 rooms is fully self-contained and well-furnished. Cathedral Square is an easy 20-minute walk away, through Hagley Park. www.annabellecourtmotel.co.nz

Turret House *** 435 Durham Street. Phone (03)365-3900.
Centrally located Turret House is a restored house dating to 1900 and now converted to a bed and breakfast. It offers guests the choice of seven rooms, each with a private bathroom. www.turrethouse.co.nz.

Windsor Hotel *** 52 Armagh Street. Phone (03)366-1503.
The Windsor is a large, rambling old-style hotel that oozes character and atmosphere. Bathroom facilities are shared, but a cooked breakfast is included in the rates. The tram stops right by the front door for easy access to all of Christchurch's downtown sights. www.windsorhotel.co.nz.

L'Hotel-Motel *** 75 Beach Road, Akaroa. Phone (03)304-7559. Akaroa is a beautiful little seaside village on the Banks Peninsula, a one-hour drive from Christchurch. This small, boutique hotel is above a popular café and directly across from the water. Each of the ten units features a kitchen and private balcony.

Airport Lodge Motel ** 105 Roydvale Avenue, Burnside. Phone (03)358-5119.
This is a standard motel set on landscaped gardens three kilometres (two miles) from the airport. Transfers are complimentary. www.airportlodge.co.nz.

DUNEDIN
Southern Cross Hotel ***** Princes and High Streets. Phone (03)477-0752. The Southern Cross is Dunedin's finest hotel. Guests enter through a spacious lobby, with a restaurant, café, casino and English-style pub off to one side. The 142 rooms are large and comfortable, with all the facilities of an international-standard hotel. www.scenic-circle.co.nz.

Cargills Hotel *** 678 George Street. Phone (03)477-7983.
Located across from the Otago Museum and one kilometre (0.6 miles) from The Octagon. www.cargills.co.nz.

Beach at the Esplanade, Kaikoura

MARLBOROUGH OR DOUBTFUL SOUNDS
Motor Yacht Galerna ***** Clifton Bay Road, Christchurch 8008, Marlborough or Doubtful Sounds. Phone (0274)994-299. Elegant motor cruising. You may join Galerna at Picton Wharf for Marlborough Sounds; at Te Anau for Doubtful Sound, or by arrangement for other cruising options. The 27-metre Norwegian-built motor yacht Galerna, constructed from oak and finished in the finest materials, is fully equipped to ply the oceans of the world. Past guests to have enjoyed the vessel's three finely appointed guest suites have included the Danish Royal family and artist Salvador Dali. The signature Prince Henry Suite features a full bathroom and sauna, while the other suites have private ensuite facilities. www.selecthotels.com/galerna.

QUEENSTOWN
Millbrook Resort ***** Malaghans Road, Arrowtown. Private Bag, Queenstown. Phone (03)441-7000. Toll Free NZ: 0800 800 604. New Zealand's premium spa facility. Luxury accommodation that combines a majestic location with outstanding facilities to create a unique and inviting destination. The historic gold-mining town of Arrowtown is a short drive away as are award-winning tourist attractions and the outdoor activities. www.millbrook.co.nz

Outrigger at the Beacon ***** 33 Lake Esplanade, Queenstown.
Toll-free 0800-555-075. Phone (03)441-0890. Situated on pristine Lake Wakatipu-just steps from the busy town centre. Spacious hotel rooms, and two- and three-bedroom apartments offer superb views of the crystal lake and picturesque Southern Alps. www.outrigger.com

The Spire Queenstown ***** 5 Church Lane, Queenstown. Phone. (03)441 0004. Ten spacious guest rooms feature stone-clad fire places, large balconies and iconic contemporary designer furniture. Located only four kilometres from Queenstown Airport. www.selecthotels.com/spire

Sofitel-Queenstown ***** 8 Duke Street, Queenstown. Phone (03)450-0045. 70 opulent and stylish deluxe rooms, ten executive suites, two penthouse suites, and 2 levels of restaurants, bars and boutique retail, fitness centre and spa, in the heart of Queenstown. The signature restaurant 'vie' overlooks a stunning landscaped garden and tranquil waterfall. Located in the heart of the city, just 15 minutes drive from the airport and 20 minutes from Coronet Peak ski fields. www.sofitel.com.

Spinnaker Bay ***** 101 Frankton Road. Phone (03)442-5050.
Each of these spacious one-, two- or three-bedroom lakefront apartments features a private balcony and everything from a fireplace to a facsimile machine. www.spinnaker.co.nz.

Parkroyal Queensland **** Earl Street and Marine Parade. Phone (03)442-7800. The Parkroyal backs onto Queenstown Gardens, a two-minute walk to downtown. Its rooms are large, modern, and well equipped. www.parkroyal.com.au.

Queenstown House **** 69 Hallenstein Street. Phone (03)442-9043.
While accommodation at this bustling resort is dominated by hotels and motels, a number of historic residences have been converted to bed and breakfasts. Queenstown House is by far the most elegant and luxurious. Each room has its own distinctive character, while modern villas and the communal lounge and deck offer unparalleled views. www.queenstownhouse.co.nz.

Lakefront Apartments *** 26 Lake Esplanade. Phone (03)441-8800.
Each of the rooms here is fully self-contained, even including laundry facilities. The private balconies overlook Lake Wakatipu, which lies directly across the road.

Recommended Reading

Most of the books recommended here are published in New Zealand. As New Zealand boasts the highest number of book-buyers per capita in the world, you find good bookshops wherever you go, and the danger is that, by the time you have to fly home, you may find yourself overweight with books. The solution is to buy some padded envelopes at the post office and send the books by surface mail at the cheap international book rate.

General Interest

Basset, Judith; Sinclair, Keith and Stenson, Marcia. *The Story of New Zealand* (Auckland: Reed Publishing, 1992). A large-format paperback written for young adults, with evocative illustrations and fast-moving, readable text. A delightful way to absorb New Zealand's rough, tough history.

Brodie, Ian. *The Lord of the Rings: Location Guide* (Auckland: HarperCollins, 2004). This revised edition of the definitive guidebook showcases the principal movie-set locations around New Zealand as seen in all three films directed and produced by Peter Jackson.

Duff, Alan. *Once Were Warriors* (Auckland: Tandem Press, 1990). Controversial but popular and essentially honest novel about the Maori as New Zealand's underclass. Originally published in 1990, the 1995 edition has pictures from the award-winning movie.

Friar, Denis and Jillian Friar. *Friar's Guide to New Zealand Gardens Open to Visit* (Auckland: Hodder Moa Beckett, 2001). A guide to over 250 private and public gardens. Includes colour photos, opening times and facilities at each.

Houghton, Bruce and others. *Eruption!* (Auckland: Viking Press, 1996). Catalogues the 1995 eruption of Mt. Ruapehu, with the text written by scientists from the Institute of Geological and Nuclear Sciences at Taupo.

Hulme, Keri. *The Bone People* (London: Macmillian Publishers, 1992). The 1985 winner of Britain's prestigious Booker Prize, this startling novel weaves magic around a cruel story and calls Aotearoa 'this shining land'. Mystical. Maori. Inspirational.

Hempstead, Andrew and Jane King. *Moon Handbooks: New Zealand* (Emeryville, California: Avalon Travel Publishing, 2002). The most complete and reliable general guidebook available. Well organized, easy to use and good on accommodation and restaurants. It is updated every three years.

King, Michael. *Wrestling with the Angel: A Life of Janet Frame* (Auckland: Penguin Books, 2001). Biography of one of New Zealand's most celebrated yet private authors.

McGill, David. *Complete Kiwi Slang Dictionary* (Auckland: Reed Publishing, 1998). Historical and contemporary slang designed to amuse and inform.

New Zealand Automobile Association. *AA New Zealand Road Atlas: Glove Box Edition* (Auckland: Hodder Moa Beckett, 2005). Available at AA offices and most bookstores, this atlas, includes information centres, unsealed roads, distance charts, and local road rules.

Reed, A. W. *A Dictionary of Maori Place Names* (Wellington: Reed Publishing, 1997). This pocketbook is sometimes hard to find, but if you see it, pick it up. Maori place names almost always commemorate an event, a slice of life or a piece of mythology, and you can learn a lot from them about life in New Zealand before the arrival of the Europeans.

Rice, Geoffrey, ed. *The Oxford History of New Zealand* (Auckland: Oxford University Press, 1993). Twenty-two essays by New Zealand's best historians.

Bird-watching

Ell, Gordon. *Seashore Birds of New Zealand* (Auckland: Bush Press, 1985). This book contains lots of descriptive information, along with photographs by Geoff Moon, New Zealand's best bird photographer.

Falla, R. A., and others. *Collins Field Guide to Birds of New Zealand* (Auckland: HarperCollins, 1993). A big, comprehensive work and an excellent reference.

Kelly, Chloe Talbot. *Collins Handguide to Birds of New Zealand* (Auckland: Collins, 1991). A well-illustrated field guide, light and handy enough to keep in your pocket.

Moon, Geoff. *Reed Field Guide to New Zealand Birds* (Auckland: Reed Publishing, 1998). Detailed descriptions of most New Zealand birds, their habitat and breeding habits, all accompanied by 330 colour photographs makes this book an indispensable tool for keen birders.

Walking

Barnett, Shaun and Rob Brown. *Classic Tramping in New Zealand* (Nelson: Craig Potton Publishing, 2000). In a wonderfully readable fashion, this book covers 12 of the best New Zealand walks, accompanied by stunning colour photography. Its companion volume, Classic Walks in New Zealand, and all of Potton's work is of the highest quality. Check out other titles at the website <www.craigpotton.co.nz>.

Burton, Robbie and M. Atkinson. *A Tramper's Guide to New Zealand's National Parks* (Auckland: Reed Books, 1999). Very useful, including all types of walks and giving precise descriptions, grades and times required for each walk. The latest edition features a foreword by Sir Edmund Hillary.

DuFresne, Jim. *Tramping in New Zealand* (Hawthorn, Victoria: Lonely Planet, 2002). The latest edition of this popular guide details 48 hikes while also offering tips on getting the best out of the tracks.

Fly-fishing

Millichamp, Ross. *Salmon Fever: A Guide to Salmon Fishing in New Zealand* (Auckland: Shoal Bay Press, 1997). Everything you'd ever want to know about salmon fishing; includes stunning colour photography.

Mossman, Sam. *How to Catch New Zealand's Favourite Fish* (Auckland: Reed Publishing, 1999). Solid tips on catching 15 common species, with detailed regional information including local tackle stores.

A magazine worth looking for is *New Zealand Fishing News*, a monthly with a special section on fly-fishing.

Golfing

Gould, Rex. *50 Top New Zealand Golf Courses* (Auckland: Reed Publishing, 1997). This book divides the country into regions, listing the best courses, including information such as course statistics, facilities, green fees and surrounding accommodations.

Schipper, Niels. Fairway to Heaven (Nelson: Craig Potton Publishing, 2005). A beautiful hardcover book that celebrates the beauty of New Zealand's golf courses.

Wine-tasting

Cooper, Michael. *The Wines and Vineyards of New Zealand* (Auckland: Hodder Moa Beckett, 1998). This big hardback contains history, a section on viticulture, and a survey of every region, with visits to the major vineyards. Exquisite photography by Robin Morrison. Also look for *Michael Cooper's Buyer's Guide to New Zealand Wines* (Hodder Moa Beckett, 2001). Both books are regularly revised classics.

Saunders, Peter. *A Guide to New Zealand Wine* (Auckland: Wine Castle Ltd., 1998). Written by one of New Zealand's foremost wine experts, this annual guide lists every winery and their latest wines in alphabetical order, as well as giving detailed descriptions of every aspect of the industry.

Williams, Vic. *Penguin Good New Zealand Wine Guide* (Auckland: Penguin Books, 2001). Lists over 1,200 wines by variety, with the best of each highlighted by a more detailed description.

Common Maori Words

Many place names in New Zealand are made up of Maori words that either describe the place or record something that happened there. The Maori language is spelled with eight simple consonants (h, k, m, n, p, r, t, w), two consonant combinations (wh—pronounced 'f'—and ng) and five vowels (a, e, i, o, u). As in all Polynesian languages (Maori and Hawaiian being amongst the most widely known), each vowel is pronounced separately, and every word ends with a vowel.

ahi	fire
ahu	mound or heap
aka	South Island form of whanga (bay, harbour)
ana	cave
ao	cloud
ara	path or road
aroha	love
ata	shadow
atua	god or demon
awa	river, valley
haere	come or go
haka	war dance
hangi	earth oven
hau	wind, famous
hoa	friend
hoe	paddle
hou	new
hua	fruit, egg
huka	foam or spray, snow or frost
ika	fish
iti	small
iwi	tribe
kahui	assemblage, gathering, flock
kai	eat, food
kainga	unfortified village
kapa	row, line, rank
ka pai	thank you

karanga	a welcome given visitors on arrival at a Maori village
kau	swim
kia ora	hello
kino	bad
kohu	mist, fog
koura	crayfish
kumara	sweet potato
kuri	dog
ma	white or clear
ma	(short for manga) stream, brook
mangu	black
manu	bird
marae	the sacred ground in front of a Maori meeting hall
mata	headland (amongst other meanings)
mate	dead
maunga	mountain
mere	type of weapon made of greenstone
moana	sea or lake
motu	island or isolated
muri	end
mutu	finished, end
namu	sandfly
nga	the (plural)
nui	big, plenty of
o	of, the place of
one	sand, mud or beach
pa	fortified village
pae	ridge or resting place
pai	good
pakeha	white person
papa	broad, flat, or ground with greenery
po	night
poi	flax ball (used by women in their dances)
puke	hill
puna	spring or water
puni	encampment

rangi	sky
rau	hundred, many
riki	small or few
rima	five
roa	long
roto	lake
rua	two
ruru	owl
tahi	one, single
tai	coast, sea, or tide
taiaha	type of weapon
tapu	sacred, forbidden
te	the (singular)
tea	white or clear
tiki	carved figurine
toa	warrior, brave
toro	explore, discover
uta	inland
wai	water
waiata-a-ringa	tribal song
waka	canoe
wera	hot or burnt
whaka	to make or cause
whanga	bay, harbour
whare	house
whata	raised food-storage platform
whenua	land or country
whero	red

Index

A
Abel Tasman National Park, 166, 171, 173–4, 175, 178
accommodation, 38–42, 192, 194, 227, 273–86
  bookings, 39
agricultural and pastoral society shows, 251
agriculture, 94, 171, 173, 191, 223,
Agrodome, 111
Ahipara village, 78
Aigantighe Art Museum, 215
air safaris, *see* flight–seeing
aircraft, historic, 60, 236
airlines and air services (*see also* flight–seeing), 272–3
  Air New Zealand, 74, 95, 105, 121, 138, 141, 151, 167, 171, 183, 203, 226, 230, 244, 250
  domestic carriers, other, 34, 151, 167, 235, 252, 258
  international, 29
airports 54, 74, 138, 151, 203, 230, 235, 236
Akaroa, 203, 212, 217–8
Albatross Centre, Royal, 262–3
Alexander Library (Wanganui), 149
Alexandra, 48
aluminium smelter, 252, 259
America's Cup, 57, 58, 59
Anaura Bay, 126, 131
Antarctic, 59, 203, 206, 210, 212
Antipodes Islands, 254
Aoraki Mount Cook, 199, 223, 226, 227
Aoraki Mount Cook National Park, 223, 237
Aparima River, 270
Aranui Cave, 99
Arrowtown, 231

art deco architecture, 128, 134
art galleries, 11, 59, 139, 145, 172, 209, 215, 246, 251
Arthur's Pass, 186, 191, 196
Arthur's Pass National Park, 191–2, 197
Arthur's Point, 231
arts and crafts, 11, 14, 104, 109, 173, 194
Arts Centre of Christchurch, 208, 217
Ashton–Warner, Sylvia (writer), 11
Auckland, 47, 48, 50, 51, 54–5, 58–63, 66
  accommodation, 274, 276–7, 279
  airport, 54
  area dialing code, 34
  town hall, 247
Auckland Art Gallery, 59
Auckland Domain, 59
Auckland Museum, 59
Auckland Observatory, 61
Auckland Zoo, 60, 63
Aupouri Peninsula, 74
Automobile Association, 37, 38, 39, 55, 273
Avon River, 206
Awarua Bay, 263

B
backpackers, 42
Banks Peninsula, 211–2
Baxter, James K (poet), 146
Bay of Islands, 47, 74, 76–8, 79
  accommodation, 279
  airport, 74
Bay of Plenty, 90, 94–5
bed and breakfast, 40–1
bicycles, 55, 206, 236
  cycling track, 210
bird–watching, 14, 15, 62–3, 100, 215, 234
birds, 18, 274, 288
  flightless (*see also* kiwis), 18, 130, 175
  North Island, 79, 100–1, 114–5, 130–1, 139, 147, 161–2,

rare birds, protection of, 148–9, 263, 267
seabirds, 85, 246–7, 262, 263
South Island, 175, 178, 197–8, 215, 237, 254, 263, 267
Blackball, 187
Blenheim, 171, 179
Bluff, 35, 251–2
Bluff Hill, 251
Bluff Hill Lookout, 128
boats (*see also* excursions)
charters, 102, 134, 218, 236, 239, 256
books and bookshops, 11, 287
botanic gardens, 139, 155, 162, 210, 246
Bounty Islands, 254
Bowen Falls, 262
breweries, 202, 271
Bridal Veil Falls, 97
bridges, natural, 100, 101, 102
Broadgreen (colonial house),173
Brooklands Park, 139
Brown, Charles Armitage, 147
Buller River, 186, 199
bungy jumping, 232, 234
Buried Village, 111
bus and coach services
buses, 35–6, 55, 91, 105, 114, 138, 141, 151, 167, 171, 183, 206, 226, 230, 235, 244, 250, 252, 258, 273
coaches, 74, 121, 167, 244
tours, 131, 136, 232, 260
Busby, James (winemaker), 28, 69
Bushy Park Homestead, 147

C

cable cars, 111, 155, 211, 230
Cambridge, 96
camper rental, 37
Campbell Island, 254
camping grounds, 42

Campion, Jane (film director),11
Cannibal Bay, 250
Cannon Point Walkway, 163
canoes (*see also* kayaking), 236
Canterbury Museum, 206, 208, 217
Canterbury Pilgrims, 206, 207, 211
Canterbury Plains, 166, 203
Canterbury Provincial Government Buildings, 210
Canterbury University, 208
Cape Egmont, 141
Cape Foulwind, 187
Cape Kidnappers, 128, 131, 134
Cape Reinga, 74, 78, 82–3
car rental, 36–7, 54, 154, 183
caravans, *see* camper rental
Carrington resort, 279
Carter Observatory, 158
cars, antique and vintage, 160, 231
Cascade Creek, 262
Castlepoint, 162
Cathedral Square, 206, 207, 209
Catlins, The, 247, 250
caves, 51, 187, 259
limestone, 75, 90, 99, 214
museum of, 98
Centennial Gardens, 128
Central Otago, 239
Centre of Contemporary Art, 209
Channell, Ian Brackenbury (sociologist), 209
Charming Creek Walkway, 198
Chatham Islands, 148, 254
Christ College, 209
Christchurch, 31, 48, 166, 203, 206–11, 215, 217
accommodation, 282–4
airport, 203
art gallery, 209
botanic gardens, 210

founding of, 207
gondola, 211
town hall, 210
Christchurch Cathedral, 206, 207, 208
Clapham Clocks (museum), 75
climate 18, 31–2, 86
clothing, 20–1, 32
Clutha River, 219
coaches, *see* bus and coach services
Coal Town, 186
Coast to Coast Walkway, 63
Cobblestones Museum, 159
Colonial Knob trail, 163
Conservation, Department of, *see* Department of Conservation
Cook, Captain James, 56, 84, 90, 121, 122–3, 134, 150
  journals, 182, quoted, 128
  landing places, 121, 126, 131, 170, 178
  statue, 210
Cook Landing Site National Historic Reserve, 126
Cook Strait, 166
Cook's Cove, 131
Coromandel, 91
Coromandel Range, 101
Coromandel Forest Park, 101
Coromandel Peninsula, 54, 91, 191
Cousteau, J (Jacques) Y, 88
Craft Habitat (art cooperative), 173
Craters of the Moon, 112
credit cards, 31, 34
Cromwell, 236–7
Cromwell Borough Museum, 237
cruise lines, 29, 170
cruises and excursions
  boats, 77, 146, 174, 212, 259–60, 262, 263
  paddleboats, 194
  paddlesteamer, 147
  steamship, 231

Curio Bay, 250
customs (service), 30, 54
cycling, 210

D

Dairyland, 141
Department of Conservation (DOC), 14, 38, 42, 55, 62
  field centres, 14, 101, 218–9, 256
Devonport (suburb), 61
dive sites, 86–9
diving (*see also* scuba diving), 86
Dobson, Arthur Dudley (surveyor and explorer), 191
dolphins, 213, 250, 262
  swimming with, 78, 95, 214
Doubtful Sound, 259–60, 267
drinks, 44
  terms, 44, 46
driving, 37–8
Driving Creek railway, 91
Duff, Alan (writer), 11
Dunedin, 31, 166, 190, 243–4, 246–7, 267–8
  accommodation, 284
  public art gallery, 246
  railway station, 246
Durie Hill, 146

E

earthquakes, 121, 128, 130, 137, 150
East Cape, 50, 121, 123–6, 130
Edwin Fox (sailing ship), 170
Eglinton River, 269
Eglinton Valley, 267
Egmont National Park, 138, 140–1, 147
electricity, 32
Eltham, 140
e–mail, 34
emergencies, 31

Enderby Island, 254
entry permits, 30
events, annual 47–8
European settlement, 51, 74, 90, 141, 182
Ewelme Cottage, 61
excursions, *see* cruises and excursions

F

Far North Regional Museum, 78
Farewell Spit, 174, 175
farmstays, 41
fax services, 34
ferry services, 35, 55, 62, 151, 167, 170, 206, 252
Ferrymead Historic Park, 211
festivals, *see* events, annual
films, 11, 230
Fiordland, 243, 258–60, 262
Fiordland National Park, 243, 258, 263, 267, 269
fireworks, 210
First Church (Dunedin), 246, 247
Firth of Thames, 100
fish, introduction of, 21
fishing (*see also* fly–fishing), 15
  big–game, 83, 95, 102
  deep–sea, 90
  licences, 23, 134
  North Island, 78, 118–9, 134–5, 149, 163–4
  season, 23
  South Island, 179, 199, 202, 219, 238–9, 269–70
Flagstaff Walk, 267
flight–seeing, 34, 112, 171, 195, 227, 234–5, 236, 260, 266
flora and fauna, 33, 124, 258
  reserve, 85
fly–fishing, 21, 178, 274, 289
  imported flies, restrictions on, 23, 30

food, 43–4, 208
  seafood, 251
  terms, 44, 46
foreign currencies, exchange, 31, 54
Founders Memorial Theatre, 96
Fox Glacier, 194, 195, 199
Frame, Janet (writer), 11
France, 69, 212
Frankton Arm Walkway, 238
Franz Josef Glacier, 194, 195, 199
Fyffe House, 214

G

gardens (*see also* botanic gardens), 59, 61, 96, 97, 105, 158, 161, 231
geography, 10
Gisborne, 121, 126, 135, 179
glaciers, 182, 194–5, 227
Glendhu Bay, 236
Glenorchy, 266
glow–worms, 51, 75, 78, 98–9, 100
Goat Island Bay, 75
Godley, John Robert (religious settler), 207
Goldfields Mining Centre, 237
gold mining, 91, 190–1, 194
gold rushes, 183, 190–1, 192, 223, 227, 232, 243
golf, 234, 274, 289–90
  clubs, 26
    North Island, 63, 66, 83, 102, 119, 135, 149–50, 164
    South Island, 179, 202, 219, 221, 239, 271
  courses, 15, 23
    North Island, 66, 83, 119–20, 135, 164
    South Island, 210, 219, 221, 239, 243, 271
  links, 23, 102, 135, 149, 164, 179, 202
Gore, 270

Government Centre, 158
Government Gardens, 105
Govett–Brewster Art Gallery, 139
Great Barrier Island, 62
greenstone, 182, 192, 194
Grey River, 202
Greymouth, 183, 187, 191
Greytown, 159
grottoes, *see* caves
gum diggers, 78, 93

H

Haast, Julius von, *see* von Haast, Julius
Haast Pass, 195, 198
Hackett, A J (bungy jumper), 232, 234
Hagley Park, 210
Hamilton, 47, 48, 90, 95–6
Hamilton Gardens, 96
handicrafts, 11
hang gliding, 235
hangi (Maori style–feast), 44, 111
Hanmer Springs, 203, 214, 218
Harihari, 202
Hastings, 121, 130
Hauraki Gulf Maritime Park, 62
Hautapu River, 164
Havelock, 171
Havelock North, 121, 130
Hawera, 140–1
Hawkes Bay, 28, 121, 135, 179
Hawkes Bay Aquarium, 130
Hawkes Bay Museum, 128
health, 31
Heaphy Track, 174
Hell's Gate, 109
Henderson Valley, 28, 66
Hibiscus Coast, 75
Hicks Bay, 124
hiking, see walking

Hillary, Sir Edmund, 57, 226
history, 68–70, 212
 events in, 56–7
Hobson, Captain William, 69
Hokitika, 48, 191, 192, 194
Hokitika Craft Gallery, 194
Hokitika River, 202
Hole in the Rock, 77
Hole in the Wall, 131
holidays, 29–30, 47
Hollyford Track, 269
Honeycomb Caves, 187
Hooker Glacier, 238
Hooker Valley, 237–8
Horonuku Te Heuheu Tukino (Maori chief), 113
horse riding, 112
hostels, 42
hot springs, 51, 97, 104, 105, 106, 112, 113, 118, 127, 203, 218
 beaches, 94, 97
 spa, 75, 105
Hot Water Beach, 94, 97
hotels, 39, 120, 227, 262,
Huapai village, 67
Huka Falls, 112
Hulme, Keri (writer), 11
Hutt Valley, 158–9
hydroelectric power, 236

I

immigration, 54
imports, restricted goods, 30
International Antarctic Centre, 210–1
Internet, 34
Invercargill, 31, 243, 250–2
Isel Park, 172
Ihimaera, Witi (writer), 11

J

Jackson, Peter (film director), 264, 266
jade, *see* greenstone
jet boating, 146, 234, 236, 266
jewellery, 192, 194
jogging, 210

K

Kahahi Falls, 109
Kahurangi National Park, 174, 175
Kaikoura, 48, 203, 213–4
Kaikoura Peninsula, 218
Kaitaia, 78, 279
Kaiti Hill Lookout, 126
Kapiti Coast, 160
Kapiti Island, 149, 162
Karamea, 187
kauri trees, 74, 92–3
   forests, 78, 79, 91
   gum, 78, 93
Kauri Museum, 79
Kawhia Harbour, 97
Kawiti Caves, 75
kayaking, 78, 171, 174, 198
Kea Point, 237
Kelly Tarlton's (theme park), 59
Kepler Track, 269
Kermadec Islands, 254
King Movement, Maori, 90, 96
Kiwi and Birdlife Park, 231
kiwis, 101, 184–5, 231, 263
Kopuaranga River, 164
Kororareka, *see* Russell
Kowhai Children's Playpark, 149
Kumeu village, 67
Kumeu River region, 28
Kupe (Polynesian explorer), 56, 122, 150

L

Lady Norwood Rose Garden, 158
Laird, Jack (potter), 173
Lake Brunner, 202
lake cruises, 111, 231
Lake Disappear, 97
Lake Ellesmere, 212, 215
Lake Grasmere, 219
Lake Hawea, 239
Lake Manapouri 258, 259, 269
Lake Matheson, 199
Lake Moeraki, 202
Lake Paringa, 202
Lake Pearson, 219
Lake Pukaki, 226, 237
Lake Rotoiti, 114, 174
Lake Rotopounamu, 115
Lake Rotorangi, 149
Lake Rotoroa, 174
Lake Ruapani, 134
Lake Tarawera, 111
Lake Taupo, 21, 23,104, 112–3, 115, 118–9
Lake Te Anau, 258
Lake Tekapo, 227
Lake Wahapo, 202
Lake Waikare, 101
Lake Waikareiti, 130, 131, 134
Lake Waikaremoana, 121, 127, 130, 134
Lake Wakatipu, 237, 238
Lake Wanaka, 238–9
Lakes District Museum, 231
lamb (meat), 43, 250
Land Wars, 50, 51, 56, 70, 124, 141
landing permits, 62, 85, 162
Langlois, Captain Jean, 56, 212
Langlois–Eteveneaux cottage, 212
Larnach Castle, 247
licences
   driving, 38
   fishing, 23

lighthouses, 78, 82, 125, 127, 141, 172, 174, 187, 250
Lincoln College, 221
Little Barrier Island, 62–3, 149, 267
lodges, 41
Lord of the Rings (film trilogy), locations, 264–6
Lower Buller Gorge, 186
Lumsden, 270
Lyttelton, 211

M

Mckenzie, Alister (golf course designer), 63
Mackenzie Basin, 223
Mahy, Margaret (writer), 11
mail service, 33
Manapouri Lake, 258
Manapouri Underground Power Station, 259
Manawatu Gorge, 161
Manawatu River, 164
Mangawhai Heads, 82
Mansfield, Katherine (writer), 11, 127, 155, 163
 quoted, 170
Manukau Harbour, 51, 62
Maori (*see also* Land Wars), 18, 109, 111, 138, 175, 182, 183, 213
 arrival of, 50, 122
 arts and crafts, 11, 14, 104, 109, 251
 cuisine, 44
 Europeans, relations with, 68, 70, 90, 150
 hunting rights, 258
 language, 144–5, 291–3
 legends, 75, 258, 265–6
 meeting houses, 76, 125, 126, 127, 251
 motto, 181
 population, 142
 queen, 96
 war canoes, 76, 96
 wood carving, 108–9

Maori Arts and Crafts Institute, 109
Maori Leap Cave 214
Maoritanga (Maori way of life), 142–5
maps
 availability, 38
marine life, 86, 213
marine studies centre, 247
Marineland (Napier), 128
maritime parks, 170
markets, 59
Marlborough, 179–80
Marlborough Sounds, 170–1, 175
Marlborough Sounds Maritime Park, 170
Marokopa Falls, 100
Marsh, Ngaio (writer), 11
Martinborough, 159, 165
Mason Bay, 263
Massey University, 161
Masterton 47, 159, 221
Mataatua, 127
Matakohe Kauri Museum, 93
Matamata, 264
Matata, 101
Mataura River, 270
mead (drink), 222
Methven, 219
Milford Sound, 243, 258, 260, 262
Milford Track, 243, 268, 269
Mimihau River, 270
mineral springs, 90, 97, 105
mining, *see* gold mining
Mirror Lakes, 262
Mitre Peak, 262
model yachts, 210
Moeraki, 247
Moeraki Boulders Scenic Reserve, 247
money, 31
Morere, 127
Morrieson, Ronald Hugh (novelist), 140

motels, 40
motor camps, 42
Motueka, 173
Mount Aspiring, 235
Mount Aspiring National Park, 223, 235
Mount Bruce, 162
Mount Bruce National Wildlife Centre, 159, 162
Mount Cook, *see* Aoraki Mount Cook
Mount Dampier, 226
Mount Eden, 60
Mount Egmont, *see* Mount Taranaki/Egmont
Mount Maunganui, 95, 101, 102
Mount Ngauruhoe, 104, 114
Mount Ngongotaha, 111
Mount Ruapehu, 104, 113
Mount Taranaki/Egmont, 137–8, 140
Mount Tarawera, 104, 109, 112
Mount Tasman, 223
Mount Tongariro, 104, 114
Mount Victoria, 154
mountaineering, 227
Mr Explorer Douglas (Pascoe), 184
Murchison, 186
Murihiku Marae (community training centre), 251
Muriwai Beach, 63
Museum of New Zealand (Te Papa Tongarewa), 154
Museum of Wellington, City & Sea, 158
museums, 75, 93, 98, 126, 128, 206, 208, 212, 246
  art, 59, 96, 105
  aviation, 236
  local history, 77, 105, 141, 170, 186, 194, 231, 237, 251
  maritime, 76, 126
  mining, 91, 192, 237
  natural history, 59, 251
  regional, 78
  sports, 161, 114
  transport, 60, 146, 159, 160, 231
music, 11
Muttonbird Islands, 258

N

Napier 47, 121, 128, 130
National Maritime Museum, 58–9
national parks (*see also under* names of parks), 51, 113, 173
Nelson, 167, 171–3, 175, 182
Nelson Lakes National Park, 166, 174–5, 179
New Plymouth, 48, 138–40, 147
New Zealand
  climate 18, 31–2, 86
  geography, 10
  population, 50, 54, 166, 191
New Zealand Fighter Pilots Museum, 236
New Zealand Maori Arts and Crafts Institute, 109
New Zealand Marine Studies Centre, 247
New Zealand Rugby Institute, 161
New Zealand Rugby Museum, 161
Ngaruawahia, 90, 96
Ngati Whatua (Maori tribe), 51
Ninety–Mile Beach 74, 78, 83
Nocturnal Park, 78, 79
North Canterbury, 214, 218
North Otago, 247
North Island, 10, 31, 50–165
Northland, 74–5
Northern Walkway, 163
Nugget Point, 250

O

Oamaru, 247
Oban, 243, 252, 256
observatories, 61, 158
Ohaki Maori Village, 102
Ohakune, 114
Ohinemutu Village, 111
Okarito Lagoon, 198
Olveston (historic mansion), 246
One Tree Hill, 60
Opotiki, 124
Orchid Garden, 105
Oreti River, 270
Otago Goldfields Park, 231
Otago Harbour, 270
Otago Museum, 246
Otago Peninsula, 246–7, 262–3
Otago Province, 166, 190
Otago Settlers Museum, 246, 267
Otari Native Botanical Garden, 162
Otorohanga, 101

P

Paekakariki, 160
Paihia, 76
Palmerston North, 161
Paparoa Mountains, 197
Paparoa National Park, 182, 187, 197, 198–9
paraflying, 235
Paraparaumu, 160
Paritutu Centennial Park, 140
parks (see also under names of parks), 59
Parliament House, 158
Parliamentary Library, 158
Parnell (suburb), 61
Parnell Rose Gardens, 61
Pascoe, John (writer), *Mr Explorer Douglas*, quoted, 184
Peel Forest Park, 218
permits (see also entry permits, landing permits), 198, 269
Picton, 170
Picton Museum, 170
Pipiriki, 146
Plane Table Lookout, 194
planetarium, 59, 61
Poho–o–Rawiri Meeting House, 126
Pollock, J S, 85
Polynesian Spa, 105–6
Pomahaka River, 270
Ponsonby (suburb), 61
Poor Knights Islands, 84–9
population, 50, 54, 166, 191
Porpoise Bay, 250
postal service, 33
pottery, 173
Pouakai Zoo Park, 139
power stations
  geo–thermal, 113
  underground, 258
Pukaha Mount Bruce, 162
Pukeiti, 139
Pukekura Park, 139
Punakaiki, 187
Purakaunui Falls, 250
Puzzling World, 236

Q

Quail Island, 211–2
Queen Charlotte Sound, 170
Queen Charlotte Track, 178
Queen Street, 58
Queen's Gardens, 172
Queen's Park, 145
Queenstown, 31, 48, 223, 227–32, 234–5, 265
  accommodation, 284–6
  airport, 230
  gardens, 231

Queenstown Hill, 238
Queenstown Motor Museum, 231

R
racehorses, 90
rafting, 234
   black–water, 99
   underworld, 186
   white–water, 186, 234
Raglan, 97
Raglan Harbour, 101
Rahui Maori village, 106
rail services, 34, 55, 95, 114, 121, 151, 167, 183, 206, 273
railways, 91, 94, 187, 246
Rainbow Springs Nature Park, 111
Rakaia Gorge, 218
Rakaia River, 215, 219
Rakiura Island, see Stewart Island
Rakiura National Park, 252
Rangaunu Harbour, 79
Rangitata Gorge, 264
Rangitikei River, 164
Rangitoto Island, 62
Read, Gabriel (gold miner), 190
Reefton, 199
Rees, William Gilbert (settler), 266
regattas, 96
rentals, see bicycles, camper rental, car rental
restaurants, 111, 194, 211, 222, 231
Ring, Charlie (gold miner), 190
Roman Catholic Cathedral of the Blessed Sacrament, 210, 247
Ross, 194
Rotoehu State Forest, 114–5
Rotorua 48, 104–6, 109, 111–2
   accommodation, 280
Rotorua Museum of Art and History, 105
Routeburn Track, 269

Ruakituri River, 134
Ruamahanga River, 164
Ruatahuna village, 127
Ruatoria, 125
Ruby Bay, 173, 182
rugby, 161
Russell, 50, 74, 77
Rutherford, Ernest (physicist), 208

S
sailing, 175
Sarjeant Art Gallery, 145, 149
Schuster, Daniel (winemaker), 221, 222
Science Alive! (interactive exhibition), 211
scuba diving, 78
seafood, 43
sea lions, 246, 250
seals, 213, 214, 246, 250, 262
Seddon, Richard John (former prime minister), 163
Shantytown, 187, 191
Shaw, George Bernard (playwright), 210
shearers, 159, 221
shearing, 231, 251
sheep, 14, 111, 220–1
sheep dogs, 231, 251
Ship Cove, 170, 172, 178
Shipwreck Museum, 76
shipwrecks, 183, 211
shopping, 46, 154
skiing, 175, 227, 235
   heli–skiing, 235
   museum, 114
Skippers Canyon, 232
Sky Tower, 58
skydiving, 112, 235, 236
Skyline Gondola, 230
Skyshow Centre, 236
Snare Islands, 254

South Canterbury, 215, 218–9
South Island, 10, 31, 166–271
   area dialing code, 34
Southeast Islands, 148
Southern Alps, 223
Southland Museum and Art Gallery, 251, 254
Southward Car Museum, 160
Speakers' Corner, 209
speed limits, 37
Split Enz (music group), 11
Staines, Richard (fishing guide), 119
Star of Canada Maritime Museum, 126
Stewart Island, 32, 35, 166, 243, 252, 256, 258, 263, 268
Stirling Falls, 262
Stratford, 140
Sugar Loaf Islands, 139–40
Sulphur Point, 114
Summit Road, 211
surf-casting, 83, 90
Suter art gallery, 172

T

Tahunanui Beach, 173
Taiaroa Head, 262
Taieri Gorge, 246
Taieri River, 270
Tairawhiti Museum, 126
Takaka, 173–4
Taranaki wars, 138
Tasman, Abel (Dutch explorer), 56, 84, 122
Tasman Glacier, 227
Taupo, 280–1
Taupo Walkway, 115
Tauranga, 94, 101
Tawhiti Museum, 141
taxi services, 55, 154
Te Ana–Au Caves, 259
Te Anau, 243, 258, 269

Te Anau Downs, 260
Te Anau Wildlife Park, 267
Te Araroa, 124
Te Arikinui, Dame Te–Ata–I–Rangi–Kaahu, 96
Te Aroha, 90, 97
Te Kaha, 124
Te Kanawa, Dame Kiri, 11
Te Kauwhata Viticultural Research Station, 102–3
Te Mata Peak, 130
Te Papa (Museum of New Zealand), 154
Te Puia Hot Water Beach, 97
Te Puia Springs, 125
Te Reinga village, 127
Te Urewera National Park, 121, 127, 131, 134
Te Wairoa village, 111
Te Whai–a–te–Motu Meeting House, 127
tea shops, 44
telephones, 34
Thames, 91
Thames School of Mines, 91
theme parks, 59
thermal springs, *see* hot springs
Tikitiki, 125
Timaru, 215
tipping, 31
Tiritiri Matangi Island, 62
Tokaanu, 119
Tokomaru Bay, 125
Tolaga Bay, 126
Tolkien, J R R (author), 264
Tongariro Crossing, 118
Tongariro National Park, 51, 113–9, 264
Totaranui, 174
Tourism New Zealand, 14, 38, 41, 272
tourist information, 38
tours, *see* cruises and excursions
trails, walking, *see* walkways

train services, *see* rail services
trams, antique, 160
Transportation and Technology, Museum of (MOTAT), 60
travel passes, 35
travellers' cheques, 31
Treaty of Waitangi 50, 56, 68–70, 76, 144
Trounson Kauri Park, 74
TSS *Earnslaw* (steamship), 231
Tuhua (Mayor) Island, 95
Tunnel Beach Walkway, 268
Turangawaewae Marae (residence of Maori queen), 96
Turangi, 113, 119
Turuturu–mokai Pa (fortress), 141
Twizel, 226, 237

U

Ulva Island, 263
Underwater World, 231
United States, Antarctic staging centre, 203, 206, 210
universities, 158, 161, 208
University of Otago, 246
Urupukapuka Island, 79

V

Victoria Forest Park, 199
Victoria Park Market, 59
Victoria Square, 210
Victoria University, 158
vineyards, *see* wineries
Virginia Lake, 146
visas, 30
Visitor Information Network (VIN), 14, 37
visitor centres
  North Island, 55, 63, 75, 96, 112, 113, 115, 118, 119, 126, 127, 128, 131, 140, 151, 160
  South Island, 170, 178, 191, 206, 212, 217, 218, 226, 230, 235, 244, 259
Volcanic Activity Centre, 112–3
volcanoes, 50, 51, 95, 104, 114, 138
von Haast, Julius (geologist–explorer), 195, 197
von Tunzelmann, Paul (settler), 266

W

Wagener Museum, 78
Wai–O–Tapu Thermal Wonderland, 109, 111
Waiau Falls, 94
Waiau River, 269
Waiheke Island, 62, 71
Waikare Lake, 101
Waikato Museum, 96
Waikato region, 90, 101
Waikato River, 113
Waikato wars, 90
Waimangu Volcanic Valley, 109
Waimauku village, 67
Waingaro, 97
Wainuiomata River, 164
Waiohine River, 164
Waipahi River, 270
Waipapa Point, 250
Waipoua Kauri Forest, 74, 79
Waipu Wildlife Refuge, 79
Wairakei Geothermal Power Station, 113, 115
Wairakei, Park 112
Wairakei Natural Thermal Valley, 113
Wairarapa, 159, 164–5
Wairau Boulder Bank, 175
Wairau River, 175, 178, 219
Wairoa, 121, 127
Waitahanui, 119
Waitakere Ranges, 63
Waitangi (*see also* Treaty of Waitangi), 50, 70, 76

Waitangi National Reserve, 82
Waitomo caves, 51, 90, 98–100, 101
   museum, 98
Waiwera River, 270
walking, 18, 234, 274
walks and walkways, 14
   classification of, 20
   legislation, 18
   North Island, 63, 82–3, 101, 115, 126,
      131, 134, 147, 163
   South Island, 174, 198, 210, 217–9, 237–8,
      243, 260, 267–8, 269, 289
Walter Peak (sheep station), 231
Wanaka, 48, 223, 235–7
   airport, 235
Wanganui, 48, 138, 141, 145–6, 149
Wanganui Riverboat Centre and Museum, 146
water sports, 175
waterfalls, 75, 97, 100, 102, 112, 115, 198, 243, 250, 262,
   thermal, 109
websites, 272–4
Wellington, 47, 48, 50, 150–1, 154–5, 158, 162–3, 264–5
   accommodation, 281–2
   area dialing code, 34
   airport, 151
   customs house, 247
   harbour, 161
Wellington Tramway Museum, 160
West Coast Historical Museum, 192
Westland, 182–3, 190–1, 194
Westland National Park, 182, 194–5, 197, 199
Westport, 186–7
wetlands, 101
Whakapapa Village, 114
Whakarewarewa, 106
Whakarewarewa State Forest Park, 114, 115

Whakatane, 95
whale–watching, 203, 213
Whangamarino Wetlands, 101
Whangamata, 94
Whanganui National Park, 146
Whanganui Regional Museum, 145
Whangarei, 74, 75
   harbour, 79
Whangarei Falls, 75
Whangarei Museum, 75
Whataroa, 202
White Island, 95
Whitianga, 94, 102
wine industry, 15, 26, 28
   research, 102–3
wine–tasting, 234, 274, 290
wineries, 26
   North Island, 66–67, 71, 83, 102–3, 135–7, 150, 164–5
   organic vineyard, 135
   South Island, 179–82, 221–3, 239, 242
wood chopping, 251
wool products, 46
writers, New Zealand, 11
Wyndham, 270
Wyndham River, 270

Y
yachting, 78
Young, Nicholas (seaman), 126
Young Nick's Head, 126
Youth Hostel Association, 42

Z
zoos, 60, 63, 139